NEW FOUNDATIONS THEOLOGICAL LIBRARY

General Editor
PETER TOON, MA, M.TH, D.PHIL

Consultant Editor
RALPH P. MARTIN, MA, PH.D

NEW FOUNDATIONS THEOLOGICAL LIBRARY

Other volumes in preparation

THE CHURCH
IN THE THEOLOGY
OF THE REFORMERS

PAUL D. L. AVIS

JOHN KNOX PRESS

ATLANTA

Library of Congress Cataloging in Publication Data

Avis, Paul D L
    The Church in the theology of the reformers.

    (New foundations theological library)
    Includes bibliographical references and index.
    1.   Church—History of doctrines—16th century.
I.   Title.   II.   Series.
BV598.A93   1980   262′.009′031   80-16186

ISBN 0-8042-3708-5

Published simultaneously in the United Kingdom by Marshall, Morgan, and Scott,
One Bath Street, London, England, and in the United States by John Knox Press,
Atlanta

John Knox Press
Atlanta, Georgia 30365

Printed in the USA

CONTENTS

PREFACE

In this book I have tried to give an account of three aspects of Reformation ecclesiology that, as far as I am aware, have not been treated in a systematic and comparative way before: the doctrine of the 'true Church' and its marks; the structure of ministry in the true Church; and the rise of protestant missionary concern—the mission of the true Church in Christendom and beyond. Part one has developed from an article in the *Scottish Journal of Theology*, Vol. xxx (1977), ' "The True Church" in Reformation Theology'.

I am grateful to Dr Peter Toon for inviting me to write on this subject for Marshalls Theological Library and for his kindness and consideration during the preparation of the book.

My wife Susan has alone made it possible for me to complete the work in a comparatively short time amid the many and varied duties of a country parson. The book is dedicated to her.

North Devon   PAUL D. L. AVIS
February 1979

ABBREVIATIONS
used in the text

WA   (Weimarer Ausgabe) *D. Martin Luther's Werke* (Weimar, 1883-).

LW   *Luther's Works* (St Louis and Philadelphia, 1955-).

BC   *The Book of Concord*, ed. T. G. Tappert (Philadelphia, 1959).

CR   ˌ*Corpus Reformatorum* (Halle, 1834-).

CO   *Calvini Opera* in *Corpus Reformatorum.*

Inst.   J. Calvin, *Institutes of the Christian Religion,* trans. H. Beveridge (London, n.d.).

TT   J. Calvin, *Tracts and Treatises,* ed. T. F. Torrance, trans. H. Beveridge (Grand Rapids, 1958).

CC   *Calvin's Commentaries* (on the New Testament), eds. D. W. and T. F. Torrance (Edinburgh, 1959-).

Schaff   *The Creeds of the Evangelical Protestant Churches,* ed. P. Schaff (London, 1877).

PS   Parker Society edition of the works of the English Reformers (Cambridge, 1840-).

HW   R. Hooker, *Works,* ed. J. Keble (Oxford, 1845).

FC   R. Field, *Of the Church* (Edinburgh, 1847).

INTRODUCTION:
THE REFORMATION CONCEPT
OF THE CHURCH

Reformation theology is largely dominated by two questions: 'How can I obtain a gracious God?' and 'Where can I find the true Church?' The two questions are inseparably related and constitute two aspects of the overriding concern of sixteenth-century men with the problem of salvation, for the truth of the old patristic watchword *Nulla salus extra ecclesiam*—no salvation outside the Church—was assumed on all sides. The unity of these two fundamental problems— the quest for a gracious God and for the true Church—can be seen with startling clarity in the theology of Martin Luther. For Luther, the answer to both questions was given with radical simplicity in the gospel of free forgiveness, of justification by the unmerited grace of God through faith alone. In speaking of a gracious God, the gospel brings the Church into being; the gospel alone, when believed, constitutes and creates the Church.

 The very existence of the reform movement and of the evangelical Churches which had broken with Rome hung upon their ability to answer the question 'Which Church is the true Church?' in a satisfactory and convincing way that would both justify their separation from the historic Western Church centred on Rome and safeguard the validity of their sacraments as means of grace and pledges of salvation. Reformation ecclesiology returns obsessively to the problem of distinguishing between the false Church and the true; the one persecuting, prosperous and triumphalist; the other weak, downtrodden, crucified and even denied the name of Church altogether. The Reformers see this theme running strongly through the Scriptures, beginning with the conflict of Cain and Abel, and the most sustained exposition of it is to be found in Luther's lectures on Genesis where Cain stands for the pope and the Turk, and Abel for the true Church of the evangelicals (LW 2. 181).

The Reformers frequently write as though simple believers of the evangelical persuasion were tormented by the claim of Rome to be the only true Church, and stung by the gibe, 'Where was your Church before Luther?' they claimed for themselves that they were one body with the ancient Church of the Fathers and that they were simply renewing and restoring the face of the Christian Church—one, holy, catholic and apostolic.

In defence of their position and to meet the challenge of Roman polemicists, the Reformers developed a doctrine of the marks of the true Church (notae ecclesiae) by which it might always be known, and insisted that it was not enough to claim to be the Church—one must also bear the marks of the Church. 'If you want to be the Church,' Luther declares, 'and bear its name, you must prove your title.' For the Christian Church is of two kinds: 'People call that the Christian Church which is not the Christian Church, and that which is the Christian Church is often not acknowledged as such. It is not a question whether one must believe the Church, or whether there is a Church; but the issue is: Which is the true Church?' All Christians, claims Luther, should be capable of 'distinguishing plainly and clearly between the alleged Church, which boasts of the name, and the true Church, which does not bear that name and yet is the true Church.' If we ask, 'But how do I know which is the true Church and which is not?' Luther replies: 'As I have said, all depends on the right knowledge of the essence of the Church and on the proper differentiation between the name and the essence of the Church' (LW 23. 289, 285, 309, 306).

What then are the outward marks that reveal where the true Church is really and essentially present? The answer— if indeed there is only one answer to be found in the teaching of the Reformers, and not several diverse or even contradictory views—will provide us with *the Reformation concept of the Church*, a concept that we can expect to find reflected also in the thought of the Reformers concerning the Church's ministry and mission.

The primary and creative impulse of Reformation ecclesiology as we find it in Luther is evangelical and christological. That is to say that the nature and essence of the Church is understood by Luther solely by reference to the

Christian gospel and the reality of the person and work of Jesus Christ. As Gordon Rupp has pointed out, the first Reformers, particularly Luther, were not concerned with defining the circumference of the Church, but with proclaiming its christological centre. They were engaged in discovering the *essentia ecclesiae*—what makes the Church the Church—not with drawing up rules and formulas relating to admission or expulsion from the Christian community. Luther himself, writes Rupp, 'was vitally concerned to determine the centre of the existence of the Church ... but it was not until after his death that protestantism really grappled with the intricate question of the circumference, and added to word and sacrament another dimension, "the Discipline of Christ" '.[1]

For Luther, the Church was created by the living presence of Christ through his word the gospel. Where the gospel is found Christ is present, and where he is present the Church must truly exist. This conviction lay at the root of the whole Reformation struggle and was shared by all the Reformers—Lutheran and Reformed, Anglican and anabaptist. They were prepared to sacrifice the visible unity of the Western Church if only by so doing they could save the gospel. Luther laid down this principle in the *Ninety-five Theses*: 'The true treasure of the Church is the most holy gospel of the glory and grace of God.' And in his *Explanation of the Ninety-five Theses* he commented: 'Nothing in the Church must be treated with greater care than the holy gospel, since the Church has nothing which is more precious and salutary.' And again: 'Christ has left nothing to the world except the gospel' (LW 31. 31, 210, 230). The gospel must shine out at all costs and at whatever sacrifice. On this principle the Reformers were immovable and undivided; it provides the distinctive Reformation concept of the Church, informing and inspiring not only the doctrine of the marks of the true Church, but also the Reformers' teaching on the ministry and their view of mission. One thing is needful; all else is secondary. To save the gospel, all outward forms of order and structure are expendable. Only thus, wrote George Downham, chaplain to James I, can we 'redeem the most precious jewel of the gospel, which is to be redeemed (if need be) with the loss of all outward things'.[2]

Luther came to realise that his understanding of the nature of the gospel implied the dispensability of the Church considered only as a visible and hierarchical structure. As the Lutheran scholar Werner Elert has put it: 'For a time it could seem that the Reformation in Luther's sense meant the destruction or abolition of the Church', for by burning the papal bull of excommunication and the corpus of canon law Luther was repudiating 'not only the existing form but any legally constituted form of the Church'. And his doctrine of the priesthood of all believers, argues Elert, 'abolishes on principle every organisational element without which the Church cannot exist as a unit above the individual'. Luther did not of course imagine that the Church would thereby cease to exist, for, if the gospel were preserved, the Church would somehow be reborn. His study of the Hussite movement had convinced him that the Church, though hidden, had continued under the papacy and would continue to survive even in the most hostile environment. But meanwhile, *abscondita est ecclesia, latent sancti*—the Church is hidden, the saints concealed (WA 18. 652). Elert points out the extremely radical consequences of Luther's position here for the Christian doctrine of the Church: 'Luther, it is true, did not absolutely destroy the Church as a supra-individual unity but he spiritualised it in such a way that when one pursues these thoughts to their logical conclusion, it is eliminated as a formative energy of history.'[3]

Luther and all the Reformers were conscious that they could be accused of diminishing the Church to a mathematical point, so to speak, and they continually had to defend the evangelical churches against the charge of being merely a *Platonica civitas*, a Platonic state, meaning not the utopian state for which Plato legislated in *The Laws* and had hoped to have seen established in Sicily (as recounted in his seventh and eighth letters), but an ideal Church enjoying a disembodied and illusory existence in the realm of pure abstractions, uncontaminated by the empirical world of space and time, place and history. Luther retorted that he did not want 'to build a church as Plato wants to build a state, which would be nowhere' (WA 7. 683). 'We are not dreaming about some Platonic republic,' asserted Melanchthon in the *Apology of the Augsburg Confession*, 'as has been slanderously alleged, but we teach that this Church actually exists, made up of true believers and righteous men scattered throughout the world and known by certain outward marks, open and visible to the eyes of men' (BC 171; cf. CR 9. 193; 12. 368, 566; 28. 409). As Caspar Cruciger also protests in 1540: 'We do not speak of the Church as a Platonic republic which does not exist anywhere.' And we find Zwingli holding that the true spiritual Church is not to be identified with the Church visible which is always 'a mixed company', and facing the immediate objection that 'such a Church no more exists than does Plato's republic! How then is it possible for there to be anywhere a Church that has neither spot nor wrinkle?' His reply is that the pure spiritual Church is hidden in Christ.[4]

Luther's teaching on the Church certainly invited the criticism that his Church, invisible and intangible, had no real existence. He had never meant to suggest, however, that the true Church is always invisible, but he was concerned to stress above all that the nature of the Church can never be adequately explained in empirical terms and that its deepest—christological—meaning is a mystery hidden with Christ in God. According to Luther, the spiritual character of the Church is entirely indifferent to matters concerned with time and place, yet not wholly independent of them. The Church is not pure disembodied spirit. Although it exists *in* the flesh *(in carne vivat)*, it does not live *according* to the flesh *(non secundum carnem vivit)*. It may be concerned with the world's concerns, but it is not to be judged by the world's standards *(Ita in loco, rebus operibusque mundi versatur, sed non secundum haec estimatur)*. For Christ abolished all restrictions of place *(omnem locum tollit)* when he taught that the kingdom of God comes not with observation, so that you cannot say, 'Here it is', or, 'There it is', for 'the kingdom of God is within you'. True, the Church cannot survive in this world without becoming involved in such mundane matters as food and drink, but, as St Paul says, the kingdom of God does not consist in food and drink. Without place and body there is no Church *(sine loco et corpore non est ecclesia)* and yet body and place are not the Church nor do they belong to it. All such matters are free and indifferent (WA 7. 719f.).

Luther is evidently speaking here of one Church in two

aspects, on the analogy of the Incarnation: in one aspect visible, tangible, identifiable; in the other invisible, elusive, mysterious. As Johann Gerhard was to put it a hundred years later in the heyday of Lutheran scholasticism: 'We do not postulate two Churches; we believe and confess one Church, and assert that this is treated in Scripture in a double way *(bifarium)*.'[5] (As we shall see, it is precisely the doctrine of the marks of the true Church or *notae ecclesiae* that forms the connection between the two aspects and bridges them.) So although the Church might be forced underground, it could never be completely invisible, for by the gospel which, according to Luther, constitutes and creates the Church, Luther understood the *preached* gospel. The Church thus emerges into visibility in the word expressed in preaching and embodied in the sacraments, but this is, as it were, merely the tip of an iceberg, for the reality of the Church remains 'a high, deep, hidden thing which one may neither perceive nor see, but must grasp only by faith through baptism, sacrament and word' (LW 41. 211; Luther's original German has a force and resonance lost in the translation: *Es ist ein hoch, tiess, verborgen Ding die Kirche* ...: WA 51. 507).

Although wholly coherent in itself, Luther's radical ecclesiology proved too paradoxical to be workable in practice and even Luther himself was ultimately both unable and unwilling to implement it. The doctrine of the Church and its marks could not be left as Luther had defined it; other Reformers attempted to develop a more comprehensive and practicable doctrine of the *notae ecclesiae*. Two tendencies developed, in both of which some consideration was given to the question of the Church's circumference.

The line of development represented by Bucer, Calvin, the early puritans, the anabaptists and English separatists stressed discipline, the use of the ban (excommunication), and moved towards the later concept of the gathered Church. Calvin himself succeeds in holding together the Church's christological centre and the circumference created by pastoral discipline because he does not include discipline or holiness of life among the marks of the true Church. Bullinger's treatment of the *notae ecclesiae*, however, with its numerous qualifications and refinements, shows that the doctrine was already under strain. In the teaching of Henry Barrow and his fellow separatists ecclesiology is totally dominated by an obsession with discipline and the gospel practically obscured by the regime under which it is preached. Separatist ecclesiology proved to be self-defeating.

The other line of development in which questions of the Church's circumference were treated is to be found in the late sixteenth-century Anglican divines Richard Hooker and Richard Field. Recognising that the concept of the *notae* had become so unwieldy as to be virtually unusable, they abandoned it and, replacing an intensive ecclesiology by an extensive one, set the reformed doctrine of the Church on a new footing. Instead of tightening the circumference of the Church, they relax it. They attempt a doctrine of the catholic circumference that does not sacrifice what Luther was essentially striving for. As we shall see, the definitely evangelical nature of the ecclesiology of Hooker and Field is brought out in the fact that it was precisely considerations concerning salvation that led them to do this. Their view, catholic and reformed, sees the gospel as *articulus stantis aut cadentis ecclesiae*—the article of a standing or falling Church—as do all the Reformers following Luther, but supplements this with a formal doctrine of the Church as a visible divine society instead of the well-worn apparatus of the *notae ecclesiae*, thus giving a new dimension to the shape of Reformation ecclesiology. In Part I we shall attempt to trace the evolution of the Reformation concept of the Church in the sixteenth century to the point where it enters this new phase.

As has already been suggested, the doctrine of the marks of the true Church is of crucial significance for our understanding of the theology of the Reformation for it provides the vital link between the two aspects of the Church as the Reformers conceived it—its invisible, spiritual reality and its physical manifestation. The difficult question then arises— and it is as well to face it at this stage—as to whether the marks are *constitutive* of the Church or merely *descriptive* of where the Church is to be found among men. In other words, do the Reformers define the nature of the true Church by reference to the marks of word and sacrament, or do they merely claim that the marks indicate where it actually exists?

First of all it must be said that the doctrine of the *notae* by no means exhausts the Reformers' teaching on the Church! For Calvin, for example, what constitutes the Church is, externally, the covenant between God and his people, and, internally and substantially, union with Christ through the Holy Spirit—and it is on this latter aspect that he lays· the emphasis. And again, if the Reformers were asked what they made of the *credal* marks of the Church—unity, holiness, catholicity, apostolicity—they would answer with the whole Christian tradition that these are the essential notes or characteristics of the Church. It is, however, important to note here that they would stress much more than Roman Catholic or Orthodox theologians that these are eschatological dimensions of the Church and to one degree or another unrealised on earth, though they are to be sought and striven for. Having accepted without question the credal marks of the Church, the Reformers would add the important qualification that it is one thing to describe the nature of the Church as holy, catholic, etc, but quite another to say where that true Church is actually to be found.

A final answer to the question, Are the marks held by the Reformers to be definitive or descriptive? must wait a more detailed account of the individual ecclesiologies of the Reformers in the chapters of Part One. It may well turn out to be the case that they are neither unambiguous nor unanimous in their statements on this point. If, however, according to the Reformers, word and sacrament are embodiments of the gospel, and if Christ is present wherever the gospel is believed in the heart, perhaps we are justified in suspecting that we are not being presented with strict alternatives here but with two aspects of one spiritual reality. As Luther says, God is veiled under the water of baptism, the bread of the sacrament and the words of the preacher.

> Behind these stands our Lord God, and they are the faces of God through which he speaks with us and works in every person individually. He baptises me; he absolves me, and gives me his body and blood through the tongue and the hand of the minister ... And *this is the presence or form and epiphany of God in these means* (LW 8. 145, my italics).

The marks are thus not arbitrary signs for any of the Reformers but reveal something of the true nature of the Church. As it has been put with reference to Calvin's doctrine of the *notae:*

> Preaching and the sacraments are not simply evidences of a reality existing independently of them: they are, from the human point of view, constitutive of that reality ... We may be led to Christ by the Spirit apart from the means, and we may have the means apart from the Spirit, and hence, without Christ, but in neither of these cases do we have the Church.[6]

In the three parts that follow, the fundamental concept of the Church in the theology of the sixteenth-century Reformers is traced through their evolving doctrine of the true Church and its marks, their view of the Christian ministry and its relation to the christological centre, and their vision of the mission of the Church as the creature and bearer of the word.

PART I

THE TRUE CHURCH

CHAPTER ONE

THE CHRISTOLOGICAL CENTRE

Luther was primarily and passionately concerned for the purity of the gospel: Calvin for the purity of the Church—the gospel had already been brought into the light of day. All the crises of Luther's life were centred on the gospel: all Calvin's on the Church. This is a distinct difference of emphasis and one which becomes apparent in their respective doctrines of the marks of the true Church. It should not, however, be exaggerated: gospel and Church were inseparably related in the thought of both Reformers and, as Jaroslav Pelikan has pointed out, a correct understanding of Luther's reformation demands that it be considered as a Church movement, 'an action which was performed in the name of one holy, catholic and apostolic Church'. Luther sought precisely to establish the Church once more upon the foundation of the gospel, 'and so to root the unity of the Church in the redemptive action of God rather than in human merit and human organisations'.[1]

For Luther the Church is built in history through the dynamic mission of the word, the gospel; it is virtually the creation of the word. He felt that his reform stood out from all previous attempts at reformation such as those of Wyclif and Huss in that it primarily concerned the integrity of the gospel. It was a reformation of doctrine from which all other practical reforms and corrections of abuses might logically follow. Others had attacked the morals of the papacy: only he had gone to the root of the matter—he alone had been called to assail the doctrine. The recovery of the word would bring the rebirth of the Church for, as Paul Althaus has written, 'only the proclamation of the word is necessary to create the Church ... The Church is nothing else than the miracle of the power of the word constantly appearing in a new form.'[2]

The existence of the Church is not open and obvious to all; it is spiritual and hidden and therefore certain marks are necessary by which the true Church may be known. 'The love and communion of Christ and all the saints are hidden, invisible and spiritual and only a physical, visible and external sign of them is given to us.' 'The Church is a high, deep, hidden thing which one may neither perceive nor see but must grasp only by faith through baptism, sacrament and word' (WA 2. 752; 51. 507). 'Christianity is a spiritual assembly of souls in one faith ... The natural, real, true and essential Christendom exists in the Spirit and not in any external thing' (LW 39. 69). Therefore 'some visible sign must be given by which we are to be gathered into one body for the purpose of hearing the word of God' (WA 7. 720).

The Church is where God is present and that presence is invisible too, but he has given certain signs to show that he is with us. In the Old Testament these were the pillar of fire, the cloud and the mercy seat; in the New Testament he gives us baptism, the Lord's Supper, the ministry of the word, 'and the like'. 'By means of these God shows us as by a visible sign that he is with us, takes care of us and is favourably inclined towards us' (LW 1. 309).

LUTHER ON THE MARKS OF A TRUE CHURCH

In his treatise of 1539 *On the Councils and the Church*, Luther enumerated seven marks by which the Church or 'holy Christian people' may be recognised. The list mentions the word of God; the sacraments of baptism and the altar, rightly administered according to Christ's institution; the offices of the keys and the ministry; public worship, namely, 'prayer, public praise and thanksgiving to God', including the use of the Lord's Prayer, the Apostles' Creed and the Decalogue; and the bearing of the cross. Supremely important, however, is the first of these marks, the Church's possession of the word of God in a greater or lesser degree of purity. Here, says Luther,

we are speaking of the external word, preached orally ... for this is what Christ left behind as an external sign by which his Church or his Christian people in the world should be recognised ... Whenever you hear or see this word preached, believed, professed and lived do not doubt that the true *ecclesia sancta catholica*, a Christian holy people, must be there, even though their number is very small.

The word alone is sufficient to identify the Church, for 'God's word cannot be without God's people and, conversely, God's people cannot be without God's word' (LW 41. 148ff.).

Luther once again deals at length with the marks of the Church in *Against Hanswurst* (1541) in which he combated the Roman claim to be exclusively the truth Church, the evangelicals having apostatised. On the contrary, Luther argues, this claim is the exact reverse of the truth, and proceeds to enumerate the characteristic marks of the reformed Church and to show that they all derive from the New Testament or the primitive Church. By virtue of the sacrament of holy baptism alone the evangelicals are part of the ancient catholic Church and in the sacrament of the altar 'we eat and drink with the whole of ancient Christendom from one table ... for we are one Church with the ancient Church in one sacrament'. The Lutherans retain the office of the keys, that is, absolution, and can claim that 'we have therefore one kind of keys and one common practice with the ancient Church. Hence we are this same ancient Church or are, in any event, in it.' They preach the word of God, inventing nothing new but holding and remaining true to 'the ancient word of God, as the ancient Church had it'. They use the Apostles' Creed, 'the ancient creed of the ancient Church', and reverence the Lord's Prayer. They honour the temporal power of the magistrate and hold the marriage bed undefiled. In their experience of suffering and persecution, claims Luther, 'our lot is like that of the ancient Church and in this we are beyond measure like it, so that we may well say that we are the true ancient Church or at least its companions and copartners in suffering'. Finally, like the early Christian martyrs, the evangelicals pray for their enemies.

Luther then proceeds to show that the Roman Church has lost or corrupted all these marks, whereas they 'cannot find anything in us that was not held in the ancient or true Church at the time of the apostles'. Among the evangelicals 'the original and ancient Church shines forth once more ... Thus we have proved that we are the true ancient Church, one body and one communion of saints with the holy, universal Christian Church ... It is out of it that we have come. Indeed, we have been born anew of it as the Galatians were of St Paul' (LW 41. 194ff.).

Here Luther is not suggesting that all these marks are necessary to make the true Church known, still less that they are all essential constituents of the Church's being. The marks are indicative, not constitutive, of the Church. As Strohl has remarked: 'The sign indicates the direction one must take in seeking the true Christians.'[3] Even as pointers they are not all equally important and Luther progressively narrows down the marks of the Church to the word and sacraments. 'If you ask where the Church is, it is nowhere in evidence. But you must not pay regard to external form but to the word and to baptism, and the Church must be sought where the sacraments are purely administered, where there are hearers, teachers and confessors of the word' (LW 6. 149). Baptism, the bread of the sacrament and the gospel itself are the three symbols, tokens and marks of Christians (*Christianorum symbola, tessare et caracteres*: WA 7. 720). It is, however, perfectly clear that the gospel itself is supremely important here and although Luther will mention the sacraments it is the gospel that dominates his thought:

> The gospel is before bread and baptism the unique, most certain and noblest symbol of the Church because through the gospel alone the Church is conceived, formed, nourished, generated, instructed, fed, clothed, adorned, strengthened, armed and preserved—in short, the whole life and substance of the Church is in the word of God (*tota vita et substantia Ecclesiae est in verbo Dei*). As Christ says, 'Man lives by every word that proceeds from the mouth of God.'... Nor am I speaking about the written word but rather the spoken gospel (*non de Evangelio scripto sed vocali loquor*) ... Only by the vocal and public voice of the gospel can it be known where is the Church and the mystery of the kingdom of heaven (WA 7. 721).

Commenting on Psalm 110.2, Luther enunciates the doctrine that will become common coin among the Reformers and their successors the puritans: Christ rules and reigns by the sceptre of his word, though for Luther this is accompanied by his presence in the sacraments. 'In his invisible essence he sits at the right hand of God; but he rules visibly on earth and works through external visible signs, of which the preaching of the gospel and the sacraments are the chief ones, and through public confession and the fruits of faith in the gospel.' In these the Church is manifested visibly, but the word remains supreme:

> These are the true marks whereby one can really recognise the kingdom of the Lord Christ and the Christian Church: namely, wherever this sceptre is, that is, the office of the preaching of the gospel, borne by the apostles into the world and received from them by us. Where it is present and maintained, there the Christian Church and the kingdom of Christ surely exist, no matter how small or negligible the number of the flock (LW 13. 272).

For the purpose of argument, Luther is even prepared to reduce that small or negligible number to only one, although this is scarcely consistent with his stress on the Church as the community: 'If I were the only one in the whole world who retained the word, I alone should be the Church and should rightly judge of the whole of the rest of the world that it was not the Church.'[4] In the preaching of the gospel, Christ's 'entire kingdom and government as far as it can be seen or grasped outwardly' consists (LW 13. 265).

When we consider the Church, we are not to look for perfection. No body of Christians is faultless and human failings do not detract from the real existence of the Church: for that, word and sacrament are enough. 'When you are minded to pass judgment on the Church, you must not look for a Church in which there are no blemishes and flagrant faults, but for one where there are people who love the word and confess it before men. Where you discover these earmarks, there you may be sure the Church exists' (LW 13. 90). The purity of the gospel virtually constitutes the purity of the Church: the Church is pure, claims Luther, when the pure gospel is preached, even though it remains full of human weakness, just as the human body is said to be sound, although it is never lacking in 'filth, matter, ulcers, spittle and excrement' (LW 6. 34). Luther develops this colourful but coarse analogy with characteristic relish, as we shall see when, at a later stage, we consider his evaluation of the Roman Church and his attempt to answer the question, Is Rome a Church or not?

In rejecting standards of holiness among believers and the effectiveness of discipline within the Church as marks of the true Church, Luther was followed by the Lutheran confessions and by Calvin, though not, as will shortly become clear, by Bucer and the puritan wing of the Reformation on the one hand, or by the anabaptists and the radical wing on the other. The *Formula of Concord*, a harmony of the Lutheran confessions published in 1580, fifty years after the *Confession of Augsburg*, expressly singles out for rejection the view 'That it is no Christian congregation in which public expulsion and the orderly process of excommunication do not take place' (BC 500, 635). As Edmund Schlink has aptly commented here: 'The mark of the Church is the preaching of the gospel—not the word that condemns but the word that liberates; not the word that expels from the Church but the word that calls into the Church.'[5]

Although, as we have seen, Luther can expound the conventional Reformation doctrine of the *notae ecclesiae*, it is more frequently the case and more truly representative of his fundamental position that he is prepared to resolve them all into the word or gospel, for the simple reason that it is the gospel alone that imparts to them their life and substance. As P. S. Watson has written: 'Just as the sacraments are constituted by the word, so it can be said that all these other marks of the Church are, in their several ways, so bound up with the word that where it is absent they entirely lose their Christian significance.'[6] This principle can be documented at length from Luther.

'Where the word is, there is faith; and where faith is, there is the true Church.' 'Wherever the word of God is preached and believed, there true faith, that immovable rock, exists; where there is faith, there is the Church, the bride of Christ; where the bride of Christ is, there are to be found all that he has betrothed to himself' (*ubi sponsa Christi, ibi omnia quae sunt sponsi*: WA 2. 208). The Church 'walks in the midst of truth. It has the genuine, legitimate, Christian sense and spirit of the word of God.' Not all who call themselves the Church are the Church; it is one thing to claim the name of Church, quite another to possess the reality. But 'if the word of God is present in its purity and is active, the Church is there' (LW 28. 302).

The sure mark by which the Christian congregation can be recognised is that the pure gospel is preached there. For just as the banner of an army is the sure sign by which one can know what kind of lord and army have taken to the field, so too the gospel is the sure sign by which one knows where Christ and his army are encamped ... Thus we are certain that there must be Christians wherever the gospel is, no matter how few and how sinful and weak they may be (LW 39. 305).

On the other hand, where the true gospel is not to be found, as in 'the synagogue of papists and Thomists' *(sicut in synagoga Papistarum et Thomistarum videmus)*, we cannot doubt that the Church does not exist for 'where the gospel is absent and human teachings rule, there no Christians live but only pagans, no matter how numerous they are and how holy and upright their life may be' (ibid. and WA 7: 721). As Luther put it in his *Large Catechism:* 'Where Christ is not preached, there is no Holy Spirit to create, call and gather the Christian Church' (BC 416). For the Church depends passively on its creation by the word: 'The Church does not make the word but it comes into being from the word' (*Die Kirche macht nicht das Wortt, sondern sie wirtt von dem Wort:* WA 8. 491).

In 1523 Luther wrote *Concerning the Ministry* for the guidance of the Hussite Church in Bohemia which was forced to maintain its episcopal orders by subterfuge.[7] He urges the Brethren to abandon this deceitful practice and to have the courage of their convictions. An episcopally ordained ministry is not necessary to safeguard the Church. The gospel and baptism remain valid without episcopal sanction or validation and they are all that is needed for Christian faith and life 'since faith alone justifies and love alone lives rightly'. The Hussites must be prepared to sacrifice the succession of their orders if this is the only way to keep the gospel. Then 'Christ without a doubt would be in their midst and would own them as his Church ... for he himself said, "One thing only is necessary", the word of God in which man has his life. For if he lives in the word and has the word, he is able to forgo all else in order to avoid the teachings and ministries of impious men. And what would it avail to have all other things but not the word by which one lives?' asks Luther, and concludes: 'The Church is nothing without the word and everything in it exists by virtue of the word alone.' It creates and builds the Church and gives life to all its ministries. 'Since the Church owes its birth to the word, is nourished, aided and strengthened by it, it is obvious that it cannot be without the word. If it is without the word it ceases to be a Church' (LW 40. 9, 11, 37).

Holding to the word alone, the true Church is oblivious of its circumstances and thrives even when outwardly brought down to the gates of hell.

The Church of God is present wherever the word of God is spoken, whether it be in the middle of the Turks' land or in the pope's land or in hell itself. For it is the word of God which builds the Church which is lord over all other spaces: where that is heard, where baptism, the sacrament of the altar and the forgiveness of sins are administered, there hold fast and conclude most certainly that there is the house of God and the gate of heaven (WA 43. 596).

The true Church is indifferent to outward things and those who grasp its true nature are not impressed by the grandiose claims of existing hierarchical ecclesiastical corporations such as the papacy. So it is foolish, asserts Luther, for the papists to claim that they are the Church, 'for the Church is not a people that should be judged on the basis of large numbers, of size, of wisdom, of power, of wealth, of prestige, of succession, of office, etc.'. The true Church knows none of these things: it is marked by the word, the promise of God, 'It is the people of the promise, that is, the people which believes the promise' (LW 4. 53). 'Thank God, a seven-year-old child knows what the Church is, namely, holy believers and sheep who hear the voice of their shepherd' (BC 315).

Ernst Troeltsch, though not always reliable as an interpreter of Luther, here takes us straight to the heart of the matter when he points out that for Luther the word provides the essential element of objectivity in the Church's existence. Although Luther was familiar with the Augustinian doctrine of illumination and the medieval mystical tradition and owed something to each, he was convinced that such a divine operation as bringing the Church into being could not be based on the subjective foundation of individual illumination or mystical insight. As Troeltsch says: 'He felt that the divine operation must be manifested in something objective, given, the same for all, something entirely authoritative, miraculous and definite, standing out in clear relief against all that is merely human.' This position underlay Luther's implacable opposition to the radicals, 'the fanatics', who, as Troeltsch puts it, 'regarded the basis of salvation and the bond of fellowship as consisting in obedience to the law of God and therefore in subjective attainment'.

For Luther, on the other hand, the concept of the word 'gathers up all the objectivity and holiness, the sense that the Church as an institution is independent of the individual and personal point of view and is, in fact, entirely objective'. Troeltsch rightly sees that the doctrine of the word decisively informs the Reformation concept of the Church and gives identity to the protestant tradition of ecclesiology. 'It constitutes the sociological point of contact, freed from the subjective element, secured quite simply, and endowed with a supernatural power of influence from which, it is held, the Church is to be reconstructed.' In this, Troeltsch perceptively comments, it forms the protestant equivalent of the Roman Catholic episcopate, centralised finally in the papacy.[8]

AMBIGUITIES OF LUTHER'S DOCTRINE OF THE CHURCH

By defining the Church in terms of the preached word, the simple gospel of sins forgiven and unmerited grace, Luther had clearly established the Church's christological centre. But his position—at once simple in concept and radical in its implications—brought obvious problems in the exercise of the cure of souls, especially when, as in sixteenth-century Germany, the Church was indissolubly bound to the temporal

power. According to Luther's ideal, true Christians have no
need of external sanctions imposed by the secular authorities,
nor even of rule and government among themselves, for all
are subject to one another. There is therefore no room for the
machinery of ecclesiastical jurisdiction or discipline supported
by sanctions within the community: mutual aid and
correction should suffice. Luther's ecclesiology does not leave
open the possibility of such discipline as would figure so
prominently in the thought of the puritans and separatists
for, as Paul Althaus has pointed out, according to Luther, 'no
earthly power can draw the boundaries of the Church and
decide who belongs to it and who does not ... The Christian
existence of the individual is beyond the reach of every
ecclesiastical organisation.'[9]

Luther's younger colleagues such as Philip Melanchthon
had never been under any illusion that it would be possible to
carry out in practical terms the Reformer's radically spiritual
concept of the Church 'with its miraculous faith which staked
everything on the power of the word' (Troeltsch). And
Luther too eventually admitted disillusionment. Writing to
Georg Spalatin, chaplain and private secretary to the Elector
Frederick of Saxony, in 1527, he confessed: 'Up to now I
have been cherishing the vain hope that men can be directed
by the gospel. But the fact is that they destroy the gospel and
wish to be constrained by law and the sword' (*volunt legibus
et gladio cogi*).[10] Persuasion was not enough to convert the
German people to the evangelical faith.

> We teach, we exhort, we adjure, we scold, and we employ
> every form of expression in order to recall the masses out
> of their smugness to the fear of God. But the world goes its
> way like an untamed beast and follows not the word but its
> own desires, which it nevertheless strives to cloak with an
> appearance of morality (LW 1. 272).

In the preface to his *German Mass* (1526), Luther prescribed
that those who earnestly desired to be true Christians and
confess the gospel by word and deed should gather themselves
together into a house Church 'to pray, read, baptise, receive
the sacrament and to practise other Christian work'. But he
sadly concluded that this could not as things stood be done:

In short, if one had the people—individuals who earnestly desired to be Christians—fitting forms and uses would soon be established. But I cannot and do not yet dare to organise or establish such a community or congregation, for I have not yet available a sufficient number of Christian people and, as a matter of fact, I do not know and see many who want it to be done (WA 19. 72f.).

Moreover, it seems that when the opportunity to translate his ideas into reality was actually presented to him, Luther was unwilling to accept it. In 1526 Francis Lambert, a former Franciscan monk converted to the evangelical faith, drew up a scheme for Church reform and ecclesiastical government in Hesse at the request of Prince Philip. Lambert's formula asserted that the word of God is the only supreme rule for the guidance and government of the Church and that canon law has no authority or relevance in such matters. Scripture teaches that it belongs to the Christian community itself to select and dismiss pastors and to exercise discipline and excommunication and to exercise authority in matters of doctrine. 'This reform', Lambert claimed,

> will have as judge the assembly of believers which alone can faithfully interpret the word of God. Any man who truly possesses the word of God has the power of the keys. All Christians are and have been since the beginning of the Church, participants in its priesthood. The priesthood of ordained priests is an institution of the devil.

The plan was approved by Philip of Hesse who then sought Luther's blessing. The proposals faithfully reflected the ideas of the early Luther who had actually written a treatise *That a Christian community or assembly has the right and the power to judge of the doctrine, to summon a preacher, to install him and to dismiss him* (1523). But having lived through the peasants' revolt of the previous year and seen his original spiritualism and congregationalism counterfeited by Müntzer and Karlstadt, Luther was in no mood to be reminded of his earlier radical views and put sufficient pressure on Philip to put a stop to the venture.[11]

Luther's concept of the Church was the ecclesiology of a

pure idealist. In actual reality, as Troeltsch points out, the vision of the progressive triumph of the word, overcoming all difficulties and bringing order out of chaos, stood in dire need of human support.

> The uniform interpretation of Scripture did not come about naturally; it had to be enforced from above. The institution of ministers in an orderly way did not come about spontaneously, neither through an outpouring of charismatic gifts nor through the voluntary exercise of love and willing submission to a charismatic ministry; a definite Church order had to be created in order to call ministers and to give them official recognition. Excommunication could not be carried out by expecting defaulters to submit to the jurisdiction of the Church of their own free will, but it needed the help of the state and the imposition of civil penalties for spiritual transgressions.

Besides all this, Luther's doctrine of the Church went no way towards providing for the regulation of the financial, administrative, civil and legal affairs of the Christian community.[12] Luther had recovered the *sine qua non* of the Church's being, but in the conditions of sixteenth-century Christendom his ecclesiology was simply not viable. Others would attempt to rationalise the doctrine.

CHAPTER TWO

THE CHURCH TAKES FORM

The second-generation Reformers, Philip Melanchthon and John Calvin, attempt to rationalise Luther's thought and to give shape and form to the evangelical doctrine of the Church. That is not to say that the dynamic nature of Reformation ecclesiology is lost or that the christological centre is obscured, but only that more formal and structural elements are added.

PHILIP MELANCHTHON

In the *Augsburg Confession* (1530) Melanchthon stated the pure Martinian doctrine: 'The Church is the assembly of saints in which the gospel is taught purely and the sacraments are administered rightly' *(Est autem Ecclesia congregatio Sanctorum, in qua Evangelium recte docetur, et recte administrantur sacramenta)*. As Edmund Schlink has pointed out, what is mentioned here is not the word of God in general, or the law, but the gospel only.[1] The German version of the *Confession* is particularly clear that the Church is constituted and defined solely by reference to the gospel. It is the gospel that is believed, the gospel that is preached and the gospel that regulates the administration of the sacraments ('The assembly of all believers among whom the gospel is preached in its purity and the holy sacraments are administered according to the gospel'—*laut des Evangelii*). The tension which would arise in the development of evangelical ecclesiology after Luther is prefigured in the combination of two distinct concepts in the formula of the *Confession*. As Doumergue has pointed out, it is striking that this definition of the Church juxtaposes a phrase characteristic of the anabaptist view of the Church, 'congregation of saints' *(congregatio Sanctorum)*, and a notion more characteristic of the formalism and legalism of the Roman Church, correct administration of the word and sacraments.[2]

Two aspects of Melanchthon's doctrine of the Church faithfully reflect the teaching of Luther. Firstly, Melanchthon holds that the visible Church is constituted by the preached word (evangelium sonans). The Church is the assembly where the voice of the gospel sounds forth entire and uncorrupt (in qua sonat integra et incorrupta vox Evangelii: CR 9. 193; cf. 12. 367f.). Melanchthon's answer to the charge of Platonising the doctrine of the Church is to cite the text from Psalm 19.5: 'Their voice has gone out into the world,' and to draw the conclusion: 'We speak therefore of a Church visible in this world' (Dicimus igitur Ecclesiam visibilem in hac vita: CR 28. 409). The preached word, publicly and visibly proclaimed (ministerium publicum et visibile), is the supreme and decisive mark of the true Church. There are and always will be, as the Apostles' Creed teaches, some saints and heirs of eternal life to be found on earth.

> And these are not to be sought under the titles of pope or bishop, but where the gospel is truly acknowledged and taught ... This word of Christ must endure: 'My sheep hear my voice'! Therefore the Church, or the true people of God, is bound to the gospel. Where the gospel is truly acknowledged, there are some who are holy.[3]

In the second place, Melanchthon echoes the thought of Luther when he asserts that the true Church lives under the cross. The Church of Christ knows nothing of the kingdom, the power and the glory in the eyes of the world (gloriam coram mundo) but is concealed under the form of the cross (est operta formis crucis) and subjected to blasphemy, sedition and persecution (CR 12. 485). It is, according to Melanchthon, the experience of suffering and the cross rather than, say, invisibility or spirituality that distinguishes the true Church.[4] Whatever other elements Melanchthon may have added, he cannot be accused of sacrificing the christological centre.

In Melanchthon's mature ecclesiology, the marks of word and sacrament figure prominently. The Church is a visible assembly which embraces and professes the pure gospel and makes proper use of the sacraments (CR 12. 431; 526; 23. 37;

28. 409). Other marks are sometimes added, such as divinely instituted ceremonies (*ritus divinitus traditos*), confession and invocation of God. All these are visible to men and serve to distinguish the Church from other communities of men (*a caeteris gentibus distinctam*: CR 12. 368). And in the *Loci Communes* of 1555 Melanchthon comments that, besides word and sacrament, some theologians would add evidences of the Holy Spirit, great virtues and miracles 'through which the name of Christ is glorified'.[5] But these do not interest Melanchthon who, as Peter Fraenkel points out, conceived of the Church 'primarily in terms of its function of administering the means of grace'.[6]

The later Melanchthon, disillusioned by theological controversy, harassed by the care of the churches and without the supporting presence of Luther, progressively strengthened the formal elements of the well-established doctrine of the *notae ecclesiae*, thus anticipating the quest among later Reformers for a rigid definition of the Church's circumference. In Melanchthon this took the form of a new stress on the ministry and its disciplinary function. Not that this was a wholly new development in Melanchthon's thought: unlike Luther, he had never conceived of the pure disembodied word going forth conquering and to conquer, but always of the word given through ministers (*per ministerium*: CR 12. 368; 431; 28. 409).

But there now takes place a distinct clericalising of Melanchthon's ecclesiology. As early as 1533 he had mentioned as one of the marks of the Church 'the obedience we owe to the ministry' (CR 12. 433). And in 1545, before the death of Luther, he had prescribed the ministry, discipline and schools as marks of the Church.[7] In the *Examen Ordinandorum* of 1554, regarded by Strohl as the definitive statement of Melanchthon's ecclesiology, a form of discipline has become one of three marks of the true Church: 'I. Agreement in the doctrine of the pure gospel, that is, in fundamentals; II. Proper use of the sacraments; III. Obedience owed, next to the gospel itself, to the ministry' (*Obedientia Ministerio debita iuxta Evangelium*: CR 23. 37). The following year, 1555, when he issued the final revision of the *Loci Communes* (Commonplaces) which had occupied him all his life, Melanchthon departed from the teaching of earlier editions with their two basic marks of the Church, word and sacrament, in adding a third, 'punishment through the ban'.[8] And finally, in his last work, *The Reply to the Bavarian Inquisition* (1559), Melanchthon once again stressed discipline as an essential mark of the true Church.[9]

In spite of these developments, Melanchthon was not moving in the direction of the gathered Church of the anabaptists and separatists; he was not envisaging a tightly defined gathering of true Christians separated from the world and with its own internal disciplinary regulations. To use Troeltsch's helpful distinction, he was not legislating for a sect-type but a church-type of Christianity. What is decisive here is that Melanchthon never denied the mixed and imperfect nature of the Church. In 1530 Article viii of the *Augsburg Confession*, drafted by Melanchthon, had asserted that 'in this life many false Christians, hypocrites, and even open sinners remain among the godly'. And in the *Apology* Melanchthon had commented: 'We concede that in this life hypocrites and evil men are mingled with the Church and are members of the Church according to the outward associations of the Church's marks—that is, word, confession and sacraments—especially if they have not been excommunicated' (BC 33. 168f.). Here the Reformers availed themselves of the old scholastic distinction between the Church 'properly speaking' *(ecclesia proprie dicta)* and the Church 'broadly speaking' *(ecclesia large dicta)*: the former being the body of Christ, the latter the mixed multitude of the Church visible (BC 170).

Twenty-five years later, Melanchthon reiterated in the *Examen Ordinandorum* that in the assembly of the Church there are many who are not saints but nevertheless assent to the doctrine of the Church *(de doctrina consentientes:* CR 23. 37). And in the final edition of the *Loci Communes* it is stated that 'hypocrites mingle in such a gathered company and are included in the confession of the true doctrine with the saints if they keep and confess true doctrine'.[10] Melanchthon's definition of the Church is echoed in the Hungarian *Confessio montana:* 'a visible assembly of those who hear, believe and embrace the pure and uncorrupted doctrine of the gospel and use the sacraments ... to which in this life are joined many who have not been born again but nevertheless are in agreement with respect to doctrine'.

It is important to see that what saves Melanchthon's ecclesiology from veering towards anabaptism and separatism is that for him, as Schlink puts it, the distinction between the real Church and the outward fellowship is 'a conceptual distinction of faith and hope but not an empirical distinction to be realised concretely'. Melanchthon was never prepared to make a certain ecclesiastical structure essential to the Church.[11] Though here he was at one with Luther, the doctrine of the nature and marks of the Church had undergone a certain transformation at his hands. The Church is no longer purely an object of faith: it has become a visible institution.[12]

JOHN CALVIN

In Calvin we find a more external and formal doctrine of the marks of the Church than in Luther. Like Luther, Calvin joins word and sacrament as *notae ecclesiae*; but whereas for Luther the word means simply the gospel or absolution, for Calvin it is more suggestive of correct doctrine and proper Church order. When pressed, however, Calvin is prepared to lay aside all other aspects of a properly constituted Church and will retreat to the word alone as the christological centre.[13]

In the *Reply to Cardinal Sadoleto* (1539), Calvin mentions doctrine, discipline, sacraments and ceremonies and argues that, whereas Rome has corrupted them all, the evangelical Churches have restored them in their purity. But here he is more concerned with those things on which the safety and well-being of the Church depends, than with the essential constituents of the true Church (TT 1. 38f.). Similarly, in the *Commentary* on the Acts of the Apostles, Calvin remarks that doctrine and fellowship, the Lord's supper and prayer (Acts 2.42) represent 'the well-ordered state of the Church' rather than the minimum that is necessary to ensure the Church's existence (CC Acts 1.84). In the definitive edition of the *Institutes* (1559), he repeatedly gives word and sacrament as the two marks of the Church: 'Wherever we see the word of God sincerely preached and heard; wherever we see the sacraments administered according to the institution of Christ: there we cannot have any doubt that the Church of God has some existence.' If churches have the ministry of the word and honour the administration of the sacraments, 'they are undoubtedly entitled to be ranked with the Church' (Inst. IV. i. 9). This represents Calvin's considered and final view, but the position had not always been so clear cut.

In the first edition of the *Institutes* (1536), Calvin had given profession of faith, an exemplary life and the sacraments as marks of the Church. Three years later, in controversy with Caroli, he had mentioned profession of faith, sacraments and discipline. The second edition of the *Institutes*, also published in 1539, reiterates the teaching of the first. In these early statements there is a discernible emphasis on discipline and standards of Christian behaviour. As well as the explicit note of discipline, there is mention of the word being 'honoured' and 'purely heard'—the subjective qualities of Christian response are integral to Calvin's view at this stage.

Calvin's mature position, however, excludes an appeal to Christian behaviour; it does not make discipline one of the essential marks of the true Church. This is all the more significant in view of the weight that Calvin normally placed on the right exercise of pastoral oversight. He undoubtedly regarded discipline as necessary to the proper functioning of the Church. Failure to get acceptance of his proposals for Church discipline had been one of the causes of Calvin's leaving the city of Geneva in 1538, and he insisted on it as a condition of his return there from Strasbourg in 1541. Excommunication has not been contrived by man for his own pleasure, Calvin remarks; it has been ordained by Christ for the government of his Church and whoever opposes it is an enemy of faith and of the Christian religion (CR 53. 123). Its removal will soon bring about the collapse of the Church (Inst. IV. xii. 1). It is simply an extension of the preaching of the gospel—the effective application of the word to the life of the individual (ibid. IV. iii. 6). Nevertheless, discipline is not of the essence of the Church: it provides the sinews of the body but the saving doctrine of Christ is its life (ibid. IV. xii. 1; CC Acts 1.5).

Calvin's overriding concern here is for the objectivity of the

Church; like Luther, he is not prepared to make its existence dependent on the subjective and fluctuating criteria of human states of soul. As Wendel remarks, it is not 'by the quality of its members, which could only give occasion for a subjective judgment, but by the presence of the means of grace instituted by the Christ, that the Church is constituted and can be objectively judged'. Discipline is not of the essence of the Church: it belongs to its organisation, not to its definition.[14] Word and sacrament are the sufficient marks of the true Church.

Even when Calvin discusses the marks of word and sacrament, he seems prepared to resolve the latter into the former. In his treatise *The Necessity of Reforming the Church* (1544), Calvin makes the doctrine of Christ constitutive of the Church and seems to mention the sacraments as an afterthought:

> It is not enough, therefore, simply to throw out the name of Church, but judgment must be used to ascertain which is the true Church and what is the nature of its unity. And the thing necessary to be attended to first of all is to beware of separating the Church from Christ its head. When I say Christ, I include the doctrine of his gospel which he sealed with his blood. Our adversaries, therefore, if they would persuade us that they are the true Church, must first of all show that the true doctrine of God is among them; and this is the meaning of what we often repeat, that the uniform characteristics of a well-ordered Church are the preaching of sound doctrine and the pure administration of the sacraments (TT 1. 213f.).

In the *Genevan Confession* of 1536, Calvin again describes the marks of the Church as word and sacrament; these constitute the Church objectively, 'even if there be some imperfections and faults, as there always will be among men'. Once more he seems to resolve everything into the word as he continues: 'On the other hand, where the gospel is not declared, heard and received, there we do not ackowledge the form of the Church.'[15] The same emphasis is found in Calvin's comment on the life of the apostolic community in the Acts of the Apostles: doctrine, fellowship, the supper and prayers 'constitute the form of the Church visible to the public eye'.

Do we seek the true Church of Christ? The picture of it is here painted to the life. He begins with doctrine which is the soul of the Church. He does not name doctrine of any kind but that of the apostles which the Son of God had delivered by their hands. Therefore, wherever the pure voice of the gospel sounds forth, where men continue in the profession thereof, where they apply themselves to the regular hearing of it that they may profit thereby, there beyond all doubt is the Church.

Here, concludes Calvin, 'The Holy Spirit pronounces that the Church is principally to be discussed by this sign: whether the simplicity of the doctrine handed down by the apostles flourishes within it' (CC Acts 1.85f.).

When Calvin refers to doctrine, he is not thinking primarily of creeds and confessions but, like Luther, of the preached word—though it is true to say that in Calvin preaching carries a stronger underlying emphasis on Church order. As Strohl suggests, for Calvin the word was constitutive not only of the Church but also of the ministry.[16] The Church, the word and the ministry are inseparably related in Calvin's thought, as we see, for example, in his remarks on 1 Timothy 3.15:

The Church is the pillar of the truth because by its ministry the truth is preserved and spread. God does not himself come down from heaven to us, nor does he daily send angelic messengers to publish his truth, but he uses the labours of pastors whom he has ordained for this purpose. Or, to put it in a more homely way: is not the Church the mother of all believers because she brings them to new birth by the word of God, educates and nourishes them all their life, strengthens them and finally leads them to complete perfection? The Church is called the pillar of the truth for the same reason, for the office of administering doctrine which God has put in her hands is the only means for preserving the truth, that it may not pass from the memory of men. In consequence, this commendation applies to the ministry of the word, for if it is removed God's truth will fall (CC Timothy 232).

In the same place Calvin describes the ministry of the word as 'the true mark of the Church'. In fact, Emile Doumergue, after tracing Calvin's teaching on the *notae* through the various editions of the *Institutes* and Calvin's other works, concludes that undoubtedly, for Calvin, the principal mark of the Church is the preaching of the word.[17]

By stressing the ministry in this way, is Calvin in danger of clericalising the doctrine of the Church and so of sapping the power at the centre of the Church's life? Calvin does not in fact intend a movement away from the christological centre of the ecclesiology of Luther and the early Melanchthon towards a clerically dominated concept of the Church, for Calvin's doctrine is to be interpreted in a christological sense—i.e., in relation to the saving knowledge of Christ, though perhaps the Christ of the law as well as of the gospel. Doumergue sees Calvin's fundamental ecclesiological principle as the reign of Christ, 'la Christocratie', and finds it expressed in the earliest edition of the *Institutes*.[18] Furthermore, the fact that Calvin is often content to join Christ and the word without going on to draw out the implications for Church order suggests that his stress on the preached word is not intended as a clericalisation of the Church.

That there is a universal Church, that there has been from the beginning of the world and will be even to the end, we all acknowledge. The appearance by which it may be recognised is the question. We place it in the word of God or (if anyone would so put it), since Christ is her head, we maintain that as a man is recognised by his face, so she is to be beheld in Christ ... But as the pure preaching of the gospel is not always exhibited, neither is the face of Christ always conspicuous. Thence we infer that the Church is not always discernible by the eyes of men, as the examples of many ages testify ... Let us hold then that the Church is seen where Christ appears and where his word is heard (TT 1. 102f.).

Calvin then refers to the good shepherd whose voice the

sheep hear and follow. In the *Reply to Cardinal Sadoleto*, he again invokes this passage which was never far from the thoughts of the Reformers when they considered the nature of the Church. We have no wish, says Calvin, to lead people away from the Church catholic and its worship. But what is the Church and where is it to be found? It is all very well for Sadoleto to speak grandly of the Spirit inspiring the universal Church but, Calvin asks,

> What becomes of the word of the Lord, that clearest of all marks *(maxima perspicua illa nota)*, and which the Lord himself, in pointing out the Church, so often recommends to us? For seeing how dangerous it would be to boast of the Spirit without the word, he declared that the Church is indeed governed by the Holy Spirit, but in order that the government might not be vague and unstable, he annexed it to the word. For this reason Christ exclaims that those who are of God hear the word of God, that his sheep are those who recognise his voice as that of their shepherd (TT 1. 35).

It is characteristic of the Reformers that, fighting on two fronts, against Rome and the sectaries, they accused both adversaries of the same error, the claim to private inspiration and prerogatives overriding the revealed word.

As a final example of Calvin's tendency to speak of the coinherence of Christ, the Church and the word, let us turn to the treatise of 1547, *The True Method of Giving Peace to Christendom and of Reforming the Church*. 'We are all in search of the Church of God,' declares Calvin. 'We all admit it to have been so propagated from the beginning as to have continued through an uninterrupted series of ages down to our day, and to be diffused at present over the whole world.' But how may we recognise it? Surely not by 'the titles of men' but by 'the truth of Christ'.

> Who of us, to recognise a man, would look at his shoes or his feet? Why then, in surveying the Church, do we not begin at its head, seeing that Christ himself invites us to do so? He says, 'where the carcase is, there will the eagles be gathered together' (Matthew 24.28). Wherefore, if we

would unite in holding the unity of the Church, let it be by a common consent only to the truth of Christ (TT 3. 266).

Calvin's position is transitional between that of Luther with its radical holding to the christological centre and that of the later Reformed and puritan tradition with its stress on discipline. Calvin's ecclesiology is distinguished from that of some of his successors by his perception that discipline, for all its importance to him, belonged not to the *esse* of the Church but to its *bene esse*, not to its being as such but to its well-being, and that it is Christ himself and not merely 'the law' that reigns in the Christian community. Calvin's doctrine of the Church was, as Ganoczy has argued, continuous with Luther's: they shared the concept of the word as the word preached, and for both Reformers the word was decisive and central to the existence of the Church. As Clavier has pointed out in his study of Calvin's doctrine of the word, the word of God is the mark and *raison d'être* not only of the individual congregation but also of the Church universal.[19]

CHAPTER THREE

PROBLEMS IN EVANGELICAL ECCLESIOLOGY

Word and sacrament were not regarded by Luther and Calvin as empirical evidence on the basis of which one could proceed, on a merely human or rational level, to deduce the existence of the Church. A leap of faith was still required. The Church is a high, deep, hidden thing which one may neither perceive nor see but must grasp only by faith. As Hans Küng has commented: 'The signs of a true Church, although they can be seen from a distance, cannot be read with objective impartiality as though they were street numbers, but only really recognised and understood in the blind leap of a trusting faith.' Word and sacrament are 'not really distinguishing features'. Only the believer knows the gospel to be the gospel, the power of God unto salvation, and the sacrament to be the sacrament, the body of Christ.

Men of the Reformation period wanted a less paradoxical way of identifying the true Church: they sensed that the *notae ecclesiae* were not watertight and foolproof criteria. As Küng has remarked: 'It cannot be denied that on the basis of these two criteria alone, it became more and more difficult to distinguish the protestant Church from the catholic Church or from enthusiastic sects.' It was precisely in relation to the problem of defining the status of Rome that the anomalies of the evangelical position manifested themselves.[1]

Luther and Calvin were driven to use frankly ambiguous language about the Church of Rome. The doctrine of the *notae ecclesiae* could not fully account for her position. Rome had baptism but had corrupted the eucharist and obscured the gospel. The Reformers can be found to say both that Rome is and is not a Church.

LUTHER'S VIEW OF THE CHURCH OF ROME

Luther acknowledges that the evangelicals have received the great Christian heritage from the papists.

> We on our part confess that there is much that is Christian and good under the papacy; indeed everything that is Christian and good is to be found there and has come to us from this source. For instance, we confess that in the papal Church there are the true holy Scriptures, true baptism, the true sacrament of the altar, the true keys to the forgiveness of sins, the true office of the ministry, the true catechism in the form of the Lord's Prayer, the Ten Commandments and the articles of the Creed (LW 41. 231f.).

The undeniable fact that the papists possess all these means of grace and yet have corrupted them all makes it impossible for Luther either to deny them the title of Church at all or to concede them the title without qualification:

> The pope declares that he is the Christian Church. We deny this, although we admit that in the papacy there are some people who are members of the Christian Church, just as there are many such among the Turks, in France or in England. They are baptised, they have the gospel, they use the sacraments properly and they are true Christians ... We are ready to concede that they are in the Christian Church, but not that they are the true members of the Church. To be sure, they have the pulpit, baptism, the ministry, the sacrament, and they are in the Church; but they are not genuine members ... You must distinguish between the genuine Christian Church, the true Church, and the Church which presumes to be the Church but is not. The false Church has only the appearance, although it also possesses the Christian offices.

As Luther accepts without reservation the mixed nature of the Church and the doctrine that the unworthiness of the minister 'hinders not the effect of the sacrament', as the *Thirty-nine Articles* of the Church of England put it, it is surprising that he should go on to assert that 'even a knave is able to baptise, read the gospel, go to the sacrament and recite the Ten Commandments. All this is and remains proper, but he remains a vile knave and is not to be called a Christian or the Christian Church.' The corrupt papists are found in the Church 'just as mouse droppings are found among the pepper or tares among the grain: they merely help to fill the bushel'. Luther's colourful imagination embroiders St Paul's analogy of the Church as a body with both noble and ignoble members: 'A body may possess fine, sound and useful members which man can employ for his various needs; but that same body may also contain perspiration, secretion from the eyes, nasal mucus, scabs, abscesses and other filth ... Filth is still a part of the body even though it stinks' (LW 23. 286; cf. 24. 206). It is solely the means of grace which preserve some semblance of a Church among the papists: 'the pope is the Christian Church in as much as he holds to baptism, the gospel and holy writ. But since he opposes the gospel and is the enemy of all true Christians, he shows that he has fallen away from Christ and baptism' (LW 23. 417).

The Reformers are brought up against this problem of the status of Rome most notably in their exposition of St Paul's epistles to the Corinthians and to the Galatians, where the apostle at one and the same time addresses them as the Churches of Christ and charges them with departing from the gospel. Once again the Reformers declare that the presence or absence of the divinely instituted means of grace is the decisive factor. So Luther, commenting on Galatians (1535), says:

> Today we still call the Church of Rome holy and all its sees holy, even though they have been undermined and their ministers are ungodly ... Although the city of Rome is worse than Sodom and Gomorrah, nevertheless there remain in it baptism, the sacraments, the voice and text of the gospel, the sacred Scriptures, the ministries, the name of Christ and the name of God. Whoever has these, has them; whoever does not have them, has no excuse, for *the treasure is still there* ... If these are preserved among a people, that people is called holy (LW 25. 24, my italics).

Therefore, Luther concludes, although the Galatians had been led astray, baptism, the word and the name of Christ still continued among them. 'Wherever the substance of the word and the sacraments abides, there the holy Church is present. The Church is universal throughout the world, wherever the gospel of God and the sacraments are present. The Jews, the Turks and the fanatics are not the Church because they oppose and deny these things' (ibid., 25f.). It is not accidental that Rome is not among those excluded from the Church. (Luther was not always consistent in totally excluding the anabaptists from the Church; a moment before he had said: 'The Church is holy even where the fanatics are dominant, so long as they do not deny the word and the sacraments; if they deny these, they are no longer the Church.')

The Reformation doctrine of justification—*simul peccator et iustus*: at the same time sinful and justified—enabled the Reformers to live with such a paradoxical position. They held that faith and the other Christian virtues could only thrive in the presence of their opposites. They took up and developed the texts of Scripture that speak of antichrist sitting in the temple of God, God reigning in the midst of his enemies, and Satan being present among the sons of God (2 Thessalonians 2.4; Psalm 110.2; Job 1.6). According to Luther, antichrist 'takes his seat not in a stable of fiends or in a pigsty or in a congregation of unbelievers, but in the highest and holiest place possible, namely, in the temple of God' (LW 24. 24f.).

To this context belongs also Luther's teaching that the true Church is concealed under its opposite. It has a double aspect: in the eyes of God it is a pure, holy, spotless dove, but in the eyes of the world 'the Church is like its bridegroom Christ: hacked to pieces, marked with scratches, despised, crucified, mocked' (LW 54. 262). What is this assembly that is called the Church? Luther asks. 'It is a tiny little flock of the most wretched, forlorn and hopeless men in the sight of the world' (LW 6. 149). The Christian Church cannot be without 'suffering, persecution and dying, yes, not without sin either' (WA 7. 684). 'The face of the Church is the face of one who is a sinner, troubled, forsaken, dying and full of distress.'[2] Luther returns again and again to this contrast in his great work on Genesis. Just as Jacob, his wives 'and his whole Church' dwelt in the idolatrous house of Laban, 'so to the end of the world the false Church will be joined to the true Church and false brethren to godly and sincere brethren. We today teach the gospel purely and faithfully, but we have an admixture of usurers, papists, heretics and sectarians, for the tares always remain mixed with the wheat' (LW 6. 32). Acceptance of the reality of the mixed nature of the Church enables Luther to speak of it on the one hand as the bride of Christ and on the other as a wretched assemblage *(armes heufflin)*. The Church seems such a worthless habitation, but to the eyes of faith it is an ivory palace enshrining the word of God (WA 49. 684, 502).

Rich, profound, paradoxical this doctrine may be, but operating within the limits of the *notae ecclesiae*, it could not account satisfactorily for the position of Rome. In his study of the Lutheran confessions, Edmund Schlink concludes: 'Taking all their statements together, we find that the confessions refer to the Roman Church both as Church and as nonchurch, and do this in a manner that leaves things unadjusted and unsatisfactory for systematic thinking. The question is left open whether the Church is still there and where it is to be found there.'[3]

CALVIN'S VIEW OF THE CHURCH OF ROME

Calvin's discussions of the matter largely follow the lines laid down by Luther and, because they take place in the context of the doctrine of the *notae ecclesiae*, are equally inconclusive. Calvin is no perfectionist; he accepts the mixed nature of the Christian community. The assemblies of the godly, he remarks, seem 'to be something like sinks and bilges holding all the dregs of society' (CC Acts 1.5). In his treatment of the Church of Rome in the *Institutes* he alternates between criticism of the papacy on principle, namely, that it has become so secularised as to be nothing more than 'a temporal court' that can have no place in the Church of God (IV. vii. 26), and condemnation of it on the grounds of the corruption and immorality of its members. Given Calvin's rejection of discipline and holiness of life as essential marks of the Church, the worldliness of the Renaissance papacy would not of itself exclude the Roman Church from the Christian fold in Calvin's view.

'Is it not surprising', he asks, 'that the title of Church should have been allowed to the Galatians who had almost deserted Christ?' Calvin's reply is far from idealistic: 'Where they professed Christianity, worshipped one God, used the sacraments and had some kind of ministry, there remained the marks of the Church' (CC Galatians 10). We may compare his remarks on the similar situation at Corinth. Why should Paul have recognised the Church at Corinth? No doubt because they preserved the word and sacraments, Calvin replies. But, recognising that as it stands this is not a full answer, he continues:

> Although some defects had crept into the administration of the supper, discipline and moral tone had greatly declined, the simplicity of the gospel was despised, they had surrendered themselves to ostentation and display, they were broken up into various parties through the ambition of their ministers: nevertheless, because they held on to the fundamental teaching—the one God was worshipped by them and was invoked in the name of Christ—they rested their confidence of salvation in Christ and they had a ministry which was not wholly corrupt. For these reasons the Church still continued to exist among them.

In conclusion Calvin again has to stretch the concept of the *notae* to breaking point: 'Hence wherever the worship of God is unimpaired and that fundamental teaching of which I have spoken persists, there we may without difficulty decide, the Church exists' (CC 1 Corinthians 17f.). A similar statement occurs in the 1539 edition of the *Institutes*: 'I hold that the Church exists where the doctrine is preached which as a foundation sustains it. And even if this preaching is strewn with blemishes *(naevis aspersa)*, so long as the fundamental doctrine is safe and sound I am satisfied that it remains entitled to the name of Church.'[4] What then did Calvin make of the position of Rome?

As early as 1539, in the *Reply to Cardinal Sadoleto*, Calvin is not prepared to write off the Roman Church as in no sense a Church of Christ. 'We indeed, Sadoleto, deny not that those over which you preside are Churches of Christ but we maintain that the Roman pontiff, with his whole herd of pseudo-bishops, who have seized upon the pastor's office, are ravening wolves whose only study has hitherto been to scatter and trample upon the kingdom of Christ' (TT 1. 50). As always, the Reformers' argument was not with the mass of the catholic faithful in their ignorance but with the hierarchical power-structure of the Roman Church centred in the papal curia. But against this the divinely instituted means of grace are effective to preserve the Christian community even though it may be hidden. As Calvin said to the perfectionists and schismatics: 'Remember that the word of God and his holy sacraments have more virtue in conserving the Church than some of its members have in dissipating it' (Inst. 1539 IV. i. 16). Even under the papacy 'some symbols of the Church still remain—symbols especially whose efficacy neither the craft of the devil nor human depravity can destroy' (Inst. IV. ii. 12).

Although Calvin can say flatly, 'Rome is not a Church of God' (CO 36. 563), he will never admit that God has totally rejected his people. If we are faithless, yet he remains faithful and will not forsake his covenant. There is then a Church among the papists, 'but hidden and wonderfully preserved' (CO 40. 354). Some are to be found 'in that labyrinth for whom God has a care ... for the disorder (confusio) of the Church is not its destruction, as God ever preserves some remnant' (CO 44. 320). 'Therefore,' Calvin writes in the final edition of the Institutes, 'while we are unwilling simply to concede the name of Church to the papists, we do not deny that there are Churches among them.' Because it is none other than the temple of God where antichrist takes his seat, 'we do not at all deny that Churches remain under his tyranny ... Churches where Christ lies half-buried, the gospel is suppressed, piety is put to flight and the worship of God almost abolished; where, in short, all things are in such disorder as to present the appearance of Babylon rather than the holy city of God'. But as the Roman Church lacks 'the true and legitimate constitution of the Church', notably the pure marks of word and sacrament 'to which we ought especially to have respect in this discussion', Calvin concludes that 'the whole body, as well as every single assembly, want the form of a legitimate Church' (Inst. IV. ii. 12). As Ganoczy has summarised: 'Ruined, deformed, enslaved, these Churches contain by the grace of God, enough vestiges of their ancient integrity still to be called the Church of God.'[5]

While not wavering from his concentration on the christological centre, Calvin, following developments in Luther's thought, is apparently moving towards a more pragmatic view of the visible Church. The doctrine of the *notae ecclesiae* is a qualitative conception: theoretically one can say without equivocation whether a certain ecclesial body possesses the marks or not. But in practice it was found to need supplementing by a quantitative concept, such as Calvin's concession that Rome contained the *vestigia* of the Church. His *French Confession* of 1559, for example, stated that in the papacy there still remained 'certain slight traces of a Church' (*il reste encore quelque petite trace de l'Eglise*: Schaff, 376). In the light of the accepted doctrine of the *notae*, the position and status of Rome would continue to be unclear: it would remain an anomaly.

THE FAILURE OF THE
'TRUE CHURCH' CONCEPT

In the teaching of Heinrich Bullinger, the successor of Zwingli in Zurich, we have a clear example of the way in which the marks of the true Church were so expounded as to die the death of a thousand qualifications. Bullinger follows Luther and Calvin in asserting that the word of God alone makes the Church. 'The Church is not built by men's decrees, but founded, planted, assembled and built only by the word of Christ ... the Church of God is undoubtedly preserved by the same word.' 'Having given teachers to the Church, our Lord God founds, builds, maintains and enlarges the Church by his word and his word alone.' There are two marks of the Church, word and sacrament. 'Therefore, being approved (*traditum*) by testimonies of the holy Scriptures, it is most certain that the outward marks and tokens of the Church are the word and sacraments. For these bring us into the society of the one body ecclesiastical and keep us there.' In one place Bullinger adds to word and sacrament 'confession of faith', but presumably this could naturally be subsumed under the word.

Now he introduces the qualifications. The mark of the word stands not simply for the essential gospel but for orthodox theology: 'But as to the perfect understanding of the marks of the Church, there belongs this also and principally: that it is not enough to brag about the word of God or about Scripture unless we also embrace and retain and uphold the true sense and that which agrees with the articles of the faith.'

Sacraments, similarly, are only a valid mark of the true Church in the context of proper Church order: 'Unless they are used orderly and lawfully, in the order in which the Lord himself instituted them, they are not marks or signs of the Church of God.' But to say this seems to impugn the validity of baptism among heretics and schismatics which the Church had always accepted, provided it conformed to the trinitarian formula of Matthew 28.19, so Bullinger finds it necessary to adduce in addition to word and sacrament (rightly understood) the inward marks of 'the fellowship of God's Spirit, a sincere faith and twofold charity' (i.e. the love of God and our neighbour according to the Decalogue and the dominical summary of the law). It is these inward qualities 'which make the outward marks to be fruitful and make men worthy and acceptable in the sight of God if for some necessary cause the outward marks are absent'.[6]

In order to close up loopholes in the received doctrine of the *notae ecclesiae*, Bullinger not only has had to rationalise and elaborate the concept until it loses all touch with Luther's radical and simple grasp of the christological centre with its twofold witness of word and sacrament, but also to sacrifice an important element in Calvin's ecclesiology whereby the quality of Christian faith and life was not made a mark of the Church. This was not the sort of clear guidance that the evangelical believer was looking for in his quest for the true Church. It is not surprising that others attempted to cut the knot of ambiguity which we have found in the thought of Luther, Calvin and Bullinger.

CHAPTER FOUR

DEFINING THE CIRCUMFERENCE

A tradition of ecclesiology from Bucer to the puritans and the anabaptists to the separatists attempted to avoid the anomalies that manifested themselves when the Reformers tried to come to terms with the position of Rome, not by broadening but by narrowing the definition of the Church, tightening its circumference by making discipline essential to its very existence. The watchword of this school is found in Bucer's remark in 1538: 'There cannot be a Church without *ein Bann* (excommunication).'[1] This was by no means a totally new departure in Reformation thought. The seeds of the later stress on discipline can be detected in Calvin and even in Luther when they state that the true Church is to be found where the gospel is purely *(pure)* preached and the sacraments rightly or correctly *(recte)* administered. Bucer and Bullinger tried to make this more explicit and, had discipline been interpreted simply as pastoral oversight, discipleship, learning the Christian way and following Christ, there would have been a more or less continuous evolution of Reformation ecclesiology rather than a rupture and the birth of a new and third type of Church—the sect type—as discipline was made a formal mark of the Church and regarded as essential to its being *(esse)*.

It was, in fact, possible to lay considerable stress on pastoral oversight as, for example, Zwingli in Zurich and Cartwright and Perkins in England did, while continuing to acknowledge the mixed nature of the visible Church, accepting the integration of Church and state and resisting separation from the mixed multitude.

NON-PERFECTIONIST ECCLESIOLOGIES

Zwingli stands with all the Reformers in affirming that the Church is constituted by the word of God. 'The Church is not where a few pontiffs meet together but where men adhere to the word of God and live for Christ; and that is clear and manifest to God alone.' In his *Reply to Jerome Emser* (later included in his treatise on true and false religion, *De Vera et Falsa Religio*), Zwingli takes Emser to task for not reckoning with the power of the divine word: 'For you will never know which Church it is that cannot lapse unless you recognise the word of God which has constituted the Church, causes it to trust in him and defends it from error, not permitting it to hear any other word.' Zwingli is of course referring here to the true spiritual Church that abides in Christ and hears the voice of its shepherd; but the Church visible is a mixed company made up of all the citizens of the state and of which the civic community provides the external structure. The magistrate is concerned only with good conduct, outward conformity and the external aspects of Church admin- istration. Thus spiritual and secular affairs can both be carried on—distinguished but not divided—within the one Christian community.

The city-state structure of Zurich society lent itself readily to Old Testament models of the godly commonwealth and medieval ideas of the *Corpus Christianum*. Zwingli's fre- quent use of the parable of the wheat and the tares underlines his acceptance of the mixed nature of the Church. It is within this mixed body that the work of reform and correction must be carried on. The Church must be reborn in blood, declares Zwingli, but, as Robert Walton has commented in *Zwingli's Theocracy*, 'there is no way of interpreting his words as expressing the ideal of a Church made up of a suffering remnant. Both those zealous for rebirth and those not in favour of it are in the Church. The Reformers therefore face oppression because of their labours within the structure not beyond it.'[2]

In England, both William Perkins, an 'establishment' puritan concerned above all for the effective cure of souls, and Thomas Cartwright, a radical puritan, proponent of presby- terian government and campaigner for implementation of the Old Testament Mosaic penal code in place of English common law, who later conformed and wrote against the separatists, held that discipline was necessary to the well- being *(bene esse)* of the Church but not absolutely indispen- sible to its existence *(esse)*. The visible Church, according to

Perkins, is 'a mixed company of men professing the faith, assembled together by the preaching of the word' in which there are to be found 'true believers and hypocrites, elect and reprobate, good and bad'. The Church is 'begun and continued' by the word of God and, in the final analysis, the word alone will ensure the continued existence of the Church, even if other aspects of a properly constituted Church are lacking.

> Indeed it is true there be three things required to the good estate of the Church—the preaching of the gospel, the administration of the sacraments and the due execution of discipline according to the word. Yet if the two latter are wanting, sobeit there be preaching of the word with obedience in the people, there is for substance a true Church of God.[3]

Cartwright, similarly, though a radical who fell foul of the authorities, was never in favour of 'disestablishment' or congregationalism. He shared the concern of the separatists for a disciplined Church and proposed that prospective members should undergo an examination by the ministers before being admitted—for the Church is not an inn but a household, not for swine but for sheep. But while, for Cartwright, discipline is necessary for the 'comely and stable well-being' of the Church, it is not essential for 'simply ... the being of the Church'. As Cartwright wrote against Harrison the separatist: 'To say it is none of the Church of God because it hath not received this discipline, me thinkes is all one with this as if a man woulde say, it is no citie because it hath no wall, or that it is no vineyarde because it hath neither hedge nor dyke.' The *esse* of the Church may exist in an imperfect body, and so the Church of England, though not a perfect Church, could not be held to be no Church at all, as the separatists claimed. Though not a properly constituted Church, it is a Church of Christ where he is owned as head, the true faith professed and where the Holy Spirit has sanctified many of its members. One truly faithful member of a Church is enough to make it a Church of God.[4]

MARTIN BUCER

Others, beginning—as far as the main stream of Reformation theology at least is concerned—with Martin Bucer, the reformer of Strasbourg, not content with this rather pragmatic, compromising approach, were in no way prepared to regard discipline as a dispensable luxury in the Church of God. Bucer is, however, first and foremost, an exponent of the authentic Reformation concept of the Church. With Luther, Melanchthon, Calvin and Zwingli he holds to the christological centre. The Church is born of the word of God and abides in the same. The gospel of Christ constitutes the Church as his living body on earth.

It is not here that the thought of Bucer diverges from that of the other Reformers. As Robert Stupperich has pointed out, Bucer's struggle to establish the foundation of the Church *(der Kampf um die Grundlage der Kirche)* was determined solely by his grasp of the creative, christological word. It is only in his struggle to secure the continued existence of the Church *(der Kampf um den Bestand der Kirche)* that a new departure is made. For this the word alone is not enough; it must be heard with joy and obeyed with zeal. The quality of Christian discipleship becomes a mark of the Church. Love and discipline must be added to word and sacrament to form the true church *(Wahre Gemeinschaft des Worts, der Sakramente, der Liebe und der Zucht)*. Bucer will define the Church, just as Luther and Calvin do, by reference to John chapter 10: 'Heed is paid to the voice of its shepherd.' And in his *Strasbourg Catechism* of 1534, he teaches that the Church consists of all who truly believe in Christ and live by his Spirit. They are assembled together by the word of doctrine *(Wort des Lehre)*, exhortation and the holy sacraments. His later ecclesiology stressed increasingly that the Church is the elect people, forming the body of Christ. This rather mystical and esoteric approach to the doctrine of the Church is, however, more than counterbalanced by a progressive formalisation and clericalisation of the Church.[5]

Bucer gives the marks of the true Church as 'the ministry of teaching ... the possession of suitable ministers ... the lawful dispensation of the sacraments ... righteousness and holiness of life'. Here discipline is tacitly included under the need for ministers and correct administration of the sacraments. Elsewhere Bucer lays it down that there cannot be a Church without the ban, and again: 'Where there is no discipline and excommunication there is no Church' *(Wo kein Zucht und Bann ist, ist auch kein Gemein).* Indeed, as Stupperich remarks, for Bucer, discipline has become the first duty of the Church. Bucer wanted to build into the Church structure a set of mechanisms designed to separate believers from the disobedient. All kinds of people, good and bad, were swept into the Church through baptism. But once they reached adulthood they became subject to the censure, admonition and discipline of the Church. To effect this Bucer created the office of ruling elder which, through the ecclesiology of Calvin who learned it from Bucer during his Strasbourg pastorate in 1538-41, was destined to have a permanent place in the polities of the Reformed Churches. Every adult member of the Church was required to demonstrate to the elders his outward moral fitness to receive the sacrament of holy communion. (We note in passing that the anabaptists, by abolishing paedobaptism, found a more tidy, more radical and more consistent way of achieving the same end, namely, a purified and disciplined Christian community.)

To sum up, for Bucer discipline became a mark of the Church, being added to the word and sacrament specified by Luther, Melanchthon and Calvin. 'The Church which lacks these aforesaid marks', Bucer declares, 'is not to be called the body of Christ. Although it may contain many members of Christ it is not a fellowship gathered by the Spirit of Christ.'[6]

As well as influencing others, notably Calvin, Bucer was himself influenced both by Oecolampadius at Basle, for whom the disciplinary authority of the Church independent of the civil power was essential to the existence of the Church, and by Wolfgang Capito who, at that time, leaned strongly towards clericalism and discipline. Capito defines the Church as existing 'where the word of the gospel is preached and the sacraments administered by the ordained ministers' *(per ministrum).* 'The Church, though born of the word,' declares Capito, 'would never grow strong without discipline.' Peter Martyr who, like Bucer, eventually settled in England, and played a part in the English Reformation, is another who always adds discipline ('brotherly correction') to word and sacrament.[7]

A distinct puritan tradition is already emerging, marked by an all-pervasive stress on discipline—though it would not do to try to *define* puritanism by reference to discipline alone: the old problem of definition, which continues to exercise historians of the puritan movement, is not so easily solved.

JOHN KNOX

The same rigorous approach is to be found in John Knox, though he does not include holiness of life among the *notae*: He remarks that St Paul addresses the congregations of Corinth, Galatia and Thessalonica as 'the trew Kirkis of Christ Jesus, in the whilk not the less wer crymis maist grevous', and concludes that therefore 'the lyfe, and conversatioun of man is na assurit note, sign or tokin of Christis visibill Kirk'. But it is no less urgent a matter to define how the true Church may be recognised:

> We must decerne the immaculat spous of Jesus Christ frome the Mother of confusioun, spirituall Babylon, least that imprudentlie we embrase a harlote instead of the cheast spous; yea, to speak it in plaine wordes, least that we submit ourselves to Sathan, thinking that we submitt our selfis to Jesus Christ.

In Knox's view of the Roman Church there is not the ambiguity that we have found in Luther and Calvin: 'I no more dowbt but that it is the synagog of Sathan, and the head thairof, called the Pape, to be that man of Syne, of whom the Apostle speakis, than that I doubt that Jesus Christ suffered by the procurement of the visible Kirk of Hierusalem.' In fact, Knox adds, Rome is more corrupt than the kirk of Caiaphas that had crucified the Messiah. He adds discipline to the marks of the Church, and no Church can flourish without it:

> As that no commoun-wealth can flourische or long indure without gude lawis, and scharpe execution of the same; so

neathir can the churche of God be brocht to puritie, neathir yit be retained in the same, without the ordour of Ecclesiasticall Discipline, whiche standis in reproving and correcting off those faltis, which the civill sweard doeth eather neglect, eather may not punische.

The doctrine of the *notae ecclesiae* becomes, therefore, according to Knox, the following: 'The nottis, signes, and assured tokenis whairby the immaculat spouse of Christ Jesus is knawin from that horrible harlote the Kirk malignant are trew preaching of the word of God ... rycht administracioun of the sacramentis ... Ecclesiasticall discipline uprichtlie ministered.'[8] We may compare the *Scots Confession* of 1560 which, to word and sacrament, adds 'Ecclesiastical discipline uprightlie ministred, as Goddis Worde prescribes, whereby vice is repressed, and vertew nurished' (Schaff, 462f.).

While it is true, as we shall see, that some of the non-puritan English Reformers can be found to give these three marks of the Church, there is surely a clear difference of emphasis discernible in the pronouncements of the puritan party. We cannot help noticing, for example, the weight which falls on the last word in this excerpt from *An Admonition to the Parliament* (1572): 'The outward markes wherby a true Christian Church is knowne, are preaching of the worde purely, ministring of the sacraments sincerely, and ecclesiastical discipline which consisteth in admonition and correction of faults severely.'[9]

THE RADICALS

The so-called Radical Reformation is wider than anabaptism; it includes movements of dissent in north Italy within the Roman Catholic Church, sacramentalism in the Netherlands which influenced both Zwingli and Karlstadt, the trial of strength in Wittenberg between Luther and the Zwickau prophets who had won over Karlstadt and begun to intimidate Melanchthon, and the violent revolutionary movement of Thomas Müntzer and the Peasants' Revolt of 1525, culminating in the terrible events at Münster in 1534-35. It is, however, anabaptism itself that is significant in the history of the doctrine of the Church. As Littell says: 'In a treatment of the anabaptists, the doctrine of the Church affords the classifying principle of first importance.'[10]

Anabaptism, as a movement concerned with the sacrament of baptism and the nature of the Church, had its birth in Zwingli's Zurich on 21 January 1525 when Conrad Grebel, a layman, baptised George Blaurock, a former priest, in the home of Felix Mantz on Blaurock's confession of sin. The first gathered Church of sectarian protestantism, as G. H. Williams puts it, came into being at this moment. 'The first true sect of the Reformation era was formed when the sacramentarian brethren separated from "the world", so defining it as to include not only the idolatrous realm (as both the sectaries and the Zwinglians saw it) of papal Christendom but also the comparatively oppressive jurisdiction of a magisterially reformed cantonal republic.'[11]

Zwingli soon recognised that what was at issue was the nature of the Church. At first, he too had been inclined to reject infant baptism, but he saw the logic of that position and where it would lead—the Church gathered by baptism on profession of faith and the maintenance of a state Church were incompatible. As Littell has pointed out, the real issue in Zurich 'was not the act of baptism, but rather a bitter and irreducible struggle between two mutually exclusive concepts of the Church'. Zwingli was irrevocably committed to the state Church with its inclusive parish system; the anabaptists, on the other hand, were out to restore apostolic Christianity as they saw it. Baptism became important because it was the most obvious dividing line between the two systems—and, incidentally, because it afforded the magistrates an excuse for suppressing the radicals by force, invoking the ancient Justinian legislation against the Donatists. Zwingli was justified therefore in declaring: 'The issue is not baptism, but revolt, faction, heresy.'[12]

Not to give a distorted picture of the radicals, it is important to stress before we go any further that, for a significant movement on the left wing of the Reformation that shared many of the assumptions of the anabaptists—particularly their vision of a pure primitive Church, its fall and the need for restitution—questions of the Church's circumference and disciplinary procedures held no interest whatever.

The spiritualists, notably Sebastian Franck, Caspar Schwenkfeld and Hans Denck, condemned all sectarianism, compulsion and attempts at discipline. Franck put the fall of the Church at the end of the apostolic age rather than, with the anabaptists, at the conversion of Constantine: 'I firmly believe that the outward Church of Christ was wasted and destroyed right after the apostles,' since when it was not to be found on earth.

> I believe that the outward Church of Christ, including all its gifts and sacraments, because of the breaking in and laying waste by antichrist right after the death of the apostles, went up into heaven and lies concealed in the Spirit and in truth. I am thus quite certain that for fourteen hundred years now there has existed no gathered Church nor any sacrament.

Franck was in no way concerned with the visible Church and its marks; he held all such matters to be irrelevant to the spiritual life. 'All outward things and ceremonies, which were customary in the Church of the apostles, have been done away with and are not to be reinstituted.' Nevertheless, their spiritual reality remains and we must therefore seek the inner, spiritual baptism, supper, ban and gathering for worship. The true Church is in heaven and we are not required to choose between the competing claims of rival Churches, all purporting to be the one true Church and so cancelling each other out. 'If Luther baptises, Zwingli and his Church does not baptise ... Therefore, either none of all the Churches baptises or only one. If only one, where, my friend, is this Church? ... I believe, nowhere.' Franck's answer to the question that so agitated the minds of six-teenth-century men, 'Where can I find the true Church?', is, in effect, There is no true Church on earth; seek it in heaven, in the Spirit. 'Only the free, nonsectarian, nonpartisan Christianity ... is from God, and its piety is not bound to sect, time, station, law, person or party.'

In a similar way Schwenkfeld refused to accept believers' baptism (or the ban), deeming it a new captivity of the conscience and declaring: 'To my mind, I am one with all Churches in that I pray for them, in that I despise none, because I know that Christ the Lord has his own everywhere, be they ever so few.' As Littell correctly points out, the radical individualism of the spiritualists constituted in fact a fundamentally different view of the Church and of Christian history from that of the *Täufer* (anabaptists).[13]

At first sight, the anabaptist movement seems to represent the main aims and tenets of the magisterial Reformers taken to their logical conclusion. This was claimed by contemporary Roman polemicists and it provided a stick with which to beat the protestants. In the sphere of Church and state, for example, the Reformers rejected the temporal jurisdiction of the papacy, believing that the Church, by its nature, could only exercise spiritual power; but they did not conceive of a complete separation between Church and state. Here the radicals went further, opposing any kind of state-Church union (with the exception of the communistic Hutterites for whom the boundaries of the civil and religious communities were identical, the millenarian and utopian protagonists of Münster, and Thomas Müntzer who urged the powers that be to put the sword at the disposal of God and his prophet). Many anabaptist leaders would not permit Christians to be magistrates or to bear arms in the service of the state.

Again, the Reformers questioned certain traditional doctrines such as merit, transubstantiation and a sacrificing priesthood, but continued to share much common ground with the Church of Rome. They all adhered to the creeds, though Calvin was critical of some of the terminology. Among the radicals, however, many fundamental Christian doctrines were denied. Some held to the notion of the celestial body of Christ, thus undermining the Incarnation. The objective doctrine of the atonement was replaced by mystical and subjective concepts such as Müntzer's theology of the personal cross. The deity of Christ and, consequently, the doctrine of the Holy Trinity were denied. Socinianism flourished at the rationalist centre of Rakow in Poland, and Socinus' *Rakovian Catechism* rejected all the main Christian doctrines.

Luther, Calvin and Zwingli aimed at the purification of the Church, distinguishing between the invisible Church of the elect, known only to God, and the visible Church which will always be imperfect. But the radicals were dissatisfied with this worldly Church and strove for perfection. The Reformers sought to restore the original purity and integrity of the sacraments, rejecting any idea of a substantial change in the elements or a meritorious value in the eucharist, giving the cup back into the hands of the laity and recovering the simple supper beneath the accretions of the mass. The radicals, characteristically, went a step further. They abolished infant baptism (which their concept of the Church could not in any case accommodate) and saw the eucharist as merely a memorial of the death of Christ rather than, with all the Reformers—including, contrary to a widespread assumption, Zwingli—as an objective means of grace. Like the Donatists of the early Church, they held the *ex opere operantis* view of the efficacy of the sacraments, believing that the validity of a sacrament depended on the spiritual state of the minister: hence their practice of rebaptism and reordination. The magisterial Reformers, on the other hand, stood with the whole catholic tradition since the middle of the third century when Cyprian had been overruled by Stephen of Rome, in maintaining that the real giver of the sacrament was Christ himself and that, therefore, the unworthiness of the minister could not detract from its objective efficacy.

Although in all these ways the radicals seemed to be simply pursuing the principles of the Reformers to their logical conclusions, there are other aspects of anabaptism that suggest that, rather than a fringe movement of protestantism, it should be regarded as a definite third Church type. Here four underlying principles of radical ecclesiology come into view: its voluntarism, its primitivism, its exclusivism, and its obsession with discipline, with defining the circumference of the Church.

1. *Voluntarism.* For the anabaptists, the Church was a voluntary association which took its spirit and its discipline from those who intentionally belonged to its fellowship. They rejected the concept of the *Corpus Christianum* or Christendom, common to both the catholic tradition since Constantine and the thought of the magisterial Reformers, in favour of the concept of the *Corpus Christi*, the body of Christ. The division between sacred and secular, virtually unknown to Augustine or Anselm, beginning to emerge in the Aristotelian

theology of Aquinas and becoming more pronounced in Renaissance and Reformation thought, became explicit in the ecclesiology of the anabaptists—most markedly in their total separation of Church and state. They replaced the state-supported Church with its parochial structure and magisterial supervision by small, tightly knit groups with internal disciplinary sanctions and specific procedures for the admission or expulsion of members.

Both Luther and Bucer had for a time courted this concept of the Church as it seemed to them the only feasible way of putting evangelical ideas of holiness and discipleship into practice—the masses would always continue in their unregenerate courses. But, as we have seen, when the opportunity presented itself to establish such Christian communities, Luther fought shy of it. It would have been inconsistent with many of the presuppositions of reformed theology according to which the minister and the magistrate were equally the servants of God, following their different callings. Luther knew that, humanly speaking, both he and his Church owed their survival to the protection of the princes. This view is to be found in an extreme form in the thought of Cranmer who was theologically convinced that the king needed ministers, both spiritual and temporal, and was supreme head in both spheres. The king's subjects were duty bound to obey his will. But the radicals polarised the church-state relationship and, without the support and sanction of the magistrate, a strict internal discipline became imperative.

2. *Primitivism.* The anabaptists harked back to the 'pure' primitive church of the Acts of the Apostles. They held that the New Testament provided a pattern not only of doctrine but also of organisation. The concept of the true Church, gathered and disciplined on the apostolic platform was the *raison d'être* of anabaptism. As Philip Schaff remarked: 'The Reformers aimed to reform the old Church by the Bible; the radicals attempted to build a new Church from the Bible.' They accused Luther and Zwingli of tearing down the old house but erecting nothing better in its place. The dominant theme of anabaptist thought was that of the recovery and restitution of the life of the early Church. They dreamed of a golden age of pacifism and communal living, of a Church

untainted by compromise with the world. They held that the fall of the Church had taken place when Constantine espoused Christianity and that the Church had continued in its fallen state right through the reforming efforts of Luther and Zwingli—until, that is, the birth of anabaptism in Zurich. (The antitrinitarians among them, it is interesting to note, believed that the early Church was non-dogmatic and dated the fall from the Council of Nicea in AD 325.)

The concern of the radicals was for *restitutio* rather than *reformatio*; unlike the magisterial Reformers, they sought a repristinisation of the Church on the apostolic model and regarded the intervening fifteen hundred years of history and tradition as a deplorable irrelevance. As Littell remarks, this was primitivism both as myth and as manifesto! But the ferment of early radicalism soon gave way to a formalised and legalistic programme claiming the authority of the New Testament and stressing exclusivism and discipline. 'After a short period of general protest, a strict Biblicism triumphed over prophetism and chiliasm in large sections of the left wing, and the restored true Church began to assume definite proportions.'[14]

3. *Exclusivism*. The anabaptists did not regard themselves as a movement within the Church—they *were* the Church on earth, the true Church of the apostles and prophets. They felt dismayed and disgusted by the failure of the magisterial Reformers to follow through the logic of evangelical theology. They looked on them as worldly compromisers, lukewarm, worse than the heathen. The radicals themselves were after perfection, both individual and corporate and, like Luther, they took the priesthood of all believers to mean that all Christians were required to follow counsels of perfection, demanding total commitment previously only expected of religious. Unlike Luther, however, they saw with consistent clarity the impossibility of achieving this except within the exclusive community of the elect. They felt acutely the stark contrast between the Church and the world, light and darkness, and the organisation of anabaptist communities was designed to accentuate this.

Separation was not, however, entirely the responsibility of the radicals themselves: they faced rejection and punishment as a self-confessed threat to the *Corpus Christianum* of the state-Church. As Littell has pointed out, the persecution to which they were subjected heightened the eschatological note, atrophied interest in the general social order and hardened the rigour with which their distinctive teachings were applied.[15]

The anabaptists disdained all association with unbelievers, that is, non-members of their communities, adherents of the state-Churches, including their unregenerate spouses. As Jacob Hutter put it: 'We have sundered ourselves from worldly society and its loathsome life and have gone out from it.'[16] 'Everything which is not one with our God and Christ is nothing other than the strife which we should avoid and flee,' declared Michael Sattler in his *Schleitheim Confession* of 1527, which describes the position of the anabaptists just as the *Rakovian Catechism* summarises what was believed (or not believed) by the rationalist anti-trinitarians.

The Reformers attributed this exclusivism to spiritual pride; more accurately, it was the manifestation of a powerful eschatological vision and sense of being the persecuted remnant. 'From the time of Cain and Abel,' writes Dietrich Philips in his treatise on the Church, 'there were two kinds of people, two kinds of children, two kinds of congregations on earth, namely, the people of God and the devil's people, God's children and the devil's children, God's congregation and the synagogue or assembly of Satan'. Throughout history the children of God have had to suffer persecution at the hands of the children of the devil; it is an inevitable fact of history that 'the congregation of Christ must be suppressed, hunted and put to death by antichrist's assembly'.[17] A profound cosmic dualism underlies the anabaptist view of the pure community, just as it does the exclusive Jewish community described in the Dead Sea Scrolls. As the *Schleitheim Confession* put it: 'Truly all creatures are in but two classes, good and bad, believing and unbelieving, darkness and light, the world and those who are out of the world, God's temple and idols, Christ and Belial, and none can have part with the other.'

The anabaptists, like the Reformers, employ the concept of the true and false Church. For the radicals, the true Church is marked supremely by the note of purity—purity of

doctrine, of usage and of life. The false Churches, asserts
Dietrich Philips,

> do not use the sacraments of Jesus Christ according to his
> word, nor according to his command and example, nor
> according to the precepts and practices of the apostles, but
> according to the world's establishment and the ideas of
> men. Besides this, they remain impenitent in the old sinful
> life ... which is a sure evidence that they have not the pure
> word of God and the true faith, with the proper use of
> baptism and the supper of Jesus Christ according to the
> Scripture.

Where this pristine purity does not pertain 'there is neither
God, nor Christ, nor Holy Spirit, nor gospel, nor faith, nor
true baptism, nor the Lord's supper. In short there is no
congregation of God.'[18] As G. H. Williams points out, the
anabaptist community, the true Church, is not projected as an
esoteric, hidden, mystical reality but is described in 'boldly
visible and mordantly moral terms'.[19]

4. *Discipline.* Without 'evangelical separation', the anabaptists held, 'the congregation of God cannot stand or be
maintained'.[20] The enforced breaking of fellowship was the
only form of compulsion that was possible within a voluntary
association. Just as their concept of the Church is the key to
the anabaptist movement as a whole, so the practice of the
ban dominates Church life among the radicals. 'If anyone
transgressed among them,' recorded a contemporary witness,
'he was banned, for there was the practice of daily excommunication among them.'[21] Members could incur the ban by
'unwillingness to be reconciled with one's brother or to
abstain from mortal sin' and the penalties involved

> exclusion and separation to such an extent that no
> fellowship is held with such a person by Christians,
> whether in speaking, eating, drinking, grinding, baking or
> in any other way, but he is treated as a heathen and a
> publican who is bound and delivered over to Satan. He is
> to be avoided and shunned, lest the entire visible Church
> be evil spoken of, disgraced and dishonoured by his

company and corrupted by his example, instead of being startled and made afraid by his punishment, so that they will mortify their sins.[22]

The ban could operate either within the community by imposing loss of privileges, or extend beyond it in the form of social ostracism or shunning *(Meidung)*. In its most severe form it was believed to entail eternal consequences. As Hubmaier writes: 'Whomever the Church binds and casts out of her assembly on earth, he is bound before God in heaven and excluded from the catholic Christian Church (out of which there is no salvation).' And elsewhere it is asserted that 'as truly as God lives, what the Church admits or excludes on earth is admitted or excluded above'.[23]

The words of Christ in Matthew 18.15ff. provided the *locus classicus* for the anabaptist view of discipline and the ban: 'If your brother commits a sin, go and take the matter up with him, strictly between yourselves, and if he listens to you, you have won your brother over. If he will not listen, take one or two others with you so that all facts may be duly established on the evidence of two or three witnesses. If he refuses to listen to them, report the matter to the congregation; and if he will not listen even to the congregation, you must treat him as you would a pagan or a tax-gatherer. I tell you this: whatever you forbid on earth shall be forbidden in heaven, and whatever you allow on earth shall be allowed in heaven' (NEB). As Littell remarks, this text was 'the beginning of every anabaptist elaboration of the problem of government within the Church.[24]

The obsessive concern of anabaptist groups with the discipline of the Church came to eclipse the primacy (as the magisterial Reformers would have held) of the word and sacraments. A pre-communion ban was prescribed in the *Schleitheim Confession* on the grounds that 'whoever has not been called by one God to one faith, to one baptism, to one Spirit, to one body, with all the children of God's Church, cannot be made one bread with them'. And Conrad Grebel, writing to Thomas Müntzer in 1524, seems to make experience of the true spiritual nature of the sacrament dependent on the ban: 'It is not to be used without the rule of Christ in Matthew 18, otherwise it is not the Lord's Supper, for without that rule every man will run after the externals; the inner matter, love, will be passed by if brethren and false brethren approach or eat it [together].' Even so, discipline was not a mere preliminary to admission to the Lord's Supper: it was needed by the elect at every stage of their Christian lives. Hubmaier laid it down that:

> After the people have received the word of God and through water baptism in the presence of the Church have put themselves under obligation to God to live according to the word, and if they are ready to walk in newness of life and henceforth not to let sin reign in the mortal body, they still have need of medicine, because men are by nature children of wrath, evil and incapable, whereby the foul and stinking flesh together with the poisoned members may be somehow cut off in order that the whole body may not be dishonoured and corrupted.

The anabaptists had made discipline the *sine qua non* of the Church: it loomed over every aspect of Christian life.[25]

THE ENGLISH SEPARATISTS

The tendency towards an exclusive rather than an inclusive definition of the Church, and with it the failure of the doctrine of the *notae ecclesiae* to provide a constructive and coherent basis for Reformation ecclesiology, reaches its term in the teachings of the English separatists of the late sixteenth century: Robert Browne, John Greenwood, Robert Harrison, John Robinson and Henry Barrow. Barrow rejects Calvin's view of the Church, having apparently given up an earlier attempt to reinterpret the arguments which, he claims, his opponents had 'corruptly sucked from Mr Calvin'. 'I have already often, and I hope, sufficiently shewed, how corruptly Mr Calvin thought of the Church, or rather how ignorant he was thereof.' Barrow held that word and sacrament were not a perpetual mark of the Church, and John Robinson that they were not a mark at all. The pride of place that Luther afforded to the gospel and Calvin to the whole word of God, Barrow undoubtedly gave to the ban. It is, he asserts, the chiefest thing of all to set forth Christ's kingdom. As Powicke

justly remarks, for Barrow discipline is almost the clearest
note of a true Church.[26]

Barrow was accused by Gifford of 'judging them to be no
true Churches which have not excommunication'. Barrow
denied this as 'a false charge', but his view of the reformed
English Church is much more extreme than the Reformers'
view of Rome. The English Church, he claims, is 'utterly
destitute of this power of Christ [the ban] and wholly
overruled by the erroneous power of antichrist in his limbes,
these bishops and their clergie'. For Barrow, discipline
exercised by the congregation is vital to the existence of the
true Church. Two or three agreeing together in the truth and
keeping separate from the wicked in their meetings, constitute
a Church, writes Barrow against Cartwright.

> Which people, thus gathered, and leading their lives
> together, are to be esteemed an holy Church and have
> power both to receave into and cast out of their fellowship,
> etc, although they have as yet obtained to have neither a
> ministerie nor sacramentes among them: alwais provided,
> that this be not by any default or negligence in them.

Here discipline is clearly set above the sacraments and the
ordained ministry, though not above the word as such for,
presumably, the members of the Church would speak the
word to each other informally.

Barrow gives a full description of the true Church; it is
dominated by the need for discipline:

> The true planted and rightlie established Church of Christ
> is a companie of faithful people; separated from the
> unbelievers and heathen of the land [i.e., professing
> members of the Church of England]; gathered in the name
> of Christ, whome they trulie worship, and redily obey as
> thier only king, priest, and prophet; joined together as
> members of one bodie; ordered and governed by such
> officers and lawes as Christ in his last will and testament
> hath thereunto ordeyned; all and each of them standing in
> and for their libertie to practise whatsoever God hath
> commaunded and revealed unto them in his holie word
> within the limites of their callings, executing the Lorde's

judgements against all transgression and disobedience which ariseth among them, and cutting it off accordinglie by the power which thier Lord and King, Christ Jesus, hath committed unto them.

Without the power and practice of discipline, 'there can be no Church, no ministerie, no communion ... al their praiers in this estate are accursed of God, and all such as participate with them in the same'. Here Barrow is excommunicating and anathematising all professing Christians outside the separatist community.[27]

Evidently this tendency could go no further; the attempt to tighten the definition of the Church proved self-destructive. The gospel, for Luther the christological centre of the Church, had become stifled by a legalistic obsession with the Church's circumference. It is not surprising that Robert Browne was expelled from his own congregation! We must now, however, turn to the second and more promising attempt to rationalise Reformation ecclesiology, represented by the writings of Richard Hooker and Richard Field, the Anglican divines.

CHAPTER FIVE

A REFORMED CATHOLICITY

The doctrine of the Church in sixteenth-century English theology tends to follow developments on the continent, with the elaboration of the *notae ecclesiae* from the two marks of word and sacrament to include eventually a form of discipline as well, until with Hooker and Field a new synthesis is achieved in which, while the distinction between the visible and invisible (or as Hooker would say, mystical) aspects of the Church is preserved and nothing is lost of the christological centre, the evangelical doctrine of justification by grace alone through faith is nevertheless set in the context of the Church conceived as a visible catholic society on earth. Hooker and Field abandon the received apparatus of the *notae ecclesiae* and—most significantly—the notion of one exclusive true Church in favour of a more open, pragmatic and realistic approach.

THE ENGLISH REFORMERS' DOCTRINE OF THE CHURCH

Thomas Cranmer, working within the stark antithesis of the Church visible and the Church invisible characteristic of early protestant theology—almost two Churches in fact—states the ecclesiological problem as the English Reformers saw it: 'If we shall allow them for the true Church of God, that appear to be the visible and outward Church, consisting of the ordinary succession of bishops, then shall we make Christ, which is an innocent lamb without spot, and in whom is found no guile, to be the head of ungodly and disobedient members.' For the visible Church of Rome, in Cranmer's view, agrees with Christ as darkness does with light, sweet with sour (PS 2. 13). The attempt is therefore made by the English Reformers to identify the true Church by its possession of the marks of word and sacrament. As Hooper writes:

These two marks, the true preaching of God's word and right use of the sacraments, declare what and where the true Church is ... Where the doctrine is sound, and no idolatry defended, that Church is of God, as far as mortal man can judge. And where this doctrine and right use of the sacraments be not, there is no Church of Christ, though it seem never so holy (PS 2. 87).

It follows that Rome, lacking these essential marks, is no true Church; so Jewel declares:

'We truly have renounced that Church wherein we could neither have the word of God sincerely taught, nor the sacraments rightly administered, nor the name of God duly called upon' (PS 3. 91f.).

The third note of discipline was added in a general hardening of theological positions both in the reign of Edward VI when the protestants saw a golden opportunity for further unimpeded reform and in the bitter days of disappointment and dispersion under Mary when the English divines came strongly under the influence of reformed theology abroad.

Nicholas Ridley identifies the true Church not only by the *triplex notae* (adding discipline), but also by the quality of Christian life (adding charity):

The marks whereby this Church is known unto me in this dark world and in the midst of this crooked and froward generation are these—the sincere preaching of God's word; the due administration of the sacraments; charity; and faithful observing of ecclesiastical discipline according to the word of God (PS 123).

And Hooper, who courted stricter puritan views, agrees in adding discipline: 'I believe that the Lord God hath given us three principle [sic] signs or marks by which we may know this his Church, that is to say, the word, the sacraments, and discipline' (PS 2. 43). Ponet's catechism of 1553 mentions

first, pure preaching of the gospel, then brotherly love ...

thirdly, upright and uncorrupted use of the Lord's sacraments, according to the ordinance of the gospel: last of all, brotherly correction, and excommunication, or banishing those out of the Church that will not amend their lives (PS *Liturgies of Edward VI*, 513).

Parker's Eleven Articles of 1559 declare 'that Church to be the spouse of Christ, wherein the word of God is truly taught, the sacraments duly administered according to Christ's institution, and the authority of the keys duly used'. Nowell's catechism regards discipline as desirable: 'yet also in the same Church, if it be well ordered, there shall be seen to be observed a certain order and manner of governance, and such a form of ecclesiastical discipline'—but, human nature being what it is, it 'can hardly be maintained in churches' (PS 174f.). While Whitgift held that discipline was certainly not an essential mark of the Church (PS 1. 185f.), his lieutenant Richard Bancroft, in a sermon at St Paul's Cross, laid it down that a Church 'which maintaineth without error the faith of Christ, which holdeth to the true doctrine of the gospel in matters necessary to salvation, and preacheth the same; which retaineth the lawful use of those sacraments only which Christ hath appointed, and which appointeth vice to be punished and virtue to be maintained' is alone a true Church. Finally, the note of discipline was incorporated into the teaching of the Anglican *Homilies*; the second part of the Homily for Whitsunday states: 'The true Church ... hath always three notes or marks whereby it is known: pure and sound doctrine; the sacraments ministered according to Christ's holy institution; and the right use of ecclesiastical discipline.'

All the English Reformers are agreed—and here they show their essential continuity with the continental Reformers—that the primary mark of the true Church is the word of God. The notes claimed by Rome—unity, antiquity and consent—may equally exist in the devil's Church; as Bradford remarks, 'idolatry among the Israelites had all those three' (PS 1. 551). It is by its possession of the word and adherence to the Scriptures that the Church is to be known. So Jewel writes: 'It behoveth us rather to search the Scriptures, as Christ hath advised us, and thereby to assure ourselves of the Church of God: for by this trial only and by none other, it may be known' (PS 3. 152; cf. Cranmer 2. 25). In his support Jewel is able to adduce the authority of Irenaeus, Chrysostom and Augustine. The hidden complexities, however, of this apparently straightforward appeal to Scripture and the word appear in remarks of Tyndale where standards of orthodoxy and holiness are seen to be involved as well:

> The Scriptures truly understood, after the plain places and general articles of the faith, which thou findest in the Scripture, and the ensamples that are gone before, will alway testify who is the right Church ... which thou shalt alway know by their faith, examined by the Scripture, and by their profession and consent to live according unto the laws of God (PS 3. 44f.; cf. Coverdale 2. 412f.).

The difficulties and incoherencies in the concept of the *notae ecclesiae* which we have already observed in the teaching of the continental Reformers are also apparent in the thought of their English counterparts: the *notae*, ostensibly a clear guide to the evangelical believer in his search for the one true Church on earth and an effective antidote to the arguments of catholic polemicists, were found to need such a degree of elaboration and qualification as to lose their value to all practical intents and purposes. Besides this, the English Reformers experienced the same difficulties as Luther and Calvin in accounting for the position and standing of the Church of Rome.

The official declarations of doctrine put out during the reign of Henry VIII had allowed that Rome was to be regarded as a part of the true Church. This followed from Henry's desire for a limited reformation on the Erasmian rather than the Lutheran pattern which would enable him to retain many of the advantages of the papal system—particularly the centralisation of power—while avoiding the revolutionary ferment of protestant theology. *The Institution of a Christian Man* (1537) and *A Necessary Doctrine and Erudition for any Christian Man* (1543), known respectively as *The Bishops' Book* and *The King's Book*, set forth a doctrine of the Church which could accommodate Rome within its scheme.

The Christian Church is a mixture of good and bad; it can err and parts of it can go into schism or heresy without ceasing to be of the Church. Even the wicked are to be accounted as true members of Christ's mystical body until the Church has pronounced its sentence of excommunication.

After the false dawn of Edward's reign and the troubled interlude or Mary's, Anglican divines returned to this more eirenic attitude to the Church of Rome. Both William Fulke's *A Retentive to stay good Christians* (1577) and Oliver Carter's *An Answere unto certaine Popish Questions and Demaundes* (1579) accepted that papists could be saved notwithstanding their errors. This view was followed in Gifford's *A Short Treatise Against the Donatists of England* (1589), which claimed that Rome was a part of the Church. Gifford had strong presbyterian leanings and after 1584 was suspended from his living for nonconformity, but his views are as moderate and tolerant as those of Hooker. 'Whosoever believeth in the Son of God shall be saved, though he be full of errors, full of infirmities and deformities, both in body and soul, labouring to be purged. ' Gifford was writing against the separatists who, he claimed, 'condemne them all as infidels and prophane, which professe the faith of Christ, because notwithstanding they do it in some weaknesse and infirmities'.

For Hooker, to whom we must look for a way out of the impasse created by the ambiguities of Reformation ecclesiology, the moral problem of the salvation of those who had lived and died within the Roman communion was a matter of passionate concern. Reflection on this gave a radically new turn to the protestant doctrine of the Church.[1]

RICHARD HOOKER

Hooker's controversy with the puritans was not merely concerned with secondary questions such as Church polity, where he sought to refute the claims of the presbyterians and to defend a moderate doctrine of episcopacy, or even with the problems of authority, where he argued for the place of reason, antiquity and consent against the exclusive biblicism of the strict Calvinists. The issue was fundamentally, as both Hooker himself and Archbishop Whitgift realised, one concerning the salvation of 'our fathers'. Englishmen who had 'lived and died' in communion with Rome in the centuries before the Reformation were to be regarded as 'not *Papists*, but *our* fathers', as Whitgift put it (HW 1. 64). The entire Western Church was not to be written off with the papacy for it was, as Field, for example, more than once points out, 'that wherein all our fathers lived and died' (FC 4. 526f.; 2. 171). If Rome were put utterly beyond the pale, being held to be no true Church, there could be, as Hooker saw clearly, no hope of salvation for 'thousands of our fathers living in popish superstitions' (HW 3. 501).

Once again, the interpretation of the Epistle to the Galatians proved crucial. Unlike Luther and Calvin, Walter Travers, Hooker's lecturer at the Temple Church and his first adversary in this debate, asserted that the Galatians were excluded from salvation (HW 1. 51n.). Against this, Hooker, who accepts with all the Reformers and his puritan opponents that the doctrine of justification is the *articulus stantis aut cadentis ecclesiae*, argues in the great sermon 'Of Justification, Works, and how the Foundation of Faith is Overthrown' that Rome errs not in the essential matter of redemption itself, but in its application. If she does overthrow the foundation of faith, it is only 'by a consequent' (HW 3. 505). Not that Hooker has any wish to exculpate Rome and her errors: 'This is the mystery of the man of sin. This maze the Church of Rome doth cause her followers to tread, when they ask her the way of justification' (HW 3. 489). Nevertheless, a distinction must be made between the leaders and the led, those who embrace heresy and error with their eyes open, as it were,. and those, on the other hand, who imbibe it unwittingly (HW 3. 499). The latter might well touch the hem of Christ's garment and be saved: 'I may, I trust without offence, persuade myself that thousands of our fathers in former times, living and dying within her [Rome's] walls, have found mercy at the hand of God' (HW 3. 503). As for the former, the theologically articulate, so to speak, who consciously maintain the official doctrine of the post-Tridentine Roman Church 'that we cannot be saved by Christ alone without works:· they do not only by a circle of consequence, but directly, deny the foundation of faith; they hold it not, no not so much as by a slender thread' (HW 3. 505).

But Hooker is not primarily concerned with these. His point is that even those who die in unconscious error may be saved by the mercy of God (Travers held that they would be saved if they repented and came to a knowledge of the truth before death; hence the significance of the oft-repeated phrase in the writings of the Anglican divines: 'lived and died'). 'What although they repented not of their errors?' asks Hooker. 'God forbid that I should open my mouth to gainsay that which Christ himself hath spoken: "Except ye repent, ye shall all perish." And if they did not repent, they perished.' But what sort of repentance is required here? 'We have the benefit of a double repentance,' Hooker points out—general as well as particular, and sins not confessed in particular may be covered by a general confession, such as those provided in the *Book of Common Prayer*. Hooker does not dispute that sin is damnable or the need for repentance to be saved; he cogently points out, however, that no confession, no matter how scrupulous and particular, will cover all actual sin. 'The least sin which we commit in deed, word, or thought, is death, without repentance. Yet how many things do escape us in every one of these, which we do not know, how many which we do not observe to be sins! and without the knowledge, without the observation of sin, there is no actual repentance.' The conclusion is inescapable, claims Hooker,

> that for as many as hold the foundation, and have all known sin and error in hatred, the blessing of repentance for unknown sins and errors is obtained at the hands of God, through the gracious mediation of Christ Jesus, for such suitors as cry with the prophet David, 'Purge me, O Lord, from my secret sins.' (HW 3. 503f.).

The view that a papist might be saved was of fundamental and far-reaching importance for the shape of Hooker's ecclesiology and, furthermore, as Sisson has pointed out, 'it was a bold position to take up in days when catholicism was treason as well as heresy, when extreme puritans were only too ready to read Rome into Canterbury and antichrist into both'.[2] But Hooker felt passionately about this: 'Let me die, if ever it be proved, that simply an error doth exclude ... utterly from hope of life. Surely, I must confess unto you, if it be an error to think that God may be merciful to save men even when they err, my greatest comfort is my error; were it not for the love I bear unto this error, I would neither wish to speak nor to live' (HW 3. 543).

This conviction led Hooker to define the visible Church in a more empirical and pragmatic way than the Reformers— both on the continent and in England—had done, by reference to its outward profession of faith, taken at its face value. That profession centres on (in the words of St Paul) the Church's one Lord, one faith, one baptism (Ephesians 4.5):

> The unity of which visible body and Church of Christ consisteth in that uniformity which all several persons therunto belonging have, by reason of that *one Lord* whose servants they all profess themselves, that *one faith* which they all acknowledge, that *one baptism* wherewith they are all initiated. The visible Church of Jesus Christ is therefore one in outward profession of those things which supernaturally appertain to the very essence of Christianity, and are necessarily required in every particular Christian man (HW 1. 339).

This definition enables Hooker to spread his net very widely. It obviously includes Rome as well as 'impious idolaters, wicked heretics, persons excommunicable, yea and cast out for notorious improbity'. These latter, though still within the visible Church, are to be regarded as 'the imps and limbs of Satan, even as long as they continue such'. Thus Hooker's doctrine of the Church is not without its own element of paradox; his rationalising of Reformation ecclesiology has not ironed out the mystery and paradox that mark authentic evangelical theology of the protestant Reformation just as they do the carefully balanced structure of Thomism or the great antinomies of Greek and Russian Orthodox theology.

In Hooker, protestant thought retains its tensions and power to disturb and perplex. For it is possible, according to

Hooker, that 'the selfsame men should belong both to the synagogue of Satan and to the Church of Jesus Christ' (though not 'unto that Church which is his mystical body').

> Howbeit, of the visible body and Church of Jesus Christ those may be and oftentimes are, in respect of the main parts of their outward profession, who in regard of their inward disposition of mind, yea of external conversation, are most worthily both hateful in the sight of God himself, and in the eyes of the sounder part of the visible Church most execrable (HW 1. 342).

It is explicit in what Hooker says that he has only excluded 'Saracens, Jews, and Infidels' from the Church.

Hooker's broad view of the visible Church as a mixed, imperfect society in which all who make the Christian profession—notwithstanding their heretical notions or schismatical tendencies—must be included until the Church has pronounced in their case, is not without precedent in sixteenth-century English theology. Closely comparable ideas were contained in the doctrinal statements of Henry VIII's reign and had been revived by earlier writers under Elizabeth. Even Whitgift, who had written his doctoral dissertation on the thesis that the pope is antichrist, held that papists and heretics are to be regarded as members of the Church unless and until they are excommunicated (PS 1. 386f.).

In the writings of Richard Hooker, however, against the background of separatism and rigorist puritanism, on the one hand, that would not acknowledge even the Church of England—let alone Rome—as a true Church, and, on the other hand, the catholic threat embodied in the papal excommunication of Elizabeth and the Spanish Armada, the claim that Rome must be regarded as part of the visible Church, however much her errors may be deplored, attained a new clarity, charity and urgency.

> Notwithstanding so far as lawfully we may, we have held and do hold fellowship with them. For even as the Apostle doth say of Israel that they are in one respect enemies but in another beloved of God; in like sort with Rome we dare

not communicate concerning sundry her gross and grievous abominations, yet touching those main parts of Christian truth wherein they constantly still persist, we gladly acknowledge them to be of the family of Jesus Christ (HW 1. 347).

RICHARD FIELD

Richard Field (1561-1616), the friend and near-contemporary of Hooker and who broadly shared his ecclesiological position, published his great treatise *Of the Church* in five books in 1606 and 1610. More systematic and scholastic than the *Ecclesiastical Polity*, it is, like Hooker's monumental work, a foundation document of Anglican theology.

Field is concerned at the outset to rescue the catholic doctrine of the Christian Church from what he sees as its corruption in separatist and puritan platforms. There are those, he remarks—Pelagians, anabaptists, separatists—who, 'possessed with a false opinion of absolute sanctity and spotless righteousness, reject the societies and companies of them in whom any imperfection may be found'. These are the most extreme. 'Others there are which, though they proceed not so far, yet deny those societies of Christians to be the true Churches of God, wherein the severity of discipline is so far neglected that wicked men are suffered and tolerated without due and condign punishment.' Here Field has in mind the rigorist puritans who sought to fence round the boundaries of the Church by stressing the note of ecclesiastical discipline. His verdict on both tendencies is the same:

These, while they seem to hate the wicked and fly from their company for fear of contagion, do schismatically rent and inconsiderately divide themselves from the body of God's Church and forsake the fellowship of the good through immoderate hate of the wicked. Both these do dangerously and damnably err ... (FC 1. 56).

Like all the Reformers, Field is deeply impressed with the way in which St Paul handles the backsliding congregations of Corinth and Galatia:

We see then the difference between the turbulent disposition of these men and the mild affection of the apostles
of Christ, who writing to the Corinthians, and well
knowing to how many evils and faults they were subject,
yet doth not thunder out against them the dreadful
sentence of anathema, exclude them from the kingdom of
Christ, or make a division and separation from them, but
calleth them the Church of Christ and society of saints.
What would these men have done if they had lived among
the Galatians ... ? (FC 1. 58).

It is significant that Field's order of exposition and
argument leads him to state, even before he comes to the
distinction between the Church visible and invisible, that the
Church is composed 'of very divers sorts' who share the
calling of God to be his people, make the outward Christian
profession and receive the means of grace. 'All these are
partakers of the heavenly calling, and sanctified by the
profession of the truth, and consequently are all in some
degree and sort of that society of men whom God calleth out
unto himself and separateth from infidels, which is rightly
named the Church.' And again:

All they must needs be of the Church whom the grace of
God in any sort calleth out from the profane and the
wicked of the world, to the participation of eternal
happiness, by the excellent knowledge of divine, supernatural and revealed verity and the use of the good, happy
and precious means of salvation (FC 1. 26f.).

Following Hooker, Field has by-passed the venerable
protestant doctrine of the *notae ecclesiae* and defined the
Church broadly enough to include heretics and schismatics.
Though it is not within human jurisdiction to judge their
hearts, it cannot be denied that they are found within the
bounds of the visible Church. For 'many were of the Church
which were not of the Christian Church, as the Jews before
the coming of Christ; many of the Christian Church that are
not of the orthodox, that are not of the catholic, that are not of
the invisible Church of the first born whose names are
written in heaven.' All these share the outward calling and

outward profession, though it is to some degree or other defective:

> For there are some that profess the truth delivered by Christ the Son of God, but not *wholly* and *entirely*, as heretics; some that profess the whole saving truth, but not in *unity*, as schismatics; some that profess the whole saving truth in unity but not in *sincerity* and singleness of a good and sanctified mind, as hypocrites and wicked men, not outwardly divided from the people of God ...

The orthodox Church must be distinguished from heretics, the catholic Church from schismatics, the invisible Church of the elect who are 'principally, fully and absolutely' of the Church from the visible, imperfect society which is only relatively the Church. 'They only perfectly and fully in respect of outward being, which profess the whole truth in unity, and they only principally, fully and absolutely are of the Church whom divine grace leadeth infallibly and indeclinably by these means to the certain and undoubted possession of wished blessedness' (FC 1. 25f.).

But Field is clear that there is and can be only one Church (FC 1. 35f.). So the schismatics, for example, 'are and remain parts of the Church of God', as do heretics such as the papists. 'The present Roman Church is still in some sort a part of the visible Church of God, but no otherwise than other societies of heretics are, in that it retaineth the profession of some parts of heavenly truth and ministereth the sacrament of baptism' (FC 4. 527). And Field has no doubt that, in the mercy of God, this was enough to ensure the salvation of its members. In words that echo Hooker's and Whitgift's, Field asserts: 'For we most firmly believe all the Churches in the world, wherein our fathers lived and died, to have been the true Church of God in which undoubtedly salvation was to be found' (FC 2. 171).

For Field, as for Hooker, the evangel recovered by Luther is the *articulus stantis aut cadentis ecclesiae*. As far as Rome is concerned, the decrees of Trent, in which justification by faith was anathematised and the necessity of good works for salvation asserted, mark a watershed. While he is willing to allow that the Western Churches 'wherein our fathers lived and died' continued 'the true Churches of God, held a saving profession of heavenly truth, turned many to God, and had many saints that died in their communion, even till the time that Luther began', though 'oppressed with Romish tyranny', Field now holds that by rejecting the evangelical reform and giving conciliar status to doctrinal errors, Rome has forfeited any claim to apostolicity and catholicity. Before Trent, erroneous doctrines may have been held by some doctors of the Church, but they were not elevated to the status of dogma. Now 'there hath been an apostasy from the catholic faith in the midst of the Church'. 'Formerly, the Church of Rome was the true Church, but had in it an heretical faction: now the Church itself is heretical. But it is still the Church' (FC 4. 526f.; 1. 174, 359f.).

Three notes—not the *triplex notae* of second-generation protestantism, nor yet the 'one Lord, one faith, one baptism' of Richard Hooker—identify the Christian Church as a visible society from the Jewish and other religions. There are, Field asserts, 'inseparable, perpetual and absolutely proper and peculiar' marks which 'perpetually distinguish the true catholic Church from all other societies of men and professions of religion in the world,' namely, doctrine, sacraments and ministry: (1) 'The entire profession of those supernatural verities which God hath revealed in Christ his Son.' (2) 'The use of such holy ceremonies and sacraments as he hath instituted.' (3) 'An union or connexion of men in this profession and use of these sacraments, under lawful pastors and guides, appointed, authorised and sanctified' (FC 1. 65). It is interesting to note that, whereas the puritan wing would have made discipline essential to the Church's existence, Field is not far from their position when he claims that 'the ministry of pastors and teachers is absolutely and essentially necessary to the being of the Church ... For how should there be a Church gathered, guided and governed, without a ministry?' (FC 1. 82).

The radical difference, however, between the ecclesiologies of Hooker and Field on the one hand and the puritans on the other, is in the failure of the latter to appreciate the eschatological and dialectical nature of truth and purity as notes of the Church. As the Anglican divines realised, the doctrine of the *notae ecclesiae*, though a useful rule of thumb in the early days of the struggle with Rome, had proved ultimately to be a blind alley. Hooker and Field no longer saw the issues in black and white; they called a halt to the rationalising process in protestant ecclesiology, and came to terms with the mixed and imperfect conditions of the Church on earth. On the question, 'How can I obtain a gracious God?', they stand with all the Reformers. But to the related question, 'Where can I find the true Church?', they were impelled by the claims of charity and catholicity to give an answer more pragmatic, more realistic and, we might add, more ecumenical.

In the first part of this book we have tried to discover the master-principle of the ecclesiology of the protestant Reformers, the Reformation concept of the Church, and to relate this to the evolving doctrine of the true Church and its visible marks. In Part II we shall consider the question that inevitably arises: If the Church is constituted solely by the Word of God, the gospel, how is that word given and received, and what place, if any, is found in Reformation ecclesiology for the traditional structures of the Church, symbolised by the figures of the bishop, the magistrate and the godly prince?

PART II

MINISTRY IN THE
TRUE CHURCH

CHAPTER SIX

THE WORD OF GOD
AND THE WORD OF MAN

The theology of the Reformation is from first to last a
theology of the word of God. The Reformers' understanding
of the Church is no exception: their ecclesiology is one that is
totally determined by the word. As the Reformers gathered at
Berne in 1528 proclaimed: 'The holy Christian Church,
whose only head is Christ, is born from the word of God and
abides in the word and hears not the voice of strangers.' What
did the Reformers of the sixteenth century mean by the
word? Was William Chillingworth—to take a famous example—echoing the thought of the Reformers when he claimed:
'The Bible, I say, the Bible only, is the religion of
protestants'?

THE INNER AND OUTER WORD

Reformation theology distinguishes between the written word
and the oral word, the inner word and the external word; but
the word of God is not thereby divided for all these forms are
manifestations of Christ the living Word. The Reformers
characteristically thought of God as a speaking God *(Deus
loquens)*, of the gospel as a tale or spoken message, of the
Bible not merely as a book but as preaching, and of the
Church as the gathering of people who listen to the word of
God being addressed to them. In 1540, an enquirer asked
Luther, 'Doctor, is the word that Christ spoke when he was
on earth the same in fact and in effect as the word preached
by a minister?' 'Yes,' replied Luther, 'because he said, "He
who hears you hears me," and Paul calls the word "the
power of God".' Then the enquirer asked, 'Doctor, isn't there
a difference between the Word that became flesh and the
word that is proclaimed by Christ or by a minister?' 'By all
means,' Luther replied, 'the former is the Incarnate Word
who was true God from the beginning, and the latter is the

word that is proclaimed. The former Word is in substance God; the latter word is in its effect the power of God, but is not God in substance, for it has a man's nature, whether it is spoken by Christ or by a minister' (LW 54. 394f.).

For the Reformers, the word is nothing less than Christ, revealing and communicating himself to us in divers ways— through the Scriptures, the preaching of the gospel, the simple formula of absolution, the comfort and counsel of a Christian brother or sister, or the visible words of baptism or communion. These are all facets of the external word. As Calvin says: 'The sacraments are to be ranked in the same place as the word; so while the gospel is called the power of God for salvation to everyone who believes, we do not hesitate to transfer the same title to the sacraments' (TT 2. 400). And again: 'Let it be a fixed point that the office of sacraments differs not from the word of God; and this is to hold forth and offer Christ to us, and in him the treasures of heavenly grace' (Inst. IV. xiv. 17). The treasure of the Church, writes Luther, is the word, for the word includes all divine gifts and graces—*Verbum, Baptismus, Eucharistia, gubernatio divina, consolatio conscienciarum, timor Dei, fiducia in Deum, pacientia Dei, imitacio Christi etc* (WA 40 II. 549f.).

It is not enough for the Church to possess and study the Scriptures: their message must be proclaimed orally, for the oral word is the original and authentic medium for the good news. As Luther says, 'The gospel must not only be written; on the contrary, it must be proclaimed with the physical voice' (WA 8. 33). It is 'not at all in conformity with the New Testament to write books about Christian doctrine'. Before committing their message to writing, the apostles had preached to the people in person and converted them 'with the physical voice'. The writing of books is therefore a necessary evil (WA 10 I. 625ff.). The Holy Spirit speaks—as Luther knew so well from his own experience of unremitting labour on the Greek text of the New Testament—to those who read the word of God as well as to those who hear it, and 'in this way, speaking and writing become identical'; but the fact remains, in Luther's view, that the oral word is more powerful than the written word. 'By means of the written word, however,' Luther admits, 'you can communicate with people more than a hundred miles distant from you' (LW

22. 473). And Calvin takes a similar view, asserting not perhaps the priority, as with Luther, but at least the indispensability of the oral word: 'Though the law was written, yet God would have the living voice always to resound in his Church, just as today, the Scripture is conjoined with preaching as by an invisible bond' (CO 24. 453).

There is, according to Luther, something inappropriate about putting the gospel into books: good news should be uttered spontaneously from the heart not entombed in ponderous tomes: 'The gospel should really not be something written, but a spoken word ... This is why Christ himself did not write anything but only spoke. He called his teaching not Scripture but gospel, meaning good news or a proclamation that is spread not by pen but by word of mouth' (LW 35. 123). Luther marvelled at the gift and power of speech:

> Speech is a great and divine gift. It is with words and not with might that wisdom rules men, instructs, edifies, consoles and soothes in all circumstances of life, especially in affairs of conscience. Therefore God provided his Church with audible preaching and visible sacraments ... The power of the oral word is truly remarkable. To think that Satan, that proud spirit, may be put to flight and thrown into confusion by such a frail word on human lips! (LW 54. 317f.).

The external oral word is dependent for its effect on the secret inner word spoken by the Holy Spirit in the hearts of men and without this it is of no avail. The Church, writes Bucer, 'is born through the word; not through the word of the outward sermon or Scripture alone, but through the living word which God speaks in the heart. This does not sound differently from the outward word, indeed, it is one and the same word, except that God has made it live in the heart.'[1] Zwingli makes the same distinction between the internal and external word. The word we hear in the sermon has not in itself the power to make us believe, 'for if we were rendered faithful by that word which is read and heard, evidently all of us should be faithful, for somewhere or other all of us have either read or heard the word, especially in these days in which all things, even woods and fields, re-echo the gospel'. It is, however, sadly all too evident that 'many both hear and see yet have not faith'. Faith is born of 'that word which the heavenly Father proclaims in our hearts, by which also he illumines us so that we understand and draws us so that we follow'. This is the word that 'resides in the minds of the faithful'.[2]

The sacraments too are dependent on the secret working of God. 'The sacraments are dead elements in our hands,' writes the English Reformer Thomas Bilson, 'and the word a deadly sound in our mouths without the Spirit that quickeneth.'[3] And as Calvin says, speaking of the sacraments, 'What the minister figures and attests by outward action, God performs inwardly.' And again:

> First, the Lord teaches and trains us by his word: next, he confirms us by his sacraments; lastly, he illumines our mind by the light of his Holy Spirit, and opens up an entrance into our hearts for his word and sacraments, which would otherwise only strike our ears, and fall upon our sight, but by no means affect us inwardly (Inst. IV. xiv. 17, 8).

According to Luther, God speaks to men in a twofold manner (*dupliciter*): firstly, through the public ministry of the word and through parental instruction; and secondly, through inward revelation (*per revelationem internam*) of the Holy Spirit. But this is very rare and confined to special occasions (WA 42. 321). Here Luther does not intend to deny that the outward word needs to be accompanied by an efficacious inner word to accomplish its mission: he is in fact thinking of 'the fanatics' who expect 'new revelations'.

Whereas the magisterial or mainstream Reformers always sought to preserve the polarity of inner and outer word, those on the left wing of the Reformation took their teaching about the inner word (itself the product of a reaction against dead formalism) to an extreme, exalting the inner spiritual word at the expense of the external physical word. 'God's word is a fountain out of which divine spirit flows into the believers and renews them and makes them a kingdom of God,'

asserted Karlstadt in 1521. Luther claimed that Karlstadt
called the external word merely a sibilant sound of the
human lips (LW 54. 318), but Luther was not quite fair to
Karlstadt here, for while it is true that he and his fellow
radicals tended to disparage all external means, he himself
did in fact believe that the preaching of the word was the one
external thing essential to the existence of the Church: 'The
Church can by no means live, exist and bear fruit without the
proclamation of God's word.'[4]

The opposite tendency developed among the English
puritans who exaggerated the importance of public preaching,
claiming it to be 'the ordinary means of grace', without which
saving faith could not normally be bestowed. Thomas Cartwright held that merely reading the Scriptures might 'set
forward' but not actually begin the work of salvation, nourish
but not engender faith in the heart. He regarded reading of
the gospel as on the level of natural theology like the
contemplation of God's wisdom in his creatures—able to
strengthen faith already present but not, unaided by
preaching, to effect salvation. Cartwright was, however,
driven to concede that exceptionally God may save through
the instrumentality of reading alone: 'that may be done by the
Lord's extraordinary working; which feedeth sometime with
quails in the wilderness'.

Richard Hooker, who took up the cudgels of controversy
from Archbishop Whitgift, Cartwright's first opponent in
this matter, cited the telling examples of Josiah's reform and
Christ's warning in the parable of Dives and Lazarus that
those who would not heed the writings of Moses and the
prophets 'were not likely to be persuaded by other means,
although God from the very dead should have raised them up
preachers'. Would the puritans really have us believe, asks
Hooker, that 'neither conversation in the bosom of the
Church, nor religious education, nor the reading of learned
men's books, nor information received by conference, nor
whatsoever pain and diligence in hearing, studying,
meditating day and night on the law, is so far blest of God as
to work this effect in any man' without 'hearing sermons'?
Hooker felt that the puritans were in danger of giving too
much glory to the wit of man; he is not happy with the
tendency of the Reformers to equate the word of God and the

word of man and he would have approved of the remark
already quoted from Luther's *Table Talk* that the word
when uttered by man bears the marks of human nature. If, he
asks,

> we did conceive that our own sermons are that strong and
> forcible word, should we not hereby impart even the most
> peculiar glory of the word of God unto that which is not
> his word? For touching our sermons, that which giveth
> them their very being is the wit of man, and therefore they
> oftentimes taste too much of that over corrupt fountain
> from which they come. In our speech of most holy things,
> our most frail affections many times are bewrayed.

Hooker added in a manuscript note:

> If sermons be the word of God in the same sense that
> Scriptures are his word, if there be no difference between
> preaching and prophecying, noe ods between thapostles of
> Christ and the preaching ministers of every congregation,
> as touching that form of delivering doctrine wch did exempt
> both the speaches and writings of thapostles from
> possibility of error, then must we hold that Calvin's
> sermons are holie Scripture.

If the puritans really do mean to identify their own effusions
with the divine word, Hooker remarks, 'let the people
applaud unto you, and when you speake, cry mainly out, The
voice of God and not of man' (cf. Acts 12.22).

Although reacting against one aspect of the Reformation
doctrine of the word of God, Hooker was more faithful than
Cartwright to the early Reformers' conviction that the word
was one and undivided in its operations when he asserted that
the word of God is the instrument of salvation whether read
in private or 'made known ... by lively voice' in public
reading or preaching.

> Belief in all sorts doth come by hearkening and attending
> to the word of life. Which word sometimes proposeth and
> preacheth itself to the hearer; sometime they deliver it
> whom privately zeal and piety moveth to be instructors of

others by conference; sometime of them it is taught whom the Church hath called to the public either reading thereof or interpreting. All these tend unto one effect ... (HW 2. 88ff.).

It was in the context of the devaluation of the external word together with the other means of grace by the radicals that the Reformers, followed by the puritans, so strongly asserted the importance of the public ministry of the word. In the ordinary way, claimed Bucer, God 'does not impart to any adult the inward teaching of the Spirit without the outward teaching that comes through ministers'. So let us banish from the Church of Christ, he continues, the strange doctrines 'that it is not by God's word that man speaks, and that the mind is able to be taught by the Spirit, and not by the outward voice, the things that are of God.'[5] Luther lays down the principle that 'you find no word of God in the entire Scriptures in which something material and outward is not contained and presented'. And again: 'God sets before us no word or commandment without including with it something material and outward, and proffering it to us.' To Abraham he gave the promise embodied in his son Isaac; to Noah the promise enshrined in the rainbow; to us Christ has given the forgiveness of sins in the water of baptism and his body and blood in the bread and wine.

God's justice in the kingdom of this world is embodied in the civil government and the sword of the magistrate. This principle underlay Luther's implacable hostility to the spiritualists and sacramentarians who, he said, think that 'the divine word must set forth nothing but spiritual things and have nothing to do with outward material things. But this is the seed of Müntzer's and Karlstadt's spirit, who also wanted to tolerate nothing outward, until they were utterly drowned in flesh' (LW 37. 135ff.).

In the thought of the Reformers, the word is all-determinative for the being of the Church. It creates and builds the Church and gives life to all its varied ministries. 'The first and foremost of all,' says Luther, 'on which everything else depends, is the teachings of the word of God. For we teach with the word, we consecrate with the word, we bind and absolve sins by the word, we baptise with the word, we sacrifice with the word, we judge all things by the word' (LW 40. 21). Without the word, the Reformers are agreed, even the sacraments of baptism and the Lord's supper remain merely water and bread and wine, dead elements. As Calvin says, 'If the word by which God enters into covenant with us be taken away, useless and dead figures will alone remain.' 'If signs only are presented to our eyes, they will be, as it were, dead images. The word of God, then, throws life into the sacraments' (CO 23. 432; 40. 63). 'If the word is not there,' remarks Luther, 'it is mere bread; but as soon as the words are added they bring with them that of which they speak.' 'For as soon as Christ says, "This is my body," his body is present through the word and the power of the Holy Spirit.' The word is a creative, effectual word and 'brings with it everything of which it speaks, namely, Christ with his flesh and blood and everything that he is and has' (LW 36. 341, 278). This conviction informed Luther's position at the Colloquy of Marburg in 1529 when he withstood Zwingli's view that the bread and wine of the sacrament do not in any sense become or even convey the body and blood of Christ but only signify them. Luther asserted:

> When the words are spoken at the command and in the name of God, then they not only signify, but also at the same time effect and offer that which they signify. Then the words are not only the sound of a man who speaks them but of God who conveys [something] to the person who eats the bread (LW 38. 41).

Preaching too is the authentic word of God orally expressed. As the *Second Helvetic Confession* (1566) put it:

> When today the word of God is proclaimed in the Church by means of preachers lawfully called, we believe that the very word of God is proclaimed (*ipsum Dei verbum annunciari*) and is to be received by the faithful, nor is there any other word of God to be invented or to be looked for from heaven (Schaff, 237).

And in the short table of contents the point is made even more bluntly: *Praedicatio verbi Dei est verbum Dei*—'the preaching of the word of God is the word of God' (not in Schaff).

According to Calvin, God has appointed pastors and ministers 'in his place, to speak as if out of his mouth' (CC Acts 2.391). The power of the word in the mouths of the ministers of God was set forth by Calvin in his *Genevan Catechism* of 1537:

Let us remember that this power attributed to pastors in the Scriptures is entirely contained in and limited by the ministry of the word; for Christ has not given this power to men as such (*proprement*), but to his word whose ministers men are. Let them brave everything, however, by the word of God whereof they are made the dispensers (*dispensateurs*); let them constrain all the virtue, glory and pomp of the world to give place to and to obey the majesty of the word; by means of it let them give commands to all from the greatest to the smallest; let them build up Christ's household; let them demolish the kingdom of Satan; let them feed the sheep, slay the wolves, instruct and exalt the humble; let them engage, confute and overcome rebels: but all this by the word of God.[6]

The oral word is the manifestation of the presence of Christ; as Luther puts it: 'To preach the gospel is nothing else than Christ's coming to us or bringing us to him' (WA 10. I. 14). It is the sole instrument of his kingly rule; as Calvin writes to the Duke of Somerset: 'It is not without cause that it is said that Christ shall strike the earth with the sceptre of his mouth and shall slay the wicked by the spirit of his lips.'[7] The Reformation had been accomplished in the beginning simply by the power of the word, and by the word alone it would be continued and completed. Luther wrote to Spalatin in 1521: 'The world has been conquered by the word; by the word the Church has been served and by the word it will also be reformed.' And later he reflected: 'See how much [God] has been able to accomplish through me, though I did no more than pray and preach. The word did it all. Had I wished, I might have started a conflagration at Worms. But while I sat still and drank beer with Philip and Amsdorf, God dealt the papacy a mighty blow.'[8]

John Jewel, the apologist of the English Reformation and the Elizabethan settlement, echoed these convictions when he wrote: 'Where this word is received, it is fire and burneth; it is a hammer and breaketh the hardness of the heart; it is mighty in operation: it cleanseth the inner man, it is a savour of life unto life, it is the means of salvation' (PS 4. 1164).

The Reformers' understanding of the word—its oral expression, its priceless value as the true treasure of the Church, its power to impart the life of God to man—is summed up in Luther's short treatise of 1521 *The Liberty of a Christian Man:*

> We must therefore be assured that the soul can do without anything but the word of God, and apart from the word of God it has no means of help. Where it has the word, however, it has no need of anything else. In the word it possesses food, joy, peace, light, ability, righteousness, truth, wisdom, freedom and all good sufficient to over-flowing ... What then is that word which gives such signal grace and how shall we use it? The answer is: It is nothing else than the preaching proclaimed by Jesus, as contained in the gospel, and this should be and is so presented that you hear God speak to you.

THE AUTHORITY OF THE MINISTRY

By virtually equating the word of man and the word of God, the Reformers exalted the ministerial office to an extent that, at least at first sight, seems incompatible with their doctrine of the priesthood of all believers. In the case of Luther, for example, his radical interpretation of the gospel as justi-fication, absolution or 'open forgiveness' gave a tremendous authority to the one who absolves, pronouncing the for-giveness of sins in the name of Christ. Here Luther's doctrine gave a power to the minister as great as that of the medieval priest who was called upon to remit or retain sins, impose penance and offer the propitiatory sacrifice of the mass for the living and the dead. According to Luther, the absolver stands in relation to the penitent as Christ does: he is Christ's representative in ministering both word and sacrament.

As the *Apology of the Augsburg Confession* puts it: those

who exercise the ministry 'do not represent their own persons but the person of Christ, because of the Church's call, as Christ testifies (Luke 10.16), "He who hears you hears me." When they offer the word of Christ or the sacraments they do so in Christ's place and stead' (*Christi vice et loco*: BC 173). In baptism, Luther claims, the minister acts 'not on his own authority but in God's stead. Hence we ought to receive baptism at human hands just as if Christ himself, indeed God himself, were baptising us with his own hands.' We should learn to 'look upon the person administering it as simply the vicarious instrument of God, by which the Lord sitting in heaven thrusts you under the water with his own hands and promises you forgiveness of your sins, speaking to you upon earth with a human voice by the mouth of his minister' (LW 36. 62f.). The human agent is purely instrumental: 'A preacher is God's servant and instrument, used by God to accomplish his work. When I preach, baptise, absolve, offer the sacrament, God uses my mouth and hand outwardly in the work that he performs inwardly' (WA 45. 310).

Luther's doctrine of the ministry is in keeping with his underlying conviction that our experience of God is not of God in his naked majesty, so to speak (*Deus nudus*), but God disguised, concealed, masked, mediated. The creator of heaven and earth stoops to speak to us through our preachers; baptises, catechises and absolves us through the sacramental ministry (WA Tischreden 4. 531). In preaching and all forms of ministry we are passive rather than active and God is working through us:

> Those things which the saints speak should be regarded as being spoken by God himself. When, for example, we teach the gospel, baptise, call men to the ministry of the word and ordain ministers, we ourselves do not preach, we do not baptise, we do not ordain, but God is speaking through us. So it is called God's word, God's sacrament, God's ministry and it is rightly said, 'God is speaking, God is baptising,' when he does it through ministers.

'Therefore,' Luther concludes, 'when we speak the word of God, it should not be taken as the word of man' (LW 6. 257). Here the identification of preaching with divine revelation comes very close to being explicit. Again: 'It is a wonderful thing that the mouth of every pastor is the mouth of Christ' (WA 37. 381). Whoever hears the minister preach, hears Christ preach (WA 49. 690). 'You ought to listen to the pastor not as a man but as God' (WA 49. 140). And as the *Augsburg Confession* puts it: absolution 'is not the voice or word of the man who speaks it, but it is the word of God who forgives sin, for it is spoken in God's stead and by God's command' (BC 61f.).

On precisely these grounds the Lutheran Confessions agree emphatically with the pre-reformation Christian tradition that the unworthiness of the minister cannot affect the validity or efficacy of the sacraments or other means of grace. We should look to the office and not to the person. Thus when Judas baptised as one of the twelve apostles his baptism was as valid as the baptism of Peter or John because Christ was baptising through him (LW 54. 47). Luther remarks: 'Christ gives the Spirit to the public office and not to a private person' (LW 54. 90). And Melanchthon states in the *Apology of the Augsburg Confession:*

> We confess that hypocrites and evil men have been mingled with the Church and that the sacraments are efficacious even when evil men administer them, for ministers act in Christ's stead and do not represent their own persons, according to the word (Luke 10.16), 'He who hears you hears me.' (BC 177).

Calvin too declares that the Christian minister stands in the place of Christ (i.e., not as his substitute but as his representative) to give word and sacrament and to pronounce the forgiveness of sins. Nothing is more commonplace in Calvin's writings than the doctrine that what the minister says Christ is saying and what the minister does Christ is doing. 'The Lord himself commands that his ministers shall be regarded just as he is (Luke 10.16). Nor is this surprising, for it is in his place that they discharge their embassy. And so they play the part of him in whose stead they act.' And again: 'He commands them to declare in his name the forgiveness of sins that he may reconcile men to God through them. In short, he alone, properly speaking, forgives sins, through his apostles' (CC Galatians 80; John 2. 207). Calvin can speak as anthropomorphically as Luther of God acting through the ministry. 'The word goeth out of the mouth of God in such a manner (*ut simul*) that it likewise goeth out of the mouth of men' (CR 37. 291). 'He deigns to consecrate the mouths and tongues of men to his service, making his own voice to be heard in them' (Inst. IV. i. 5). 'The glory of God so shines in his word that we ought to be so much affected by it, whenever he speaks by his servants, as though he were nigh to us, face to face' (CR 44. 95).

Calvin draws the same conclusion from this as Luther and Melanchthon—we should look beyond the person of the preacher or minister to Christ the giver of all grace. We should

> not esteem God's word according to the worth of those who bring it to us. For one of the common artifices which the devil uses to diminish reverence for God's word is to place before our eyes the persons who bring it ... Let us take note then that when men come to bear testimony to the forgiveness of our sins and the salvation we ought to hope for, our faith must rise up higher and not stand questioning whether such a man is worthy to be heard or not, or enquiring what manner of person he is. Let us content ourselves with the thought that God by that means intends to draw us to himself.[9]

Other Reformers share this exalted view of the ministerial office. According to Bucer, for example, ministers do not simply announce remission of sins: they themselves remit. They are not like the messenger sent by a prince who tells a prisoner he can go free; they are like the envoy who, in the name of his prince, takes the prisoner by the hand and leads him out of the dungeons to daylight and freedom. His word is fully effectual.[10]

The English Reformers from Cranmer to Jewel and Hooker do not dissent from this view. Hooker's teaching belongs to a different theological ethos to that of the earlier reformed divines, but it faithfully reflects the theology of the Reformation: 'Whether we preach, pray, baptise, communicate, condemn, give absolution, or whatsoever, as disposers of

God's mysteries, our words, judgments, acts and deeds are not ours but the Holy Ghost's' (HW 2. 462f.). Whatever Hooker's criticisms of the tendency of the Reformers and puritans to identify the effusions of the preacher with the voice of God speaking from heaven, he has no reservations about the divine authority of the Christian minister in performing the sacramental functions of his office:

> The power of the ministry of God translateth out of darkness into glory; it raiseth men from the earth and bringeth God himself down from heaven; by blessing visible elements its maketh them invisible grace; it giveth daily the Holy Ghost; it hath to dispose of that flesh which was given for the life of the world and that blood which was poured out to redeem souls; when it poureth malediction upon the heads of the wicked they perish; when it revoketh the same they revive (HW 2. 456).

The Reformers give the highest sanctions to the ministry in its office of dispensing word and sacrament. Luther's revolution was, however, to claim in his doctrine of the priesthood of all believers that this power was the possession of every baptised Christian.

CHAPTER SEVEN

THE UNIVERSAL PRIESTHOOD

The doctrine of the universal priesthood or the priesthood of all believers was at the heart of Luther's reform. It figured more prominently in his popular pamphlets than the doctrine of justification by faith alone. It is not an appendage to evangelical theology; it is nothing less than a paraphrase of the Reformation concept of the Church. In the protestant tradition, the universal priesthood has sometimes become merely a shibboleth, invoked to cast a cloak of spurious sanctity over abuses of the right of private judgment. As Gordon Rupp has remarked: 'The priesthood of all believers never means for Luther what it has sometimes meant in degenerate protestantism, the secularisation of the clergy, the doctrine that we are all laymen.'[1] Here, however, it is important to distinguish between the views of the various Reformers.

For Calvin, the universal priesthood is understood as expressing the relation between the believer and his God. It refers to the freedom of the Christian to come to God through Christ without human mediation; no third party need or may come between the individual and his maker. Christ is himself prophet, priest and king and bears these offices on our behalf: his priesthood is shared with his people.

> Christ now bears the office of priest, not only that by the eternal law of reconciliation he may render the Father favourable and propitious to us, but also that he may admit us into this most honourable alliance. For we, though in ourselves polluted, in him being priests (Rev. 1.6), offer ourselves and our all to God and freely enter the heavenly sanctuary, so that the sacrifices of prayer and praise which we present are grateful and of sweet odour before him (Inst. II. xv. 6).

And again: 'Those to whom Christ has appeared in the

gospel have obtained more than their fathers in as much as they are all endued with priestly and royal honour and can, therefore, trusting to their mediator, appear with boldness in the presence of God' (Inst. II. vii. 2). Conceived of as the ministry of all Christians, as the relation between the believer and his brother, the doctrine of the universal priesthood does not interest Calvin. It is probably Calvin's interpretation rather than Luther's that has been dominant in post-Reformation protestantism.

At the other extreme of Reformation theology, for Karlstadt, the anabaptists and the English separatists, the doctrine of the universal priesthood stands, above all, for the liberation of the layman in the Church. Karlstadt, who took several of Luther's ideas to their logical conclusion, granted laymen the right to perform all the duties normally reserved to the clergy. They could, he claimed, hear confession and grant absolution as a matter of course, celebrate the eucharist and interrupt the sermon if they had something revealed by God to contribute. Laymen could judge matters of doctrine and attend general councils. 'Faith in Christ makes all believers priests or pastors and the pastors receive nothing new when they are consecrated. Rather they are merely elected to the office and to service.' Karlstadt renounced his orders and spoke of 'us laymen' (uns layeen).[2] The radicals rejected not only the Roman priesthood but the ministries of the evangelical Churches as well. So Sebastian Frank declared:

> I believe and am certain that at the present time not a single true and natural word of the Lord Jesus Christ, the Son of God, is acknowledged on earth ... No one, I say, in the whole of Germany, nay more, in the whole world—I speak of those who sound forth their falsified word from their pulpits to the common people, that is, of the swine and the dogs—no one has been called or sent ... they are not sent of God but instead retch out the word solely according to the letter, soiled with human filth, not according to the divine sense.[3]

In the anabaptist communities, the practice of mutual admonition and discipline depended upon a radical implementation of the evangelical doctrine of the universal priesthood. By what right, Hubmaier asks, may one brother exercise admonitory authority over another? 'By the baptismal vow, which subjects everyone to the Church and all its members, according to the word of Christ.'⁴ Henry Barrow, the separatist, wanted members of the gathered Church to take part in 'all the actions of the Church', and approved of ordination by laymen. We have all been 'inlightened with that bright morning star, that sun of righteousness', he said.⁵ In the radical theology of the sixteenth century, the universal priesthood preached by Luther was taken as the charter of the liberation—almost the apotheosis—of the layman. But what was Luther's own understanding of the doctrine?

LUTHER ON THE UNIVERSAL PRIESTHOOD

Luther's statement of the universal priesthood derives directly from his fundamental concept of the Church. The gospel is the Church's true treasure and the source of its life; it is expressed and embodied in the preached word and the sacraments (visible words); the gospel is the possession of every true believer. Thus all Christians are constituted priests by the gospel in its twofold form of word and sacrament, for all partake of these. If we have Christ's word, Luther asserts, we have Christ himself and all that is his, so sharing in his priesthood. 'Now he who has faith and is a Christian also has Christ; now if he has Christ, so that everything Christ has is his, he also has the power to forgive sins; and if a Christian has the power to forgive sins, he also has the power to do everything a priest can do.'

Entrusted with the gospel, a Christian must offer it wherever it is needed, especially in bringing comfort and reassurance to distressed consciences. 'What is the difference', Luther asks, 'between saying, "Thy sins are forgiven thee" and preaching the gospel?' (WA 10 III. 394f.). All this is purely by virtue of the word: 'When we grant the word to anyone, we cannot deny him anything pertaining to the exercise of his priesthood' (LW 40. 21). 'No one can deny that every Christian possesses the word of God and is taught and anointed by God to be priest' (LW 39. 309). Karlstadt, who hastened to adopt and exploit Luther's doctrine of the priesthood of all believers, put it thus: 'God's word is a fountain out of which divine spirit flows into the believers and renews them and makes them a kingdom of God.'[6]

The word of the gospel is embodied in the sacrament of baptism and this is the source of the believer's priesthood on which Luther lays most stress. 'In baptism we proffer the life-giving word of God which renews souls and redeems from death and sins' (LW 40. 23). The fact that all Christians have received baptism invalidates the division between the spiritual estate (the clergy) and the temporal estate (the laity) which was fundamental to medieval society. In his *Appeal to the Christian Nobility of the German Nation* of 1520, Luther attacked the three walls erected by the papists around their privileges to prevent the reform of the Church, the first of which was precisely this distinction between the spiritual and temporal estates which carried with it such dubious consequences as, for example, benefit of clergy.

It is pure invention that pope, bishop, priests and monks are called the spiritual estate while princes, lords, artisans and farmers are called the temporal estate. This is indeed a piece of deceit and hypocrisy. Yet no one need be intimidated by it, and for this reason: all Christians are truly of the spiritual estate and there is no difference among them except that of office ... This is because we all have one baptism, one gospel, one faith, and are all Christians alike; for baptism, gospel and faith alone make us spiritual and a Christian people ... we are all consecrated priests through baptism, as St Peter says in 1 Peter 2, 'You are a royal priesthood and a priestly realm' (LW 44. 127).

When in 1523 Luther wrote to the Hussites advising them to dispense with episcopal ordinations which they could only obtain by subterfuge, he based his recommendation on the principle that in the New Testament a priest was not made but was born, not ordained but created (*non fit sed nascitur; non ordinatur sed creatur*). 'He was born not indeed of flesh, but through a birth of the spirit, by water and Spirit in the

washing of regeneration. Indeed, all Christians are priests ...'
(WA 12. 178).

Christian priesthood rests not only upon the word and
baptism but also upon a divine commission. Luther often
assumes that the ministry is divinely instituted but he stresses
the point that it is the ministry of all Christians that is
divinely ordained. As Werner Elert remarks, 'Precisely
where Luther declares expressly that the office of preaching
was founded, instituted, commanded and established by
Christ, the statement recurs that this pertains to all
Christians.'[7] Christ's commission to the apostles embraces the
whole Church. 'This power is not given solely to the clergy,'
asserts Luther (WA 11. 96; cf. 12. 521; 49. 139). 'The
ministry of the word is the highest office in the Church ...
and belongs to all who are Christians, not only by right but
by command' (LW 40. 23).

What sort of ministry does Luther envisage all Christians
as exercising? What exactly does the power of priesthood
entail? First of all, Luther is in no doubt that it includes the
power to administer the sacraments of baptism and the
eucharist (WA 6. 566; 15. 720). Secondly, priesthood implies
the authority to judge doctrinal questions (*iudicare de
doctrina*: WA 15. 720) and the right and duty of teaching the
faith (*Omnes Christiani ius et officium habent docendi*: WA
8. 423). Luther supports this aspect of the universal
priesthood by reference to a parent's responsibility to teach
the gospel to his family (WA 17 I. 509), just as he supports
the right of administering the sacrament from the common
practice of having midwives baptise infants in an emergency
(LW 40. 23). Thirdly, the universal priesthood is empowered
to exercise the keys, the granting of absolution to the penitent.
But this is understood as an aspect of the ministry of the
word. Luther speaks of the keys 'or ministry of the word, for
these must not be separated' (LW 3. 124). And elsewhere he
says:

The ministry of the word belongs to all. To bind and loose
clearly is nothing else than to proclaim and to apply the
gospel. For what is it to loose, if not to announce the
forgiveness of sins before God? What is it to bind, except
to withdraw the gospel and to declare the retention of

sins? ... The keys are an exercise of the ministry of the word and belong to all Christians (LW 40. 27f.).

Fourthly, the priesthood is an office of intercession before God for the needs of the brethren. Like Calvin, Luther sees the priesthood of all believers as giving access to God's presence, but this is linked in Luther's thought primarily to the ministry of prayer and intercession for the needs of others. 'To appear before God on behalf of others' is the key concept and the constantly repeated refrain in Luther's statements on this matter (*coram deo apparere pro aliis orare; für Gott treten, eyner für den andern bitte*: WA 7. 54; 12. 307). As must already be clear, for Luther the pastoral nature of the universal priesthood is supreme.

Fundamentally, his priesthood means that any Christian can stand in the place of Christ to minister spiritual counsel to a brother. The 'mutual conversation' (*mutuum collo-quium*) and 'consolation of the brethren' (*consolatio fratrum*) are ways indicated by Luther in which the gospel is at work 'offering counsel and help against sin' within the Christian fellowship (BC 310). A Christian's authority resides in the gospel itself. Any one may relieve his neighbour of a vow which has brought him into bondage and 'Christ has given to every one of his believers the power to absolve even open sins.' All brothers and sisters should be permitted 'most freely to hear the confession of secret sins, so that the sinner may make his sins known to whomever he will and seek pardon and comfort, that is, the word of Christ, by the mouth of his neighbour' (LW 36. 79, 88). Luther recommends that you go first to the priest or pastor but, failing that, to any godly brother or sister. The priest has no superior authority in this matter. Luther often explicitly refers to the priest or pastor as our neighbour or brother and says, 'I admonish you not to confess anything privately to a priest because he is a priest but only because he is a brother and a Christian' (WA 8. 184). The office of priesthood is thus one of mutual service, counsel and comfort in which the message of the gospel is shared between Christians according to their various needs and troubles. (It also involves proclaiming the gospel to unbelievers—but this is a point to be deferred until we come to consider the mission of the Church in the thought of the Reformers.) The universal priesthood means, says Luther,

> that I may go to my good friend and say to him, 'Dear friend, this is the trouble and the difficulty that I am having with sin,' and he should be free to say to me, 'Your sins are forgiven, go in the peace of God.' You should absolutely believe that your sins are forgiven as though Christ himself were your father-confessor—as long as your friend does this in the name of God (WA 10. III. 395).

The priest or your neighbour will give absolution in the name of Christ: 'then you have the word and what they are doing, Christ is doing' (*quando ipsi faciunt, Christus fecit*: WA 41. 546).

To sum up Luther's doctrine of the priesthood of all believers: We note, firstly, that the concept refers not to status but to service, not to privilege but to obligation. As Althaus has pointed out, 'The universal priesthood expresses not religious individualism but its exact opposite, the reality of the congregation as a community.'[8] Secondly, the doctrine focuses attention on a fact that should not be overlooked, namely, that the Reformation was a movement of liberation and its theology a liberation-theology. (The radicals were not alone in recognising this: their significance is that they seized on the social implications of what was originally a purely religious programme of liberation.)

When we have grasped the truth of this doctrine, claims Luther in *The Babylonian Captivity of the Church*, 'then our joyous liberty will be restored to us; we shall realise that we are all equal by every right. Having cast off the yoke of tyranny, we shall know that he who is a Christian has Christ, and that he who has Christ has all things that are Christ's and can do all things' (LW 36. 117).

> Here we take our stand: there is no other word of God than that which is given to all Christians to proclaim. There is no other baptism than the one which any Christian can bestow. There is no other remembrance of the Lord's Supper than that which any Christian can observe and which Christ has instituted. There is no other

kind of sin than that which any Christian can bind or loose. There is no other sacrifice than that of the body of every Christian (LW 40. 34f.).

The doctrine of the universal priesthood, as Luther defines it, might seem to open the door to anarchy in the Church. It appears to be a charter for the abolition of order, a recipe for fragmentation and chaos. But, true to the dialectic method that pervades Luther's thought, there is a balancing factor: Luther is as concerned as any other Church leader with safeguarding order in the church.

THE REACTION AGAINST LUTHER'S EARLY VIEW

Among second-generation Reformers, there was a marked reaction against the spontaneity and liberty of the early years: a turning away from charismatic ministries, a stress on structure at the expense of spirit, a growing clericalisation of the evangelical Churches. Even for Melanchthon, so close to Luther himself, 'the idea of the universal priesthood had only minor significance'.[9] At the Diet of Augsburg in 1530, Melanchthon advised against discussion of the priesthood of all believers, relegating it to the category of 'odious and inessential articles which are commonly debated in the schools', and the doctrine is not mentioned in the *Augsburg Confession*.

Melanchthon's position is the antithesis of Luther's. For Melanchthon, it has been said, the ministerial office is the living nerve of the Church, on which all depends. The universal priesthood stands unquestionably in the background of his thought, having little constitutive significance for his doctrine of the ministry.[10] He goes as far as to say that, just as the Church cannot be without the gospel, so it also cannot exist without the ministry: 'To be without pastors would be tantamount to being without the keys, the gospel and the forgiveness of sins' (CR 8. 430). God does not save except through the ministers he has ordained; if the ministry ceased the Church would not exist (CR 12. 490). Where there is no ministry, there is no Church (*Non est ecclesia, ubi non est verbum ministerium*: CR 14. 892; cf. 21. 832).

The theology of Martin Bucer exhibits a strange progress from Martinian to Philippian views on the priesthood and ministry. In Bucer's early writings, the priesthood of all believers is so strongly present that it is not always clear whether he is talking about the ordained minister or the ordinary believer. The power of the keys—understood in Luther's sense as the ministry of the word of reconciliation—can be exercised by all. When making your confession, it is unnecessary to consider whom the bishop has appointed for this purpose, but only whom God has authorised by his word and spirit to console, admonish and advise you. As Jacques Courvoisier has remarked, 'The ministry of the Church here disappears behind the ministry of the individual Christian.'

From 1536 onwards, however, Bucer's ecclesiology becomes much more clerically orientated. The fourfold office of ministry now appears (later to be adopted by Calvin) and the power of the keys is extended to embrace all the administrative and supervisory duties of the pastorate. The ordained ministry becomes essential to the life of the Church. It is impossible to come to faith and eternal life, asserts Bucer, unless one hears the gospel—the gospel administered by a man. In fellowship with the minister, we are in fellowship with God. Theoretically, Bucer does not retract his earlier statements: the keys still belong to all Christians, but the crucial qualification is added that their exercise is confined to ministers. 'This power belongs to all the Church, but the authority of the ministry belongs to bishops and pastors, just as in Rome of old, power and dominion belonged to the people and authority to the senate.'

Bucer cannot deny that any Christian, by virtue of his priesthood, can give absolution, but points out that 'it is preferable to consult those who are regularly invested with the ministry of the Church as more suitable to profitably hear confession'. As for discipline and oversight, this is in principle the right and duty of every Christian; by virtue of our priesthood we should all care for our neighbour and we ought to recognise that brotherly admonition is given with the authority of Christ. In practice, however, Bucer observes that individuals are prone to neglect this duty: elders and deacons must make up for their negligence![11]

Even the anabaptists were not immune from the general

clericalising tendency. The early communities were apparently purely democratic. An observer noted: 'They have no rulers; one is like the other, all equal in the service of one another ... When they are together, it is their custom to speak of the word of God and to admonish one another in a brotherly fashion.' But this was a state of affairs that could not last and a struggle between inspired and elected leadership ensued, between charismatic and regular ministries. 'As the centre of authority in the movement shifted from the protesting individual conscience to the newly gathered congregations governed by the Holy Spirit in the midst, a new principle of leadership came to the fore.'[12] This development reflected a shift of emphasis throughout the Churches of the Reformation—not least in the theology of Luther himself.

In the medieval Church, order had been secured by the hierarchy and episcopate, the source and focus of all ecclesiastical order and discipline. In the thought of Martin Luther, the same end is secured by the doctrine of the call of the Church. Luther himself often fell back on his call to be a doctor of theology as his warrant to proclaim the gospel, come what may. In the local congregation the same principle applies: the individual Christian must receive the call of the congregation to preach. In this way, Luther—and not only Luther but the other magisterial Reformers too—made a fundamental distinction between priesthood, on the one hand, which belongs to all Christians, and the ministry, office or call, on the other hand, which is bestowed on selected individuals within the congregation.

Luther lays down the simple but far-reaching rule that what is common to all (i.e. the priesthood), no individual may presume to take upon himself without the consent of all. Though all have the same power, he says in *The Babylonian Captivity*, 'no one may make use of this power except by the consent of the community or by the call of a superior. For what is the common property of all, no individual may arrogate to himself unless he is called.' Priests or pastors have the ministry committed to them, asserts Luther, only 'with our common consent' and consequently 'have no right to rule over us except in so far as we freely concede it' (LW 36. 116, 112). And again, this time in the *Appeal to the Christian Nobility*:

Whoever comes out of the waters of baptism can boast that he is already a consecrated priest, bishop and pope, although of course it is not seemly that just anybody should exercise such office. Because we are all priests of equal standing, no one must push himself forward and take it upon himself, without our consent and election, to do that for which we all have equal authority. For no one dare take upon himself what is common to all without the authority and consent of the community.

What then, for Luther, is the purpose of ordination? It is simply an ecclesiastical ceremony (*ritus ecclesiasticus*) by which the call and election of the minister is ratified. In the *Appeal,* Luther goes on to say:

And should it happen that a person chosen for such office were deposed for lack of trust, he would then be exactly what he was before. Therefore a priest in Christendom is nothing else but an office-holder. As long as he holds office he takes precedence; where he is deposed he is a peasant or a townsman like any body else. Indeed a priest is never a priest when he is deposed ... It follows from this argument that there is no true, basic difference between laymen and priests, princes and bishops, between religious and secular, except for the sake of office and work, but not for the sake of status. They are all of the spiritual estate, all are truly priests, bishops and popes. But they do not all have the same work to do (LW 44. 129).

It follows that 'what we give him today, we can take away tomorrow' (*possumus ein hodie commendare, cras iterum adimere*: WA 15. 721). In a sermon on royal priesthood, Luther gathers several of these points together:

Those who are now called priests would all be laymen like the others and only a few officiants would be elected by the congregation to do the preaching. Thus there is only an external difference because of the office to which one is called by the congregation. Before God, however, there is no distinction and only a few are selected from the whole group to administer the office in the stead of the congregation. They all have this office, but nobody has any more authority than the other person has. Therefore, nobody should come forward of his own accord and preach in the congregation. No, one person must be chosen from the whole group and appointed. If desired, he may be deposed (LW 30. 55).

There is, however, another factor in Luther's teaching on this matter: beside the principle that no individual may make free with what is the property of all, there is the practical consideration that everything must be done decently and in order: 'otherwise there might be shameful confusion among the people of God and a kind of Babylon in the Church where everything should be done in order, as the apostle teaches' (LW 40. 34). As preaching is a public matter, some people—women, children and other 'unqualified persons' (*untüchtige Leute*)—are excluded straight away as unfit to hold any public office (WA 10 III. 171; 50. 633). And if all were to preach, it would be 'like women going to market'—no one would listen for all would be talking at once (WA 10. III. 397). All must be done *secundem ordinem*, in an orderly manner.

It may be helpful at this point to try to understand what lay behind Luther's exclusion of women from the public ministry. There is no need to point out that women share equally with men in the universal priesthood; they too partake of the royal priesthood that Christ imparts to his people. Luther supports this from the common practice of women administering baptism: 'When women baptise, they exercise the function of priesthood legitimately and do it not as a private act but as a part of the public ministry of the Church which belongs only to the universal priesthood' (LW 40. 23). 'A woman can baptise and administer the word of life by which sin is taken away, eternal death abolished, the prince of the world cast out, heaven bestowed; in short, by which the divine majesty pours itself forth through all the soul' (LW 40. 25). When Luther grants women the power to administer baptism, he recognises that this carries with it all other priestly functions for, according to Luther, the sacrament of baptism includes the ministry of the word and is, moreover, superior to other priestly offices. 'In baptising we proffer the life-giving word of God which renews souls and redeems from death and sins. To baptise is incomparably greater than to consecrate bread and wine for it is the greatest office in the Church—the proclamation of the word of God' (LW 40. 23). There is then no suggestion in Luther's thought that women are somehow incapable of bearing the priestly 'character'.

It is not unknown for Luther to exclude women from the public ministry on grounds of principle (namely, a doctrine of creation) rather than mere expediency. Their created constitution is better adapted to domestic than to public affairs. Women were 'not destined by God for government in the state or Church where the greatest strength of character and wisdom is required' but rather for care of the home. And Luther adds: 'For the longer they deliberate about important and difficult matters, the more they complicate and obstruct the business' (LW 6. 60).

This is as near as Luther comes to providing a theological basis for an exclusively male ministry—it is significant that his statement here turns out to be a rationalisation of experience. The logic of Luther's overall position in fact dictates that the question of whether women should be ordained to the ministry should be answered purely in terms of social expediency. They could not be denied the essential priesthood, but in the light of the sixteenth-century social structure they would inevitably have been regarded as 'unqualified persons' to exercise any public office, not only in the Church but in society at large. It is highly revealing that Calvin, who was not enthusiastic about Luther's concept of the universal priesthood, nevertheless saw the logic of the doctrine and was opposed to the administration of baptism by women in any circumstances (Inst. IV. xv. 20ff.).

As Luther worked through his doctrine of the Church, he was led to develop a fundamental distinction between priesthood which is universal and ministry which is particular. 'One must distinguish between the preaching or ministerial office and the common priesthood of all baptised Christians—the former office is none other than a public ministry and so something that must be authorised by the whole community in which all are alike priests' (WA 41. 210). The same distinction between priesthood and ministry is to be found in Zwingli and Calvin. Zwingli states: 'It is true that we are all fully ordained to the priesthood which in the New Testament offers sacrifices, which means nothing else but that everyone offers himself (Rom. 12). But we are not all apostles and bishops.'[13] And as Calvin rather tartly remarks in the same vein, 'If priesthood is common to all Christians, ministry is not.'[14] Calvin is characteristically concerned that all things should be done decently and in order and thus that 'no one shall assume a public office in the Church without a call' (Inst. iv. ii. 10). Calvin has no room for a charismatic ministry. Wherever there is a Church of God with its own laws and rule of discipline, he says, 'no one should thrust himself in, so as to exercise the prophetic or pastoral office, though he equalled all the angels in sanctity' (CO 38. 432).

The *Second Helvetic Confession* of 1566, drafted by Heinrich Bullinger, Zwingli's successor in Zurich, sums up in measured terms both the doctrine of the universal priesthood in the low-key form that had come to prevail and the corresponding need to safeguard order in the Church:

> The apostles of Christ indeed call all believers in Christ priests, but not by reason of a ministerial office (*sed non ratione ministerii*), but because through Christ all the faithful, having been made kings and priests, are able to offer spiritual sacrifices to God. Accordingly, there are great differences between a priesthood and a ministry. For the former is common to all Christians, as we have just now said, but this is not so with the latter. And we have not removed the ministry out of the midst of the Church when we have cast the papistical priesthood out of the Church of Christ (Latin text in Schaff, 281).

CHAPTER EIGHT

THE REFORMED EPISCOPATE

The first and most decisive task of Reformation ecclesiology was to establish the centre of the Church's existence. Not only Luther but all the mainstream Reformers pointed to the gospel as the Church's christological centre, the spiritual reality which makes the Church the Church. But the Reformers accepted that the Church had a visible, empirical aspect too: it was bound up with certain structures of life in this world; it needed to be organised and governed and its relations with the civil power regulated. In this chapter we shall enquire how the reformed Church with its overriding concern to preserve the christological centre came to terms with one of the more dominant of these structures, the monarchical episcopate of catholic Christendom.

There is remarkable agreement among the Reformers both on the continent and in England, for all their differences of emphasis, that the primary task of the Church is the preaching of the gospel and that this task is constitutive of the Christian ministry. Questions of polity or of Church order are therefore definitely secondary, peripheral and even indifferent (*adiaphora*). As far as the situation in England was concerned, however, there was an evident hardening of positions when, under the influence of Theodore Beza, Calvin's successor in Geneva, the English puritans began to make exclusive claims for presbyterianism and provoked a corresponding escalation of claims on behalf of episcopacy by defenders of the Elizabethan settlement.

LUTHER'S VIEW OF BISHOPS

Luther and Melanchthon make a fundamental distinction between the pastoral office which includes the preaching of the gospel, the cure of souls and the exercise of the keys (absolution) on the one hand and matters of polity and order on the other. The latter is concerned with the *externa forma*

Ecclesiae, the entire visible, institutional structure and shape of the Church, in fact all outward aspects of Church life—not only matters concerned with ecclesiastical jurisdiction and visitation but even ceremonies and ordination. The Church is solely concerned with preaching the gospel: external aspects of Church life which involve the civil power, the magistrate, are peripheral to the real existence of the Christian community. The Church is bound only to the gospel and can sit lightly to all other matters. It is in keeping with the most fundamental principles of Luther's theology that his attitude towards questions of polity should have been entirely neutral and pragmatic. What he feared above all in this connection was that Church polity might become a new legalism, destroying the liberty of the gospel. The preaching of the gospel is essential: the rest is indifferent. As Melanchthon puts it:

> It is necessary to distinguish from the episcopal polity, bound to place person and due succession, offices and human regulations—the ministry of the gospel instituted by God and continually restored by his great mercy which perpetually serves the Church and is not bound to certain places, persons and human laws but to the gospel (CR 5. 627; cf. 559).

In its possession of the gospel, the Church has all that it needs; all the means of grace are simply manifestations of the gospel 'for God is surpassingly rich in his grace' and his gospel is mediated to us in many ways:

> first, through the spoken word, by which the forgiveness of sin (the peculiar function of the gospel) is preached to the whole world; second, through baptism; third, through the holy sacrament of the altar; fourth, through the power of the keys; and finally, through the mutual conversation and consolation of brethren: Matt. 18.20: 'Where two are gathered' (*Smalkald Articles* III. iv: BC 310).

Secure in its grasp of the gospel, the christological centre, the Church could, in exceptional circumstances, survive without an ordained ministry at all. The universal priesthood would provide the ministry of the word and every father would act as pastor to his own family. In these terms Luther counselled the Hussites whose ministry had to be maintained by subterfuge:

> I would confidently advise that you have no ministers at all. For it would be safer and more wholesome for the father of the household to read the gospel and—since the universal custom and use allows it to the laity—to baptise those who are born in his home and so to govern himself and his according to the doctrine of Christ, even if throughout life they did not dare or could not receive the eucharist. For the eucharist is not so necessary that salvation depends on it. The gospel and baptism are sufficient since faith alone justifies and love alone lives rightly (LW 40. 9).

For Luther, the Church clearly precedes the ministry in the logic of divine grace. The Church is not dependent on the ordained ministry, as in traditional catholic theology; rather, the ministry is dependent on the Church. It is possible to find statements in Luther's vast output that seem to contradict that—for example, in the *Sermons on John* of 1537: 'If the office of the ministry were not constantly being administered in Christendom and the Holy Spirit did not hold sway, it would be impossible to retain baptism, the sacrament and the knowledge of Christ. Who could preserve these if it were not done by the exercise of the public ministry?' (LW 24. 131).

But this seems to be a momentary aberration; Luther consistently and characteristically lays the emphasis not on the office but on the gospel that creates the office. Christ's authority and commission and the power of the keys are given to the apostles (John 20.21; Luke 10.16) only as representative of the whole Church. 'Wherever the Church exists, the right to administer the gospel also exists' and the right to proclaim the gospel carries with it all other necessary authority, for all the various ecclesiastical functions are subservient to that of preaching the gospel. The Church is therefore empowered to ordain ministers for itself and can by-pass the bishops to whom the power of order is normally reserved. 'Wherefore, when the bishops are heretics or refuse to administer ordination, the Churches are by divine right compelled to ordain pastors and ministers for themselves.' 'Where the true Church is, therefore, the right of electing and of ordaining ministers must of necessity also be' (BC 331f.).

It is one thing for presbyters to ordain without a bishop: it is going much further for a congregation itself to confer ordination without the presence of other ministers, for here the principle of transmitted authority as it has normally been understood in the Christian tradition is absent altogether. But this is, nevertheless, a procedure envisaged by Luther in special circumstances. The possibility derives from the fundamental evangelical doctrine that the gospel is all-sufficient and is entrusted to the whole Church together with the authority to administer it. Even where bishops are retained in the reformed Church, their office must be interpreted in the light of this fundamental concept. When a bishop ordains, therefore (writes Luther in his *Appeal to the Christian Nobility of the German Nation* of 1520), it is simply that 'in the place and stead of the whole community, all of whom have like power, he takes a person and charges him to exercise this power on behalf of the others' (LW 44. 128). And where there is no bishop and no ordained minister, the power to institute a ministry rests with the congregation by virtue of its possession of the gospel and with it the spiritual priesthood. Thus,

> suppose a group of earnest Christian laymen were taken prisoner and set down in a desert without an episcopally ordained priest among them. And suppose they were to come to a common mind there and then in the desert and elect one of their number ... and charge him to baptise, say mass, pronounce absolution and preach the gospel: such a man would be as truly a priest as if he had been ordained by all the bishops and popes in the world (ibid.).

The various divisions of the ministerial office, into bishops, priests and deacons, for example, are a purely human arrangement, a helpful man-made system that ought to be retained as long as it serves a useful purpose. Luther's view is put in the *Smalkald Articles*:

If the bishops were true bishops and were concerned about the Church and the gospel, they might be permitted (for the sake of love and unity, but not of necessity) to ordain and confirm us and our preachers, provided this could be done without pretence, humbug and unchristian ostentation.

And as Melanchthon expresses it in his *Apology*:

On this matter we have given frequent testimony in the Assembly [the Diet of Augsburg] to our deep desire to maintain the Church polity and various ranks of the ecclesiastical hierarchy, although they were created by human authority. We know that the fathers had good and useful reasons for instituting ecclesiastical discipline in the manner described by the ancient canons ... Furthermore, we want at this point to declare our willingness to keep the ecclesiastical and canonical polity, provided that the bishops stop raging against our Churches.

As the last remark indicates, the Lutheran Reformers objected to episcopacy on pragmatic grounds only. The bishops had not only failed in the performance of their pastoral duties but had actually opposed the evangelical reform. So Luther writes: 'They neither are nor wish to be true bishops. They are temporal lords and princes who are unwilling to preach or teach or baptise or administer communion or discharge any office or work in the Church. More than that, they expel, persecute and condemn those who have been called to do these things.' And as Melanchthon says in the *Apology*:

The bishops either force our priests to forsake and condemn the sort of doctrine we have confessed or else, in their unheard of cruelty, they kill the unfortunate and innocent men. This keeps our priests from acknowledging such bishops. Thus the cruelty of the bishops is the reason for the abolition of canonical government in some places, despite our earnest desire to keep it.

In a similar way, the *Torgau Articles* (1530) reject the

validity of episcopal jurisdiction only because of its abuse in practice and then try to justify the assumption of this jurisdiction by the sovereign. In the sixteenth century, as Luther, Melanchthon and the English Reformers realised, the alternative to episcopal jurisdiction was the assumption of this power by the magistrate, the godly prince (BC 214f., 314; CR 26. 178f.).[1]

CALVIN ON CHURCH POLITY

Calvin follows the German Reformers in holding that polity is a secondary matter. Contrary to a common assumption, the doctrine of the divine right of presbytery stems not from Calvin but from his successor Beza. Calvin's fourfold offices of pastor and doctor, elder and deacon, are derived from an analysis of the needs of the Church and the requirements of pastoral oversight; only then are they provided with scriptural justification and authority. His teaching at this point is marked by a not uncharacteristic moderation, flexibility and commonsense approach.[2] Calvin indeed lays down the general principle that 'no form of government is to be drawn up in the Church by human judgment, but that men must wait for the command of God' (CC Hebrews, 61). And again: 'The whole government of the Church depends so entirely upon his decree that men are not permitted to interfere with it' (CO 25. 230).

Here, however, Calvin is concerned with what is 'of faith' or necessary to salvation and his remarks in the commentary on Hebrews, just now quoted, are directed against the institution of the sacrificing priesthood under the papacy. Unlike Beza, Cartwright and other puritans, Calvin himself does not claim that the structures of the Church have been divinely prescribed in detail. Provided the christological centre—the preaching of Christ and saving faith—is secured, Calvin is prepared to be flexible and to admit distinctions within the ministerial office so long as they are not contrary to Scripture. 'Political distinction (*politia distinctio*) is not to be repudiated, for nature itself dictates this in order to take away confusion.' Calvin does, however, lay down the proviso that the glory of Christ (as in the papacy) and the fraternity and equality of ministers (as in *monarchical* episcopacy) must not be obscured (CO 24. 445). In the New Testament, bishops and presbyters are synonymous, but it was inevitable, Calvin thinks, that a moderatorial system should have developed whereby one of the presbyters presided over his brethren. Calvin dislikes the word 'hierarchy' but revealingly adds: 'If, disregarding the term, we look to the thing, we shall find that the ancient bishops had no wish to frame a form of Church government different from that which God has prescribed in his word' (Inst. IV. iv. 4; cf. iv. 2, iv. 8; CC Tit., 357ff.; Acts 2. 183; Phil., 227).[3]

THE REFORMED EPISCOPATE IN ANGLICAN THEOLOGY

Among Anglican divines, there was agreement on the secondary importance and variable nature of Church polity until, in the 1590s, it became necessary to counter the presbyterian challenge. A study of Anglican statements on ecclesiastical polity reveals several significant factors underlying this view.[4]

(1) Like Luther and Melanchthon, the English Reformers held that the power of jurisdiction (as opposed to the power of order or sacramental power) derived from the prince not the pope or the apostolic succession. If the bishops' power of jurisdiction was held from his sovereign, it became unnecessary to attempt to bolster that authority by recourse to a theory of apostolic succession with its attendant doctrine of the indispensability of episcopal ordination for a valid ministry and valid sacraments. The weight that Anglican Reformers laid on the concept of the godly prince weakened the role of the episcopate in the doctrine of the Christian ministry.

(2) The English Reformers made no exclusive claims for episcopal polity, holding as they did that no such binding pattern of Church order was contained in Holy Scripture. Whitgift, for example, attacked the English puritans for their 'very popish conclusion' that a particular form of polity was a necessary mark of the Church. 'I find no one certain and perfect kind of government prescribed or commanded in the Scriptures.' But it is equally true, he adds, that nowhere has Christ ordered that all ministers should be equal, as presbyterians would have it—let the puritans prove the contrary if

they can (PS 1. 184f.; 2. 227f.; 395; 3. 406). Whitgift's claim
for episcopacy is not that it is of divine right, or that it is of
dominical institution, but that it is an historical, useful form
of government that is not contrary to Scripture and,
moreover, is established by the sovereign.

(3) The English Reformers did not regard episcopacy as
essential to the life of the Church for the simple reason that
they held with all the Reformers that the Church is constituted by the gospel expressed in word and sacrament: while
these are necessary to salvation, any particular form of polity
is not. Hooker, for example, clearly distinguishes between
things necessary to salvation and things indifferent, and
makes much play of the fact that—contrary to the tenor of all
reformed theology—Cartwright asserted that matters concerning polity and discipline belonged to the former category.
This enabled Cartwright to claim that Holy Scripture must
provide a blueprint for Church government (HW 1. 352ff.).

The apologists of the Anglican settlement did not regard
polity as of the *esse* of the Church. It is, however, true that
even according to the English divines 'the substance and
matter of government', as Whitgift puts it, 'must indeed be
taken out of the word of God'. But this substance 'consisteth
in these points: that the word be truly taught, the sacraments
rightly administered, virtue furthered, vice repressed and the
Church kept in quietness and order'. It does not include any
particular structure of Church government; how these aims
are met is a thing indifferent. 'The offices in the Church,
whereby this government is wrought', continues Whitgift, 'be
not namely and particularly expressed in the Scriptures, but
in some points left to the discretion and liberty of the
Church.' A kind of government 'is not so much a part of the
essence and being of the Church but that it may be the
Church of Christ without this or that kind of government.'
Polity cannot therefore be a matter pertaining to salvation. It
if were, Whitgift remarks, it would have been prescribed and
commanded in Scripture—which it evidently is not (PS 1. 6,
184f.).

(4) Finally, the English Reformers pointed out that a
definitive form of polity could not have been laid down in the
New Testament for all time because the Church's circumstances change from age to age. The practice of the

apostles was not intended as an immutable precedent and could not be followed now without 'preposterous zeal' (Whitgift). 'It is manifest that Christ hath left the government of his Church, touching the external polity, in sundry points in the ordering of men, who have to make orders and laws for the same as time, place and person requireth', provided only that 'nothing be done contrary to his word' (Whitgift PS 1. 416; 2. 90; cf. 1. 6, 471, 493; 2. 109; 3. 444; FC 3. 150f.). According to Richard Hooker, polity is alterable, doctrine unchangeable: mere ecclesiastical arrangements are not on the same footing as the exposition of divine truth.

All things cannot be of ancient continuance which are expedient and needful for the ordering of spiritual affairs: but the Church being a body which dieth not hath always power, as occasion requireth, no less to ordain that which never was than to ratify what hath been before ... The Church hath authority to establish that for an order at one time which at another time it may abolish and in both may do well. But that which in doctrine the Church doth now deliver rightly as a truth, no man will say that it may hereafter recall and as rightly avouch the contrary. Laws touching matter of order are changeable, by the power of the Church; articles concerning doctrine not so (HW 2. 33).

The Church has been endowed with the authority to make laws to meet changes in circumstances, provided only that it does not attempt to contravene divine law, that is, laws ordained by God, rooted and grounded in the nature of things and applicable to all times and circumstances. Even the laws of the apostles themselves, according to Hooker, may be set aside if they are merely positive laws, that is, regulations to deal with various contingencies, applications of divine law to particular occasions. 'The whole body of the Church hath power to alter, with general consent and upon necessary occasions, even the positive laws of the apostles, if there be no command to the contrary and it manifestly appears to her that change of times have clearly taken away the very reasons of God's first institution' (HW 3. 164; cf. Whit. PS 2. 90f.;

Rogers PS 183ff., 316; FC 2. 526). (It is highly significant and revealing of the real consensus of Reformation theology, that the continental Reformers and particularly Calvin do not dissent from this account of the power of the Church in external matters not binding on the conscience: cf. Inst. IV. x.)

On these four grounds—the role of the magistrate in Church government, the absence of New Testament authority for any essential form of polity, the sufficiency of word and sacrament for the being of the Church, and the power of the Church to make laws for itself according to circumstances—the Anglican divines held that matters of polity were secondary and variable; only the gospel (the word) and sacraments (visible words) were primary and unchangeable. This is the early Anglican view of the relation of centre and structure in the Church. Several consequences for Anglican ecclesiology followed.

(1) The Anglican divines of the sixteenth century accepted without question the non-episcopal ministries of other reformed Churches. As Field remarks: no one has the right to condemn all those worthy ministers who were ordained by presbyters at a time when bishops opposed the truth (FC 1. 321ff.). And Bancroft points out in 1610 that ordination by presbyters must be lawful where bishops could not be had—or else the position of all the reformed Churches would be jeopardised! The point has been conclusively established by the researches of Norman Sykes: surveying developments from the mid-sixteenth to the mid-seventeenth centuries, he summarises thus:

> Under the pressure of a century of acute controversy, the Anglican divines had developed a positive, constructive and consistent apologetic for episcopacy as retained in the Church of England. It was held to be not of dominical but of apostolic appointment and as *divino jure* only in that sense; as necessary where it could be had, but its absence where historical necessity compelled did not deprive a Church of valid ministry and sacraments. It was necessary to the perfection or integrity of a Church, though not to its essence; and on the ground of its historic continuance in the Church, its restoration in the foreign non-episcopal Chur-

ches was much to be desired ... Thus Anglican apologetic
for episcopacy, as necessary where it could be had but its
lack not unchurching those Churches deprived of it by
historical circumstances, adopted the principle of episcopal
government and ordination as being of the *plene esse*
rather than of the *esse* of the Church.[5]

Agreeing on the christological centre, they could afford
amicable disagreement on questions of structure.

(2) The Anglican Reformers believed in the fundamental
equality of ministers. Although they retained the threefold
ministry of bishops, priests and deacons, they did not,
generally speaking, maintain that the power of ministry was
derived from the episcopal succession. Being therefore under
no obligation to uphold the indispensability of sacramental
grace transmitted through apostolic succession, they were free
to assert the basic equality of the orders of ministry. There is
a range of views to be found on this question among the
Anglican divines, as might be expected on a question held to
be of secondary importance. They are, however, agreed that
bishops and presbyters are equal in power of ministry at least
(as distinguished from power of jurisdiction and power of
order). As Pilkington puts it: 'God's commission and commandment is like and indifferent to all, priest, bishop,
archbishop, prelate, by what name soever he be called: "Go
and teach, baptising in the name of the Father, the Son and
the Holy Ghost" ' (PS 493). The inequality between bishops
and presbyters, says Whitgift, is 'not in respect of the
ministry of the word, but of order and polity' (PS 2. 101).
Hooker makes the same distinction when he states that
bishops and presbyters are equal *quoad ministerium* but not
quoad ordinem et politiam (i.e., as far as ministry is concerned, but not when it comes to order and polity):

A bishop is a minister of God, unto whom with permanent
continuance there is given not only power of administering
the word and sacraments, which power other presbyters
have; but also a further power to ordain ecclesiastical
persons, and a power of chiefty in government over
presbyters as well as laymen, a power to be by way of
jurisdiction a pastor even to pastors themselves. So that this

office, as he is a presbyter or pastor, consisteth in those things which are common unto him with other pastors, as in ministering the word and sacraments: but those things incident unto his office, which do properly make him a bishop, cannot be common unto him with other pastors (HW 3. 148).

Taken alone and out of context, this statement may seem to indicate an essentially unreformed view of episcopacy. If bishops have a superior power both of jurisdiction and of ordination, both of which are essential to the life of the Church, how can it be claimed that Hooker's is a reformed ecclesiology according to which only the gospel is of the *esse*? Does not such a statement reveal that Hooker does not in fact share the Reformation concept of the Church? Here it is important to take note of two qualifications in Hooker's thought.

Firstly, while it is true that Hooker does indeed stress that bishops alone have the power of order, he admits that others do not share this view. There are some, he says, 'which hold that between a bishop and a presbyter, touching power of order, there is no difference'. (We shall be taking note of some of these views in a moment.) Hooker recognises that their position is founded on a sure grasp of the Reformation doctrine that only the gospel is essential to the Church and that the ministry is constituted by the gospel. 'They see presbyters no less than bishops authorised to offer up the prayers of the Church, to preach the gospel, to baptise, to administer the holy eucharist.'

But what they do fail to recognise, according to Hooker, is that in doing these things, presbyters are exercising a delegated authority. 'They considered not withal as they should, that the presbyter's authority to do these things is derived from the bishop which doth ordain him thereunto, so that even in those things which are common unto both, yet the power of the one is as it were a certain light borrowed from the others' lamp' (HW 3. 169). Hooker's is clearly a doctrine of transmitted authority, but the force and finality of this principle is severely curtailed when Hooker concedes that, under certain circumstances, the Church may dispense entirely with a corrupt episcopate. (The point can only be asserted here: it will be substantiated directly.) The reservation of the power of order to bishops alone and with it the principle of transmitted authority is thus revealed to be definitely *penultimate* in Hooker's thought.

Secondly, as far as the bishop's power of jurisdiction is concerned, Hooker's claims are far more moderate. He points out that the consecration of a bishop bestows only the power of order, not of jurisdiction as such. The *potestas ordinis* is universal: in this respect a bishop is a bishop of the whole Church; the *potestas jurisdictionis*, however, is strictly limited to certain territorial responsibilities. In view of this fact, Hooker remarks, 'it might be well enough said that presbyters were that way authorised to do, in a manner, even as much as bishops could do' (HW 3. 177). Hooker's claims for the inherent superiority of bishops are thus reduced to the power of order only; the drastic restriction even on this is something to be taken up shortly.

Other Anglican divines, writing before the 1590s, lay more stress than Hooker does on the fundamental equality of ministers. Leaning heavily on St Jerome's account of the origins of the episcopate, Cranmer, Jewel and Field hold that bishops have a superiority over priests more by custom than by irrevocable divine command. Some go further in claiming, as Cranmer does, that bishops and presbyters were originally synonymous, or at least equal: 'the bishops and priests were one at one time and were not two things but both one office in the beginning of Christ's religion' (*Remains*, PS 117). Field even goes as far as to deny that 'the power of order which is given in ordination is less' in presbyters than in bishops (FC 4. 150). Field was par excellence the spokesman of the Hieronymian theory of episcopacy, maintaining that bishops and presbyters fundamentally constitute one order. As A. J. Mason remarks, 'No first-rate English Church divine has so thoroughly identified himself with this opinion.'[6] And it is significant that Whitgift argues for a degree of inequality on purely pragmatic grounds: 'There ought to be degrees of superiority amongst ministers also, because they labour of imperfections as well as other men do, and especially of pride, arrogancy, vain-glory, which engenders schisms, heresies, contentions ...' (PS 2. 263).

(3) The third and related consequence of the reformed

doctrine of the ministry held by the English divines of the sixteenth century (namely, that the gospel alone is the true treasure of the Church, essential to, and constitutive of its being) is that the episcopate was held to be dispensable in certain circumstances. The power of order in the Church would not fail with the failure of the bishops. 'Succession of good bishops is a great blessing of God,' remarks Pilkington, 'but because God and his truth hangs not on man nor place, we rather hang on the undeceivable truth of God's word in all doubts, than on any bishops, place or man' (PS 599f.). And Jewel asserts that the English Church is not dependent on its own or any other bishops: 'if there were not one neither of them nor of us left alive, yet would not therefore the whole Church of England flee to Louvaine' (i.e., to receive Roman orders: PS 3. 335). Bishops alone, says Field, have the power of ordination only in so far as 'no man may regularly do it without them' (FC 4. 150f., 322). Hooker too countenances the abolition of the episcopate if this is the will of the Church, for its permanent continuance has no direct divine sanction:

> Bishops, albeit they may avouch with conformity of truth that their authority hath thus descended even from the very apostles themselves, yet the absolute and everlasting continuance of it they cannot say that any commandment of the Lord doth enjoin; and therefore must acknowledge that the Church hath power by universal consent upon urgent cause to take it away, if thereunto she be constrained through the proud, tyrannical and unreformable dealings of her bishops, whose regiment she hath thus long delighted in, because she hath found it good and requisite to be so governed (HW 3. 165).

In such a case, and in other extreme circumstances, the Church retains the power of order apart from the episcopate and this inherent power may be exerted 'when the exigence of necessity doth constrain to leave the usual ways of the Church, which otherwise we would willingly keep'.

> Where the Church must have some ordained, and neither hath nor can have possibly a bishop to ordain; in case of such necessity, the ordinary institution of God hath given

oftentimes, and may give, place. And therefore we are not simply without exception to urge a lineal descent of power from the apostles by continued succession of bishops in every effectual ordination' (HW 3. 231f.).

It has seemed desirable to deal at greater length with the views of the Anglican Reformers up to and including Hooker and Field in order to establish the unmistakably reformed character of their doctrine of the ministry, notwithstanding their retention of the threefold ministry with the power of order normally reserved to bishops. Whether this reformed ecclesiology survives the outburst of controversy on the doctrine of the ministry in the 1590s is a question that must now be considered.

After the death of Calvin, the reformist Elizabethan puritans looked to Theodore Beza for advice on matters that troubled their consciences, notably the use of 'popish' vestments and the retention of bishops. On the former point Beza counselled moderation: on the latter he was less accommodating. As Patrick Collinson has written: 'The responsibility for elevating polity to the rank of protestant dogma and for anathematising episcopacy, name and thing, lies with Calvin's successor.'[7]

Beza's position was set out in a letter of advice to Glamis, Lord Chancellor of Scotland, in 1576, in which he distinguishes three forms of oversight (*De Triplici Episcopatu*). There is, first of all, *Divinus Episcopatus*—divinely instituted oversight, i.e., presbyterianism. Secondly, there is *Humanus Episcopatus*—the form of Church government set up by man: here Beza is thinking of the bishops of the early Church and the reformed Church of England. Finally, there is *Satanus Episcopatus*—the Roman hierarchy—and this is of the devil. It is the second of these three forms that concerns us here.

Beza asserts uncompromisingly that this human episcopate has no authority from Scripture: 'The New Testament does not contain a single word which might refer in the slightest degree to any such thing.' He counsels, however, that it should be tolerated—though reluctantly—provided certain conditions are met; but the Church will never truly flourish until the divinely ordained presbyterate is established in its place. *Humanus Episcopatus*

> could indeed be tolerated provided only that the old, pure rules, instituted for the prevention of oligarchy, should again be enforced. But apart from the fact that this, in view of the changed circumstances in the world, would cost an infinite deal of trouble, the experience of so many centuries also shows that, unless this institution too is eradicated root and branch, the same fruits flourish anew ...

Beza's view is echoed in John Udall's *A Demonstration of Discipline* which asserts the divine right of presbytery: 'God doth describe perfectly unto us out of his worde that forme of government which is lawfull and the officers that are to execute the same; from which it is not lawful for any Christian Church to swarve.'[8] The argument was taken further by Cartwright who claimed that Scripture is prescriptive of every detail of Christian life ('The word of God containeth the direction of all things pertaining to the Church, yea of whatsoever things can fall into any part of man's life.') and that discipline and government in the Church were matters 'of faith', pertaining to salvation (Whit. PS 1. 18, 225f., 417; 3. 444; HW 1. 287ff.).

It was this claim to which Whitgift and Hooker addressed their argument. It is highly significant that they do not attempt to meet it by asserting the divine right of bishops to match the puritan doctrine of the divine right of presbytery. Their refutation proceeds along historical rather than dogmatic lines and is informed by a grasp of the evangelical doctrine of the liberty of a Christian man and the characteristically Anglican sense of what is morally fitting.

The teaching of Whitgift and Hooker is echoed by George Downham at the beginning of the seventeenth century when he writes:

> The episcopal government hath this commendation above other forms of ecclesiastical government, that in respect of the first institution it is a divine ordinance; but that it should be such a divine ordinance as should be generally,

perpetually, immutably, necessarily observed, so as no
other form of government may in no case be admitted, I did
not take upon me to maintain.[9]

Hooker knows that it would strengthen his own position to
be able to match the presbyterian claim of divine right and
New Testament authority with a similar claim for the
episcopal polity of the English Church. But he rejects the
temptation to attempt this. Firstly, he does not concede that
the puritans have any scriptural warrant for their platform:
'Our persuasion is that no age ever had knowledge of it but
only ours; that they which defend it devised it; that neither
Christ nor his apostles at any time taught it, but the
contrary.' Secondly, in rejecting any such pretensions for the
form of polity he is defending, he tacitly casts aspersions on
both the methods and the motives of presbyterian apologetic:

> If therefore we did seek to maintain that which most
> advantageth our own cause, the very best way for us and
> the strongest against them were to hold even as they do,
> that in Scripture there must needs be found some parti-
> cular form of Church polity which God hath instituted and
> which for that very cause belongeth to all Churches, to all
> times. But with any such partial eye to respect ourselves
> and by cunning to make those things seem the truest which
> are the fittest to serve our purpose, is a thing which we
> neither like nor mean to follow (HW 1. 390f.).

Other Anglican polemicists at the end of the century were
not content with Hooker's moderate claims.

A new note is first sounded in Richard Bancroft's sermon
at St Paul's Cross in 1589, though the significant departure
in Anglican ecclesiology is not at all easy to detect. Bancroft
did not explicitly state that episcopacy was of divine
institution nor that it was the only legitimate form of Church
government. He simply asserted that the Church had been
governed by bishops ever since the times of the apostles. In
retaining the threefold ministry, therefore, the English
Church was accepting the authority of antiquity. As Cargill
Thompson pointed out, the revolutionary implications of
Bancroft's sermon lay in what it omitted to say. Whereas the

important qualification in Whitgift's view of episcopacy had been to add that the Church was not tied to any one particular form of government, Bancroft omitted any reference to the moderating concept of *adiaphora* (things indifferent). Nevertheless, neither in this sermon nor in his *Survey of the Pretended Holy Discipline* of 1593 did Bancroft advance an exclusive theory of episcopacy or assert direct divine sanction for it.[10]

A similar emphasis is found in Hadrian de Saravia's treatise of 1590 *De Diversis Gradibus Ministrorum Evangelii* which also appealed to antiquity: 'That which we read to be done of all Churches from the apostles' times and of the fathers throughout the compass of the whole earth and the same continued even unto these our days, I do always hold as a sacred canon of the apostles, not to be repealed.' 'Against the constant and consonant conclusions of the ancient Church we ought not to attempt or admit any innovation without a plain commission from God's holy writ.' Saravia traced the distinction between bishops and presbyters back to the distinction made by Christ between the Twelve and the Seventy. But Saravia does not make the Church dependent on the episcopate—the hierarchical structure is not allowed to eclipse the christological centre. Church government, he points out, is not a question of faith or salvation and the reformed Churches are not the less true Churches for lacking the episcopate, for the times were such, he remarks, that to escape 'the captivity of Babylon, I do not see indeed how the true bishops could have been restored.' He adds, however, as a rebuke to the dogmatic presbyterians; 'Shall that which was done extraordinarily, and that but in a certain few places, and that but in our age only, prescribe a law to the world besides?'[11]

In 1593 Thomas Bilson took the logical next step of claiming that episcopal ordination is necessary to a valid ministry in a work significantly titled *The Perpetual Government of Christ's Church.* Bilson's treatise is described by E. T. Davies as 'the most exhaustive treatment of episcopacy in sixteenth-century Anglican literature as well as one of the most important defences of episcopacy in the English language.' Bilson too is profoundly impressed by the argument from the antiquity of the episcopate. He holds that

Christ had foreshadowed it in separating the Twelve and the Seventy and that the apostles had established bishops in the early Christian Churches. Bilson refuses to allow that the Church has the power to alter the threefold ministry which has the sanction of Christ and the apostles. But even Bilson is a reformed divine: he does not therefore go so far as to assert that the episcopate is constitutive of the Church or belongs to its *esse*.[12]

'By the early 1590s,' Cargill Thompson has commented, 'it is possible to detect a marked change in the character of the Anglican attitude to episcopacy; the old emphasis on the idea that Church government was ultimately a "thing indifferent" was giving way to a new concern with the historic and Scriptural claims of episcopacy.' But he adds a word of caution against exaggerating the significance of this shift:

> In the first place, the concept of 'divine right' had a much vaguer connotation in the sixteenth century than it came to have later: to say that an institution was "divine" did not necessarily imply that it owed its origin to God himself; it could mean no more than that it was presumed to have divine sanction ... Secondly, even the most ardent adherents of the divine right of bishops did not yet go so far as to condemn all other forms of Church government.[13]

Our rather protracted discussion of the delicate question of polity in the Anglican Church has established the reformed nature of Anglican ecclesiology—though, as far as certain trends towards the end of the sixteenth century are concerned, not securely or unambiguously so, for these contained the seeds of later developments in Caroline and Tractarian theology.

CATHOLICITY AND APOSTOLICITY ACCORDING TO THE REFORMERS

To return now from our excursus on the Anglican divines to the mainstream of Reformation thought: The concept of the Church which was fundamental to the thought of the Reformers (including of course the Anglicans)—namely, that only the gospel was of the *esse*—had profound implications for the doctrine of succession and with it the key concept of catholicity, one of the four credal attributes of the Church. Here a radical reinterpretation was effected. In traditional catholic theology, the catholicity of the Church was guaranteed by the apostolic succession through which the grace of holy orders was transmitted and by virtue of the power of orders sacramental grace was imparted. By making the gospel alone the power at work in the Church through the Holy Spirit, the Reformers did away with the necessity of a doctrine of apostolic succession, replacing it with the notion of a successtion of truth. Correspondingly, the gospel of truth was held to be sufficient to secure the catholicity of the Church. The Reformers believed with all of Christendom that the Church was one, holy, catholic and apostolic, but this was understood in a radically new sense in which the gospel itself became the decisive and dominant criterion.

How little external, hierarchical and structural unity meant to Martin Luther is revealed when, writing to Duke Albrecht of Prussia in 1532 about the eucharist, Luther claims that there has been a unity of faith and truth on this point throughout Christian history. The true doctrine, he says,

> has been believed and held harmoniously in all the world ever since the beginning of the Christian Church up to this hour, as the books and writings of the dear fathers, both in Greek and in Latin prove ... For it is dangerous and terrible to hear or to believe anything against the harmonious testimony, faith and doctrine of the holy Christian Church which has now endured harmoniously in the whole world for more than 1,500 years (WA 30. III. 552).

For Luther, catholicity was spiritual not empirical: it was defined in relation to the holy gospel alone. What is handed on in succession is not place or power but the word of God. 'If you ask the pope, Why are you the people of God? he replies, Because I sit in the seat of the apostles Peter and Paul, I am their successor ... But a dog or a pig can sit in the seat of Peter. But to have vocation, that is, believe the word, over and above that succession, this constitutes the Church and the sons of God' (WA 43. 387; cf. Melanchthon, CR 24. 402). And again:

> We have the calling of God, for he revealed himself to us, that we should have God visible, sensible and apprehensible. We have the word, baptism, the keys and we still suffer ... Our heirs (*posteri*), who are really ours, will abide even here on earth, as from time to time the other prophets have had their abode from the beginning of the world, and as with a kind of hereditary right handed over to us the voice of God (*quasi jure nobis vocem Dei tradiderunt*: WA 43. 404).[14]

Calvin, as we have already noted, is not opposed to episcopacy on principle and on the Roman claim of apostolic succession he goes so far as to say: 'Would that the succession which they falsely allege had continued until this day: with us it would have no difficulty in obtaining the reverence which it deserves. Let the pope be the successor of Peter, provided he performs the office of an apostle' (TT 3.265).

In criticising the notion of apostolic succession, none of the Reformers is rejecting the doctrine of a continuous visible community of faith and teaching. Indeed, the Reformers strenuously maintain this as an article of faith. As Calvin says: 'We certainly deny not that the Church of God has always existed in the world; for we hear what God promises concerning the perpetuity of the seed of Christ. In this way too we deny not that there has been an uninterrupted succession of the Church from the beginning of the gospel even to our day.' What the Reformers do emphatically deny is that this succession, tradition or continuity is dependent on the episcopate. So Calvin goes on: 'But we do not concede that it was so fixed to external shows that it has hitherto always been, and will henceforth always be, in possession of the bishops.' The apostolic succession is a hollow boast unless it is primarily a succession in truth and faith. 'If the Church resides in the successors of the apostles, let us search for successors among those only who have faithfully handed down their doctrine to posterity.' And to sum up: 'We deny the title of successors of the apostles to those who have abandoned their faith and doctrine' (TT 3. 264f.; cf. Inst. IV. ii. 2).

The sixteenth-century Anglican divines followed the continental Reformers in holding that the true succession of the apostles lay in the faithful handing on of their doctrine. Rome had failed to do this and her claim to possess an unbroken episcopal succession from the apostles was therefore spiritually worthless. So Jewel writes against Harding: 'Succession, you say, is the chief way for any Christian man to avoid antichrist. I grant you, if you mean succession of doctrine' (PS 3. 348). And Whitaker asserts: 'We regard not the external succession of places or persons but the internal one of faith and doctrine.'[15] And Philpott writes to the Archbishop of York (Nicholas Heath) in 1555: 'If you put to the succession of bishops succession of doctrine withal (as St Augustine doth), I will grant it to be a good proof of the catholic Church; but a local succession is nothing available' (PS 139). How lightly the English Reformers sat to apostolic succession is revealed when, in 1560, Archbishop Parker wrote to Calvin that the Church of England would continue to adhere to episcopacy since she derived it not from the Roman Church but from Joseph of Arimathea![16]

It follows that, for the Anglican divines, catholicity is defined in relation to truth not to the universal jurisdiction of the hierarchy or of the pope. Inward possession of truth was set above the outward imposition of unity. As Latimer remarks; 'We ought never to regard unity so much that we would or should forsake God's word for her sake' (PS 1. 487). Mere unity is neutral; to be valuable it must be unity in truth. On this point, the English Reformers excel themselves: 'There was the greatest consent that might be amongst them that worshipped the golden calf and among them who with one voice jointly cried against our Saviour Jesus Christ, "Crucify him!" ' (Jewel, PS 3. 69). 'Eve and Adam and the serpent were all of one mind' (Sandys, PS 94). For the Reformers—and here the English divines are merely representative—universality is only equivalent to catholicity when it is joined with truth. Unity must be in verity. (See also Jewel, PS 3. 137, 622f.; Sandys, PS 95; Bradford, PS Sermons, 394.)

CHAPTER NINE

THE GODLY PRINCE

As we acquaint ourselves with the thought of the protestant Reformers, we are from time to time brought up sharply against aspects of their outlook which particularly jar against our own assumptions. The campaign by some Reformers and puritans for implementation of the Mosaic penal code in place of the common law of the land; the obfuscation of eucharistic doctrine by pre-Copernican cosmology as Reformers argued about the precise location of Christ's glorified body; and the equation of heretical opinions with treason against the state are cases in point. With a feeling of culture-shock we realise that we are dealing with a world of thought whose continuity with our own is far from being direct or unproblematical. As often as we seek to return to the fountainhead of Reformation theology, the problem of its contextuality and relativity confronts us. The doctrine of the godly prince or magistrate, modelled on the kings of ancient Israel, while it rings strangely in modern ears, dominated the Reformers' thinking on the nature of the Church and its ministry.

As Norman Sykes has said: 'At this distance of time and amid such different conditions of ecclesiastical and political development, the Reformation apotheosis of "the godly prince" strikes an unfamiliar, if not actually uncongenial, note on our ears; and there is a strong resultant tendency to discount the prominence and centrality of this theme in the theology no less than the ecclesiology of the sixteenth century. Yet there can be no doubt that the rediscovery in the historical books of the Old Testament of "the godly prince", and the argument therefrom a a fortiori to the authority of the Christian sovereign, was one of the most important and significant themes of the Reformers, alike Lutheran, Calvinist and Anglican.'[1]

Two points in Norman Sykes' remarks deserve emphasis: first of all, the role of the magistrate in Church government was not, needless to say, confined to the Church of England (though the Royal Supremacy is its most explicit form and the one that will particularly concern us), but was common to all the Churches of the Reformation. Secondly, the doctrine of the godly prince was a biblically-based, profoundly religious concept, held in the fear of God. As J. J. Scarisbrick has pointed out:

> Early sixteenth-century scriptural scholarship may have been elementary and knowledge of early Christian history flimsier still, but they were sufficient to convince men of integrity that kings had been called by God to be his vicars on earth and endowed by him with the sacred duty of nursing the spiritual as well as the temporal lives of their subjects. It was not only expediency, or anger, or hope of gain which caused Englishmen to abandon their allegiance to the old order. Though the doctrine of the Royal Supremacy seems remote and uncongenial now, and evidence which supported it suspect, we must remember that, to such as Cranmer and doubtless many others, it was real and compelling—both a revelation and a liberation—and that for them the king's headship was a holy thing which demanded obedience as to a father in God.[2]

It is essential not to think anachronistically of the Church's dependence on the magisterial structure of society in the sixteenth century. For one thing, the Reformers are not adumbrating a theory of the state at all (least of all, of the modern secular state): theirs is a view of society, not of the state; of Church government, not of political theory. The background is the theocratic *corpus Christianum* of the medieval synthesis of Church and commonwealth. The theory of the godly prince was not what it may appear to us to have been—an appeal from Church to state in what was essentially a religious matter. It was an appeal from one officer to another within a single society, the Christian commonwealth. This is not giving Caesar the things that belong to God, because the things of God, according to evangelical theology, are the inward and eternal things: all else, being outward and temporal, must be Caesar's. So Melanchthon writes in the *Apology of the Augsburg Con-*

fession: 'Christ's kingdom is spiritual; it is the knowledge of God in the heart, the fear of God and faith, the beginning of eternal righteousness and eternal life' (BC 222f.). Not being essential to salvation, external and temporal matters are *adiaphora*, things indifferent, and the Church is content to let them be administered for her.[3]

PRINCE VERSUS POPE

There were only two sources of authority and jurisdiction in the sixteenth century—the pope and the prince—and the former was as much a temporal ruler as the latter. As Pollard wrote:

> The whole jurisdiction of the Church was derived in theory from the pope; when Wolsey wished to reform the monasteries he had to seek authority from Leo X; the Archbishop of Canterbury held a court at Lambeth and exercised juridical powers, but he did so as *legatus natus* of the Apostolic See and not as Archbishop, and this authority could at any time be superseded by that of a *legatus a latere*, as Warham's was by Wolsey's. It was not his own but the delegated jurisdiction of another. Bishops and archbishops were only the channels of a jurisdiction flowing from a papal fountain.

Pollard's ensuing remarks bear closely on the theme of our study:

> There were in truth two and only two sources of power and jurisdiction, the temporal sovereign and the pope; reformation must be effected by the one or the other. Wolsey had ideas of a national ecclesiastical reformation, but he could have gone no further than the pope, who gave him his authority, permitted. Had the Church in England transgressed that limit, it would have become dead in schism and Wolsey's jurisdiction would have *ipso facto* ceased. Hence the fundamental impossibility of Wolsey's scheme; hence the ultimate resort to the only alternative, a reformation by the temporal sovereign, which Wycliffe had advocated and which the Anglicans of the sixteenth century

justified by deriving the Royal Supremacy from the authority conceded by the early fathers to the Roman emperor—an authority prior to the pope's.[4]

While, in the nineteenth century, the pope could be dismissed by a British politician as 'a foreign prince of no great power', this could not have been said in the sixteenth century when the papacy, by virtue of alliances backed by spiritual sanctions which were still worth many battalions, constituted a power to be reckoned with. Even in the English tradition, as recently as the late fifteenth century, Sir John Fortescue had upheld the conservative view that the pope wielded both the temporal and the spiritual swords and could intervene in the internal affairs of a catholic country should the king mistreat his subjects. Acceptance of the Royal Supremacy meant repudiating the temporal as well as the spiritual power of the pope. The *Act extinguishing the authority of the Bishop of Rome* in England (1536) accuses the pope of using spiritual pretensions as a cloak for power politics and of threatening the temporal well-being of the king's subjects: The pope, it says,

did obfuscate and wrest God's holy word and testament a long season from the spiritual and true meaning thereof to his worldly and carnal affections, as pomp, glory, avarice, ambition and tyranny, covering and shadowing the same with his human and politic devices, traditions and inventions, set forth to promote and stablish his only dominion, both upon the souls and also the bodies and goods of all Christian people, excluding Christ out of his kingdom and rule of man his soul as much as he may, and all other temporal kings and princes out of their dominions which they ought to have by God's law upon the bodies and goods of their subjects; whereby he did not only rob the King's, Majesty, being only the supreme head of this his realm of England immediately under God, of his honour, right and preeminence due unto him by the law of God, but spoiled this his realm yearly of innumerable treasure, and with the loss of the same deceived the King's loving and obedient subjects ...[5]

When Elizabeth came to the throne, it was necessary for Parliament to reaffirm the abolition of the papal jurisdiction which had been restored under Mary. This it did by the *Act of Supremacy* (1559) which, in a similar way, linked together the temporal and spiritual power of the papacy.

To the intent that all usurped and foreign power and authority, spiritual and temporal, may for ever be clearly extinguished and never to be used nor obeyed within this realm ... may it please your Highness that it may be further enacted by the authority aforesaid that no foreign prince, person, prelate, state or potentate, spiritual or temporal, shall at any time after the last day of this session of Parliament use, enjoy, or exercise any manner of power, jurisdiction, superiority, authority, preeminence or privilege spiritual or ecclesiastical within this realm.

All office-holders in the Church had to take an oath of allegiance to the effect that 'the Queen's Highness is the only supreme governor of this realm ... as well in all spiritual or ecclesiastical things or causes as temporal, and that no foreign prince, person, prelate, state or potentate hath or ought to have any jurisdiction ... ecclesiastical or spiritual within this realm.'[6]

Hooker too points out against puritan critics of the Royal Supremacy that it is intended to exclude foreign powers (HW 3. 343). What, in the statute book of Henry VIII, may appear to be mere rhetoric, was transformed into dire reality when, by the Bull *Regnans in excelsis* of 1570, the pope excommunicated Elizabeth and catholic subjects were incited to rise against her.

THE LIBERATION OF THE LAITY

It ought to be stressed, furthermore, that the crucial role assigned to the magistrate in the Churches of the Reformation was in keeping with one of the fundamental principles of evangelical theology: the Reformation had been an attempt to throw off clerical domination and to give the laity a significant share in the government of the Church. Luther had appealed to the nobility of the German nation in 1520 as members of the universal priesthood to take in hand the reform of the Church. The course of the English Reformation under Henry VIII was decisively influenced by Henry's consistent anticlericalism. The Royal Supremacy was opposed both by catholics such as Thomas More and puritans such as Cartwright precisely because it made a layman head of the Church. When, under Elizabeth, Parliament was brought in to share, as it were, the Supremacy, the caesaropapism of Henry gave way to the ascendancy of the laity. The Supremacy of Henry had been largely a personal attribute which Parliament had been merely called upon to endorse: that of Elizabeth was a corporate supremacy of the lay members of the Church of England represented by the Queen-in-Parliament.

G. R. Elton characterises this development as 'the unquestioned triumph of the laity over the clergy.'[7] The *Act of Supremacy* of 1559 gave Parliament the power to judge in matters of doctrine and to determine heresies. The Queen, it said,

> shall not in any wise have authority or power to order, determine or adjudge any matter or cause to be heresy but only such as heretofore have been determined, ordered or adjudged to be heresy by the authority of the canonical Scriptures, or by the first four General Councils or any of them, or by any other General Council wherein the same was declared heresy by the express and plain words of the said canonical Scriptures, or such as hereafter shall be ordered, judged or determined to be heresy by the High Court of Parliament of this realm with the assent of the clergy in their Convocation.

This statement is important, not only as affirming the appeal of the reformed English Church to holy Scripture and the first four General Councils, but also as expressing the presupposition of the Reformation movement that the clergy have no monopoly of insight where Christian doctrine is concerned.

Richard Hooker, whose eighth book the *Laws of Ecclesiastical Polity* is the definitive statement of the Royal Supremacy, also defends the rights of the laity. 'Now the question is,' he says, 'whether the clergy alone so assembled ought to have the whole power of making ecclesiastical laws, or else consent of the laity may thereunto be made necessary ...' Until either papists or puritans are able to prove 'that some special law of Christ hath for ever annexed unto the clergy alone the power to make ecclesiastical laws, we are to hold it a thing most consonant with equity and reason, that no ecclesiastical law be made in a Christian commonwealth without consent as well of the laity as of the clergy ...' (HW 3. 399). The mind of the laity is expressed through Parliament which is not, in Hooker's view, a purely secular body concerned only with temporal and material affairs: it should take counsel for the spiritual well-being of the nation and ideally work in cooperation with the Convocation of the clergy:

> The Parliament of England together with the Convocation annexed thereunto is that whereupon the very essence of all government within this kingdom doth depend; it is even the body of the whole realm; it consisteth of the king and of all that within the land are subject unto him: for they all are there present, either in person or by such as they voluntarily have derived their very personal right unto. The Parliament is a court not so merely temporal as if it might meddle with nothing but only leather and wool.

The papists, on the other hand, assume that as a lay body Parliament has no competence in ecclesiastical affairs and that 'there is no more force in laws made by Parliament concerning the Church affairs than if men should take upon them to make orders for the hierarchies of angels in heaven'!

According to Hooker, no friend of absolute monarchy (his eighth book could not have been written under Henry), the whole realm has voluntarily entrusted the care of its affairs, both temporal and spiritual, to the prince. The laws made for the government of the realm do not therefore receive their force from any power which the king may condescend to devolve upon Parliament, 'but from power which the whole body of this realm being naturally possessed with, hath by free and deliberate assent derived unto him that ruleth over them ... So that our laws made concerning religion do take originally their essence from the power of the whole realm and Church of England, than which nothing can be more consonant unto the law of nature and the will of our Lord Jesus Christ' (HW 3. 408, 412).

Thus, in sixteenth-century thought, the role of the magistrate, the godly prince, as governor of the Church is a defence against both papal imperialism and clerical domination.

CHURCH AND STATE

A fundamental presupposition of the reformed doctrine of the godly prince was the almost universal identification of Church and commonwealth. For the Reformers, these represented two aspects of one social entity. In no school of sixteenth-century thought—except some varieties of anabaptism—were Church and commonwealth actually opposed: they were distinguished but not divided. 'I perceive no such distinction of the commonwealth and the Church,' declares Whitgift, 'that they should be counted as it were two several bodies governed with divers laws and divers magistrates.' And again: 'I make no difference betwixt a Christian commonwealth and the Church of Christ' (PS 1. 21; 3. 312). The Christian commonwealth was modelled on ancient Israel where godly kings took in hand the reform of the Church. So Cranmer urged the young Edward VI to be a second Josiah:

> Your majesty is God's vice-gerent and Christ's vicar within your own dominions, and to see, with your predecessor Josiah, God truly worshipped and idolatry destroyed, the tyranny of the bishops of Rome banished from your subjects and images removed. These acts be signs of a second Josiah, who reformed the Church of God in his days. You are to reward virtue, to revenge sin, to justify the innocent, to relieve the poor, to procure peace, to repress violence and to execute justice throughout your realms (PS *Remains* 127: speech at the coronation of Edward VI).

The second canon of 1604 credits the monarch with 'the same authority in causes ecclesiastical that godly kings had amongst the Jews and Christian emperors in the primitive

Church.' It is interesting that Cartwright, who would only
accept the Royal Supremacy in a qualified sense, asserted
that Old Testament kings exercised ecclesiastical jurisdiction
not as kings but because they were also prophets of God—or,
if not prophets themselves, they received a special commission
through the prophets.[8]

Hooker begins his defence of the Royal Supremacy with
the statement:

> It was not thought fit in the Jews' commonwealth that the
> exercise of supremacy ecclesiastical should be denied unto
> him to whom the exercise of chiefty civil did appertain; and
> therefore their kings were invested with both ... According
> to the pattern of which example, the like power in causes
> ecclesiastical is by the laws of this realm annexed unto the
> crown.

Those who oppose this, Hooker points out, must either
assert the sole rule of the clergy and the incompetence of the
laity in all ecclesiastical affairs or make a radical separation
between Church and commonwealth. His own assumption is
that every body politic maintains some religion (he cannot
conceive of a purely secular society) and that the Christian
Church is the body politic that maintains the true religion.
'Truth of religion' is therefore the decisive criterion whereby
'a Church is distinguished from other politic societies of men'.
The Church of Jesus Christ, Hooker concludes, 'is every such
politic society of men as doth in religion hold that truth which
is proper to Christianity. As a politic society it doth maintain
religion; as a Church, that religion which God hath revealed
by Jesus Christ' (HW 3. 327ff.). He is of course assuming
that there can be no such thing as a secular state and that
'pure and unstained religion ought to be the highest of all
cares appertaining to public regiment' (HW 2. 13f.). The
identity of Church and commonwealth is made explicit:
'There is not any man of the Church of England but the same
man is also a member of the commonwealth; nor any man a
member of the commonwealth which is not also of the
Church of England.'

For Hooker, the logic of his position is inescapable: 'For if
all that believe be contained in the name of the Church, how

should the Church remain by personal subsistence divided from the commonwealth, when the whole commonwealth doth believe?' There is indeed a difference of nature between Church and commonwealth, just as there is between Christian and citizen, but there need not be a difference of person: the same individual may be both Christian and citizen and the same society both Church and commonwealth. (Could it be that Hooker is aware of the analogy here with the doctrine of the Incarnation in which two natures are united in one person?) Temporal and spiritual affairs are but 'several functions of one and the same community'. This being so, kings are responsible for both the temporal and spiritual welfare of their subjects. 'A gross error it is to think that regal power ought to serve for the good of the body and not of the soul; for men's temporal peace and not for their eternal safety: as if God had ordained kings for no other end and purpose but only to fatten up men like hogs and to see that they have their mast' (HW 3. 330-6, 363).

Only a short step was needed for the clergy to be seen as ministers of the king and the magistracy as a sort of priesthood. The parallel between the king's clerical and civil servants is explicitly made by Cranmer:

All Christian princes have committed unto them immediately of God the whole cure of all their subjects as well concerning the administration of God's word for the cure of souls, as concerning the ministration of things political and civil governance. And in both these ministrations they must have sundry ministers under them ... The ministers of God's word under his majesty be the bishops, parsons, vicars and such other priests as be appointed by his highness to that ministration ... All the said officers and ministers, as well of the one sort as of the other, be appointed, assigned and elected in every place by the laws and orders of kings and princes ... And there is no more promise of God that grace is given in the committing of the ecclesiastical office than it is in the committing of the civil office (PS *Remains*, 116).

Two convictions (common to all the Reformers to one degree or another) underlie Cranmer's concluding remark here that equal grace is given to civil and ecclesiastical ministers.

Firstly, Cranmer held with Luther that ordination is merely the outward and public recognition of the essential inward call to the ministry. He raises the question, 'Whether in the New Testament be required any consecration of a bishop and priest, or only appointing to the office be sufficient?' and answers it by saying that, in the New Testament, 'he that is appointed to be a bishop or priest needeth no consecration ... for election or appointing thereunto is sufficient.' It follows that, in Cranmer's view, the magistrate may appoint to the priesthood:

> A bishop may make a priest by the Scripture and so may princes and governors also, and that by the authority of God committed to them, and the people also by their election: for as we read that bishops have done it, so Christian emperors and princes usually have done it; and the people, before Christian princes were, commonly did elect their bishops and priests (PS ibid., 117).

Secondly, it followed from the evangelical doctrine of vocation and the abolition of the medieval distinction between the temporal and spiritual estates that the magistrate and the priest were equally servants of God following their different callings.

Henry VIII consistently maintained that the spirituality were ministers of the crown—*his* clergy, exercising an authority delegated by him.[9] Whitgift spoke habitually of the queen's double cure, spiritual and temporal: 'as she doth exercise the one by the lord chancellor, so doth she the other by the archbishops' (PS 2. 246). Robert Some declared in 1588 that the magistracy was an order or ministry in the Church, for 'by a ministry, I understand not only the ministry of the word and sacraments ... but that ministry which concerneth the relief of the poor and the civil government.'[10] It is not fortuitous that Hooker too refers to those who bear the administration of justice as 'priests' (HW 2. 13).

'ERASTIANISM'

A final note before we leave introductory matters and go on to sketch the views of the Reformers on the place of the magistrate in the ministry of the Church: In the history of ideas—as indeed in any other context—labels can be misleading. The terms 'deism' and 'deistic', for example, are common coin in describing religious thought—irrespective of the fact that possibly the only pure form of deism is to be found in the speculations of Aristotle regarding the 'unmoved mover' of all things. Other views often labelled 'deist', such as the thought of Lord Herbert of Cherbury, known as the 'father of English deism', merely evince deistic tendencies or contain deistic elements and are really, to varying degrees, forms of Christian theism. In a similar way, the Reformation concept of the godly prince has often been labelled 'erastian' after Thomas Liebler, known as Erastus (1524-83). But to call the doctrine of the office of the magistrate in the Church 'erastian' confuses the issue by ignoring two fundamental points.

Firstly, Erastus himself did not in fact hold the views that now go by his name. He did not actually teach that the Church was the creature of the state. What he did hold was that, in a Christian state, the magistrate is the proper person to punish all offences, including religious ones, and that coercive power ought to be taken out of the hands of officers of the Church. He did not empower the magistrate to excommunicate or give him authority in matters of doctrine. As J. N. Figgis has pointed out, Erastus' main aim was 'not to magnify the state nor to enslave the Church, but to secure the liberty of the subject'.[11]

Secondly, the views commonly known as 'erastianism' are not to be found in their fully developed form in sixteenth-century political or religious thought. They came to their full expression in the teaching of Thomas Hobbes' *Leviathan* (1651) on the all-powerful and all-embracing state, embodied in the absolute sovereign holding office by divine right—*jure divino*. Hobbes shares the assumption of the English Reformers on the identity of Church and commonwealth: all forms of sovereign power, 'whether monarchs or assemblies', are the representatives of a Christian people and therefore representatives of the Church, 'for a Church and a commonwealth of Christian people are the same thing'. Hobbes' absolute power is free of the restraints of law—natural, positive and customary—and Parliament, which received such stress from sixteenth-century English writers on polity. Hobbes empowers the sovereign to judge what doctrines are to be taught its subjects and to appoint and remove pastors:

> Seeing then in every Christian commonwealth, the civil sovereign is the supreme pastor, to whose charge the whole flock of his subjects is committed, and consequently that it is by his authority that all other pastors are made and have power to teach and perform all other pastoral offices; it followeth also that it is from the civil sovereign that all other pastors derive their right of teaching, preaching and other functions pertaining to that office and that they are but his ministers ... If a man therefore should ask a pastor, in the execution of his office, as the chief priests and elders of the people (Matt. 21.23) asked our Saviour, 'By what authority doest thou these things and who gave thee this authority?' he can make no other just answer but that he doth it by the authority of the commonwealth, given him by the king, or assembly that representeth it.

'All pastors,' Hobbes concludes, 'except the supreme, execute their charges in the right, that is, by the authority of the civil sovereign, that is, *jure civili*. But the king and every other sovereign executeth his office of supreme pastor by immediate authority from God, that is to say, in God's right or *jure divino*.' Bishops are—equally with civil servants—employed 'on his majesty's service'.[12] Hobbes is here trying to put the clock back to the days of Henry VIII. He differs from Elizabethan thought in making the monarch absolute, and from Jacobean and Caroline doctrines in denying the divine right of bishops. Pure 'erastianism'—if we want to use the word at all—finds its ultimate statement in the *Leviathan*: it does not accurately describe the teaching of the sixteenth-century Reformers in England or anywhere else.

Let us now consider the views of Luther, Calvin and the English puritans on the Church and the magisterial structure of society. The complex question of the English Reformers and the Royal Supremacy will be reserved for a separate chapter.

LUTHER AND THE TWO KINGDOMS

Luther's view of the relation between the Church and the magistrate represents a reinterpretation of medieval ideas in the light of Reformation principles. The great dream of the middle ages had been of a Christian civilisation, a *corpus Christianum*, in which there were two complementary sources of authority, the emperor to rule men's bodies and the pope to rule their souls. The emperor wielded the power of the sword, the pope the power of the keys: the one could bestow temporal benefits, the other eternal life. According to this ideal, there was no question of a clash between Church and state: there was not yet any such thing as the state considered in abstraction from the Church. There was only the one Christian commonwealth, ruled by the magistrate and the priest.

As far as the background to Luther's thought is concerned, however, two developments served to profoundly modify this ideal. The first was the assumption of temporal power by the papacy—a claim to wield both swords—upsetting the balance of medieval society and provoking a groundswell of resentment culminating in the great revolt of the sixteenth century. The second was the large extent to which the German nobility already exercised almost proprietory rights over the Church through patronage (*Eigenkirche*). So when Luther called upon the nobility to take upon themselves the reform of the Church, and when the Diet of Speyer of 1526 enunciated the principle *cuius regio, eius religio* (that citizens should follow the religion of their ruler), they appeared merely to be conforming to a well-established tradition.

Luther thought of society in medieval terms: he accepted the ideal of the *corpus Christianum* with its two complementary sources of authority and developed it into his dominant doctrine of the Two Kingdoms (*Zwei Reiche*), substituting, however, the gospel for the pope. What exactly Luther meant by the Two Kingdoms is a complex and much disputed question and there is no need for us to enter upon it at any length. We ought to note, however, that the phrase

'Two Kingdoms' is misleading by itself. Luther did indeed think of two kingdoms or spheres, being influenced here by Augustine's *The City of God*—the kingdom of this world and the kingdom of heaven, and even the devil's kingdom and Christ's kingdom. But, more importantly, Luther is concerned not with two separate and opposed entities but with two types and sources of authority or regiment—spiritual and temporal.

The spiritual authority of the Church is authority over the soul only. It is persuasive not coercive. As the Lutheran formularies make abundantly clear, Christ's kingdom is spiritual—the knowledge of God in the heart and the life of faith. The power of the keys is purely the power to preach the gospel, to forgive or retain sins and to administer the sacraments (BC 81). The temporal authority of the magistrate, on the other hand, is authority over the bodies and goods of men, not over their souls. It is coercive rather than persuasive. It is concerned not with saving righteousness in the heart but with external, civil righteousness in conduct and is based on the second table of the decalogue only. 'Temporal authority is concerned with matters altogether different from the gospel. Temporal power does not protect the soul, but with the sword and physical penalties it protects body and goods from the power of others' (BC 82). It is therefore of the utmost importance that the two kingdoms or regiments are not 'mingled or confused' (BC 83). Luther's fundamental criticism of the papacy with its machinery of canon law was that it had hopelessly confused the two kingdoms, to the destruction of souls.

The temporal power has no say in matters of doctrine. 'When temporal princes and lords in a high-handed manner try to change and be masters of the word of God and decide themselves what shall be taught and preached—a thing which is as forbidden to them as to the meanest beggar—that is seeking to be God themselves ... like Lucifer' (WA 51. 240). On the other hand, however, while they cannot decide doctrine, they ought to see that it is upheld. 'The chief members of the Church, the kings and princes,' should ensure that 'errors are removed and consciences are healed' (BC 329). Their first duty is to advance the glory of God. In this vein Melanchthon appeals to the emperor, Charles V:

Therefore, gracious Emperor Charles, for the sake of the glory of Christ, which we know you want to extol and advance ... It is your special responsibility before God to maintain and propagate sound doctrine and to defend those who teach it ... [Kings] should take care to maintain and propagate divine things on earth, that is, the gospel of Christ, and as vicars of God they should defend the life and safety of the innocent (BC 236).

Here the Lutheran formularies seem to approximate to the Calvinist view of the magistrate as the executive of the Church. But the stress which the doctrine of the universal priesthood received in Luther's thought prevented any such lopsidedness developing—indeed the tendency was all the other way, towards magisterial domination of the Church. While in one sense the two kingdoms must be kept unconfused, in another, the magistrate is himself a member of the Church and shares in the universal priesthood.

On precisely these grounds, Luther was able to appeal to the German nobility in 1520. And when, in 1527, Luther and other Wittenberg Reformers invited the Elector of Saxony to undertake a visitation of the parishes, it was stressed that as a magistrate he had no such obligation but should act out of Christian love and for the sake of the gospel. He would be an emergency bishop, a bishop in time of need (*Notbischof*).

In practice, however, the strict separation of the two kingdoms was not maintained—there were too many anomalies in the confused circumstances of Reformation Germany: bishops holding temporal authority and magistrates seeking to fulfil their duties in the light of their personal religious convictions. As Cargill Thompson sums up the matter:

Technically Luther had managed to preserve the distinction between the regiments. He continued to hold that the magistrate had no *ex officio* authority in the Church and that he could act only in his capacity as an individual Christian. But the distinction was tenuous, and he had in fact opened the way to the eventual domination of the Church by the state which was to become an almost universal feature of Lutheranism.[13]

CALVIN AND PURITANISM

Calvin and the English puritans came closest to asserting the separation of Church and commonwealth. For Calvin, they were distinct realms that should not be confused. There are echoes of Luther's doctrine of the Two Kingdoms when Calvin declares in the *Institutes*: 'He who knows how to distinguish between the body and the soul, between the present fleeting life and that which is future and eternal, will have no difficulty in understanding that the spiritual kingdom of Christ and civil government are things very widely separated.' But they are not, he hastens to add, opposed to each other. The civil government 'is in the sight of God not only sacred and lawful but the most sacred and by far the most honourable of all stations in mortal life'. Calvin speaks of the magistracy as 'this sacred ministry' and uses the same language of the magistrate as he does of the minister of the word: 'they have a commission from God, they are invested with divine authority and, in fact, represent the person of God as whose substitutes they in a manner act.' Like Luther, Calvin looks on the magistrate as God's executioner. In inflicting punishment he 'acts not of himself, but executes the very judgments of God'.

The magistrate is responsible not only for morals but for the maintenance of religion; he must see that both tables of the law are followed. His duty is 'to foster and maintain the external worship of God, to defend sound doctrine and the condition of the Church, to adapt our conduct to human society, to form our manners to civil justice, to conciliate us to each other and to cherish common peace and tranquility'. His task, Calvin repeats, is to ensure that

> no idolatry, no blasphemy against the name of God, no calumnies against the truth, nor other offences to religion break out and be disseminated among the people; that the public quiet be not disturbed, that every man's property be kept secure, that men may carry on innocent commerce with each other, that honesty and modesty be cultivated; in short, that a public form of religion may exist among Christians and humanity among men' (*Inst.* IV. xx. 1-10).

We see that the concept of the godly prince figures as prominently in Calvin's thought as in that of the English Reformers. The difference is, however, that Calvin would never give the magistrate authority to decide questions of doctrine or to initiate acts of ecclesiastical jurisdiction. His role was merely executive. This is an aspect of Calvinist thought that becomes more explicit in the teaching of Thomas Cartwright in England.[14]

It is a remarkable fact that both puritans, like Cartwright, who denied that the kings of the Old Testament—*as kings*—held any ecclesiastical jurisdiction, and separatists, like Barrow, who held that reform should not tarry for the magistrate, were apparently happy to take the oath recognising the Royal Supremacy. Obviously, this they could do only by putting their own construction on the doctrine. For while Barrow held that it was 'the duty of every Christian, and principally of the prince, to enquire out and renue [*sic*] the laws of God and stir up all their subjects to more diligent and careful keeping of the same', the extent to which he was actually prepared to recognise the queen's supremacy in ecclesiastical matters is revealed in his remark that he acknowledged her as supreme governor of the whole land 'and over the Church also, *bodies and goods*' (my italics). It was, paradoxically, over temporal aspects of the spiritual body that she governed. This should not be dismissed as an eccentric view, for, as we shall see, it has support in the Anglican divines, who also, however, gave the magistrate authority in doctrine.

Cartwright too saw the sovereign as competent in temporal aspects of Church affairs but qualified this not with power over doctrine but with the notion of the prince as the executive of the Church, i.e., the clergy. According to Cartwright, the Church is not to be regarded as the commonwealth in its spiritual aspect but as a separate, self-contained and independent society ruled by its ministers.

But in the sixteenth century it did not follow from this that the state was a purely secular body and that there should be no kind of interaction between Church and state. On the contrary, the state, no less than the Church, is subject to immutable divine law of which the clergy are the authorised interpreters. The magistrate has the duty to carry out a religious reformation where necessary and at all times to maintain true religion.

> The prince and civil magistrate hath to see that the laws of God, touching his worship and touching all matters and orders of the Church, be executed and duly observed and to see that every ecclesiastical person do that office whereunto he is appointed and to punish those which fail in their office accordingly.

But he is not to usurp the authority of ministers or to dictate to the Church about its own internal affairs.

> As for the making of the orders and ceremonies of the Church, they do (where there is a constituted and ordered Church) pertain unto the ministers of the Church and to the ecclesiastical governors; and that, as they meddle not with the making of civil laws for the commonwealth, so the civil magistrate hath not to ordain ceremonies pertaining to the Church.

As a member of the Church, the king is himself subject to ordinary ecclesiastical discipline. 'That princes should be excepted from ecclesiastical discipline and namely excommunication, I utterly mislike,' says Cartwright. Now, as Hooker pointed out, Cartwright's view of the prince as the executive of the Church and subject to its discipline was precisely that of the papists. This is why so much of Hooker's argument in the eighth book of the *Ecclesiastical Polity* applies equally to both his puritan and papist opponents and enables him to deal with both positions simultaneously.

Not that Hooker believes that princes should be exempt from all discipline. Here it is important to bear in mind the traditional distinction between lesser excommunication or refusal of admission to Holy Communion on the one hand, and greater excommunication which entailed civil penalties on the other. Hooker denies that Christian princes are subject to the latter and that 'ecclesiastical judges should have authority to call their own sovereign to appear before them into their consistories, there to examine, to judge, and by excommunication to punish them, if so be they be found culpable'. But as far as lesser excommunication is concerned, 'such as is only a dutiful, religious and holy refusal to admit notorious transgressors in so extreme degree unto the blessed communion of saints, especially the mysteries of the body and blood of Christ, till their humbled penitent minds be made manifest: this we grant every king bound to abide at the hands of any minister of God wheresoever through the world' (HW 3. 454).[15]

CHAPTER TEN

THE ROYAL SUPREMACY

In the Royal Supremacy of the English sovereign, the evangelical Church of the Reformation became most closely involved with the magisterial structure of society. Precisely what powers in Church affairs were claimed by the sovereign? How far were these powers accorded by the English Reformers and what restrictions were placed upon their exercise? How did the concept of the godly prince evolve in England in the sixteenth century?

HENRY VIII

There is evidence that Henry VIII himself toyed with claims of unrestricted authority in ecclesiastical matters. His arrogation of supreme power in the spiritual sphere was both symbolised and initiated in 1533 when he took his divorce case out of the hands of the pope and asserted the competence of the English Church and parliament to settle it. 'By so doing,' it has been justly claimed, 'he committed England to a course the every advance of which was unprecedented, illegal and momentous.'[1] By a series of measures from 1534 to 1545 Henry transferred to himself as sovereign all the powers and prerogatives of the papacy within his realm. The king was invested with plenitude of power in both temporal and spiritual jurisdiction. England was an empire and its Christian emperor—another Constantine—could be subject to no external authority. As the *Act of Appeals* claimed in 1533:

Where by divers sundry old authentic histories and chronicles it is manifestly declared and expressed that this realm of England is an empire, and so hath been accepted in the world, governed by one supreme head and king having the dignity and royal estate of the imperial crown of the same, unto whom a body politic, compact of all sorts and degrees of people divided in terms and by names of spiritualty and temporalty, be bounden and owe to bear next to God a natural and humble obedience; he being also institute and furnished by the goodness and sufferance of almighty God with plenary, whole and entire power, preeminence, authority, prerogative and jurisdiction to render and yield justice and final determination to all manner of folk resiants [residents] or subjects within this realm, in all causes, matters, debates and contentions happening to occur, insurge or begin within the limits thereof, without restraint or provocation to any foreign princes or potentates of the world ...

It is only as a corollary of the supreme jurisdiction of the sovereign that the independence of the Church and its councils can be claimed, for the document goes on:

the body spiritual whereof having power when any cause of the law divine happened to come in question, or of spiritual learning, then it was declared, interpreted and shewed by that part of the said body politic called the spiritualty, now being usually called the English Church, which always hath been reputed and also found of that sort that both for knowledge, integrity and sufficiency of number, it hath been always thought and is also at this hour sufficient and meet of itself, without the meddling of any exterior person or persons, to declare and determine all such doubts and to administer all such offices and duties as to their rooms spiritual doth appertain.[2]

The Royal Supremacy approved by parliament entailed the king's right to license all new canons of Church law; to undertake visitations of ecclesiastical institutions and to delegate the power of visitation to his civil ministers (Thomas Cromwell, notably); and to appoint bishops for due election by cathedral chapters on pain of *praemunire* (i.e., contempt).[3]

The *Act of Supremacy* of 1534 explicitly gave the king the power to reform errors of doctrine. It deserves to be quoted extensively, both as a summary of the powers of the Supremacy and because the exact wording is crucial to an understanding of the debates that ensued during the next half-century and more.

> Be it enacted by authority of this present parliament that the king our sovereign lord, his heirs and successors kings of this realm, shall be taken, accepted and reputed the only supreme head in earth of the Church of England called *Anglicana Ecclesia*, and shall have and enjoy annexed and united to the imperial crown of this realm as well the title and style thereof, as all honours, dignities, pre-eminences, jurisdictions, privileges, authorities, immunities, profits and commodities, to the said dignity of supreme head of the same Church belonging and appertaining. And that our said sovereign lord, his heirs and successors kings of this realm, shall have full power and authority from time to time to visit, repress, redress, reform, correct, restrain and amend all such errors, heresies, abuses, offences, contempts and enormities, whatsoever they be ... [4]

More extensive quotation from this Act would reveal the significant fact that—ostensibly at least—parliament did not claim to be creating the Royal Supremacy of the Christian emperor, but merely to be recognising and ratifying a state of affairs with its roots in remote antiquity.

As J. J. Scarisbrick remarks, Henry was his own theologian—he never doubted either his ability or authority to put learned divines right about Christian doctrine. The fact that they did not always accept his proposals does not affect Henry's own estimate of himself.[5] In a speech in parliament in 1545, Henry implied that he had the right to forbid the reading of the Scriptures and, where their meaning was doubtful, alone decide the correct interpretation. As Allen puts it: 'The secular ruler, it appears, is to decide all controverted questions of doctrine, to determine what of tradition is sacred and what worthless, to decide in fact what are the essentials of the Christian religion.'[6]

Such unlimited aspirations received support from the Tudor civil lawyers who were prepared to see the king acquire unrestricted powers of jurisdiction in spiritual causes provided that civil causes were safeguarded from royal interference by natural, positive and customary law. They were only alerted to the dangers of royal absolutism when it began to appear that even ecclesiastical jurisdiction might make inroads into the common law.

The writings of Christopher St Germain reflect step by step every stage of Henry's breach with Rome and incorporation of ecclesiastical power in himself. According to St Germain, the authority to interpret Scripture belongs to the Church as a body; the clergy are only a part of the Church. It is 'emperors, kings and princes with their people' who comprise the Church catholic. Since, however, it is obviously impossible to gather the entire Church together to expound the Scriptures, 'it seemeth that kings and princes, whom the people have chosen ... have the whole voices of the people' and may 'with their counsel spiritual and temporal make exposition of such Scripture as is doubtful'. This was published in 1535 and Henry, while greedily accepting the power it gave him to interpret doctrine, would not have welcomed the implication that kings held their thrones by popular consent.[7] Tudor political theorists, remarks F. Le Van Baumer,

> set up a veritable cult of royal authority and proclaimed the essential sinfulness of resistance to the king under any circumstances. They asserted the superiority of the king in parliament over canon, statute, municipal and even at times customary law. They fell short of enunciating a theory of unlimited royal sovereignty, it is true. Nevertheless, the king, in consequence of their labours, emerged from the conflict with Rome with a prestige greatly advanced and with an aureole of sanctity around him reminiscent of the Roman emperors.[8]

THE SPIRITUAL COMPETENCE OF
THE SOVEREIGN

The Anglican Reformers were prepared to allow the king authority in doctrinal questions and in the appointment of bishops. They granted him supreme jurisdiction in Church as well as commonwealth though, as we shall see, they attempted to set limits to his power. What none of them was prepared to admit under any circumstances was that the

king's headship could in any way detract from the headship
of Christ. King Henry VIII, explained Cranmer, was head
'of all the people of England as well ecclesiastical as temporal ... The king is head and governor of his people, which
are the visible Church ... there was never other thing meant'
(PS 2. 224). When the king's power is termed supremacy,
remarks Hooker, 'what man is there so brain-sick as not to
except in such speeches God himself, the king of all the kings
of the earth?' (HW 3. 342).

At Cranmer's examination in 1555, the revealing dialogue
went as follows:

Questioner: 'You denied that the pope's holiness was
    supreme head of the Church of Christ?'
Cranmer: 'I did so.'
Q.   'Who say you then is supreme head?'
C.   'Nobody.'
Q.   'Ah! Why told you not king Henry this ... ?'
C.   'I mean not but every king in his own realm and
    dominion is supreme head, and so was he supreme head
    of the Church of Christ in England.'
Q.   'Is this always true? and was it ever so in Christ's
    Church?'
C.   'It was so.'
Q.   'What say you then by Nero? He was the mightiest
    prince of the earth, after Christ was ascended. Was he
    head of Christ's Church?'
C.   'Nero was Peter's head.'
The interrogator, not liking the suggestion that the pope
was subject to the emperor, repeats:
Q.   'I ask, whether Nero was head of the Church or
    no ... ?'
C.   'Nay, it is true, for Nero was head of the Church,
    that is, in worldly respect of the temporal bodies of men,
    of whom the Church consisteth; for so he beheaded
    Peter and the apostles. And the Turk too is head of the
    Church of Turkey.'
Q.   'Then he that beheaded the heads of the Church and
    crucified the apostles was head of Christ's Church; and
    he that was never member of the Church is head of the

Church, by your new-found understanding of God's word' (PS 2. 219).

Cranmer's replies certainly shed light on what was meant by the Royal Supremacy among the Anglican Reformers, but the question remains how headship of the Church 'in worldly respect of the temporal 'bodies of men' is consistent with the king's authority in matters of Christian doctrine. The ambiguity and confusion here persists at least as far as Whitgift. It is, however, to some extent resolved by taking an overall view of Reformation theology, according to which— by virtue of the universal priesthood—authority in doctrine ceased to be the exclusive preserve of the clergy and was shared with the laity, the king being their most eminent representative. This is not to say, however, that clear-cut theological principles were present in the minds of the Reformers every time they defended the Royal Supremacy.

It is interesting that Cardinal Allen, writing in defence of the Jesuits and seminarists, the recusant priests of Elizabeth's reign, argues that, just as the Church in ancient Rome was spiritually independent of Nero's jurisdiction and the Church of present-day Turkey free of interference by the Caliph in its spiritual affairs, so she ought always to be a free, spiritual society with her own spiritual head, namely, the pope, whether she lives amongst heathens or Christians. In reply, Richard Hooker grants that (in the reigns of the pagan emperors) 'the commonwealth of Rome was one society and the Church of Rome another', but argues that the conversion of Constantine and the establishment of Christianity as the state religion introduced a radically new situation. Under those circumstances, the only way that Church and commonwealth could be distinguished would be by defining the Church as the clergy exclusively.

But when whole Rome became Christian, when they all . embraced the gospel and made laws in defence thereof, if it be held that the Church and the commonwealth of Rome did then remain as before: there is no way how this could be possible, save only one, and that is, they must restrain the name of the Church in a Christian commonwealth to the clergy, excluding all the residue of believers, both prince and people.

Within this realm of England, Hooker concludes, we differ both from the pagans, in that with us one society is both Church and commonwealth, and from the papists, in that 'our Church hath dependency upon the chief in our commonwealth.' 'In a word, our estate is according to the pattern of God's own ancient elect people, which people was not part of them the commonwealth and part of them the Church of God, but the selfsame people whole and entire were both under one chief governor on whose supreme authority they did all depend' (HW 3. 331-4, 340).

Evidently play was made by Roman controversialists of the admission by Cranmer and others that in a sense even a pagan sovereign was head of the Christian Church within his realms. But in what precise sense this could be said was explained by Fulke:

> That an ethnic prince or Turk may be supreme head of our Church, we utterly deny to any such the name of an head which cannot be a member: but even an ethnic prince or Turk may be chief magistrate over the faithful and make laws for the maintenance of Christian religion, as an hypocrite Christian may' (PS 2. 262).

Hooker too is careful to distinguish the Royal Supremacy from the transcendent headship of Christ over his Church: a different 'kind of dominion' is meant. 'Christ is head as being the fountain of life and ghostly nutriment, the well-spring of spiritual blessings poured into the body of the Church.' Other earthly governors are heads 'as being his principal instruments for the Church's outward government: he head as founder of the house; they as his chiefest overseers' (HW 3. 386).

Hooker is not prepared to go as far as earlier divines in according the sovereign authority in doctrinal questions. Cranmer, for example, drawing up his views on some disputed points for the consideration of the king, appends the revealing postscript: 'This is mine own opinion and sentence at this present, which I do not temerariously define, and do remit the judgment thereof wholly unto your majesty' (PS *Remains*, 117). Whitgift asserts that 'the continual practice of Christian Churches, in the time of Christian magistrates, before the usurpation of the bishop of Rome, hath been to give to Christian princes supreme authority in making ecclesiastical orders and laws, yea and that which is more, in deciding of matters of religion, even in the chief and principal points' (PS 3. 306). Hooker, however, stigmatises as 'absurd' the suggestion that the English Church holds the view.

> that kings may prescribe what themselves think good to be done in the service of God; how the word shall be taught, how sacraments administered; that kings may personally sit in the consistory where bishops do, hearing and determining what causes soever do appertain unto those courts; that kings and queens in their own proper persons are by judicial sentence to decide the questions which rise about matters of faith and Christian religion; that kings may excommunicate; finally, that kings may do whatsoever is incident unto the office and duty of an ecclesiastical judge (HW 3. 431).

The extent of the king's authority in spiritual affairs was understood in the light of the traditional distinction between *potestas ordinis*, the purely spiritual power of a priest to consecrate and administer sacraments and to give absolution and benediction in the name of God, and *potestas juris- dictionis*, the power of jurisdiction, the authority to make and enforce orders for the government of the Church. Henry VIII neither overtly claimed nor tacitly enjoyed the power of order, although it should be recognised that Henry's extreme anticlericalism may in due course have led him so to devalue the office of priesthood that some of its functions came within his grasp. The fact is, however, that this did not happen, nor would it have been tolerated by either parliament or Church. It is true that parliament gave to the king absolute ecclesiasti- cal jurisdiction and the power to interpret doctrine but, as Baumer says, 'they stopped short of making him a spiritual person with the right to consecrate bishops, to preach and to administer the sacraments. Henry VIII was made supreme head, but not high priest.'[9]

The Anglican formularies are quite unambiguous about this. *The Bishops' Book* of 1537 stated: 'We may not think that it doth appertain unto the office of kings and princes to preach and teach, to administer the sacraments, to absolve, to excommunicate, and such other things belonging to the office and administration of bishops and priests.' *The Thirty-nine Articles of Religion* (1562) echo this when they declare:

Where we attribute to the king's majesty the chief government, by which titles we understand the minds of some slanderous folks to be offended, we give not to our princes the ministering either of God's word or of the sacraments ... but that only prerogative which we see to have been given always to all godly princes in holy Scriptures by God himself; that is, that they should rule all estates and degrees committed to their charge by God, whether they be ecclesiastical or temporal, and restrain with the civil sword the stubborn and evildoers.

Hooker points out more than once that 'to lead men unto salvation by the hand of secret, invisible and ghostly regiment or by the external administration of things belonging unto priestly order (such as the word and sacraments are): this is denied unto Christian kings' (HW 3. 363; cf. 356f.). The monarchs not only did not attempt to exercise *potestas ordinis* themselves, but they did not attempt to inhibit the bishops in exercising it.[10]

The *potestas jurisdictionis* was traditionally divided into two parts: the *jurisdictio poli*, the right of dispensation in the matter of vows and penances, i.e., concerning a man's spiritual life and relation to God, which was denied to the king as being closely bound up with the power of order; and the *jurisdictio fori*, the power of jurisdiction in external ecclesiastical matters but including, significantly, authority in doctrine. By canon law all these powers, not only of order but also of jurisdiction, were reserved to the clergy. In the light of fundamental Reformation principles, however, the English parliament set aside canon law and vested certain of these powers in the king, a layman.

As far as appointments to the episcopate are concerned, there are, if we follow Hooker, three aspects to be

distinguished: a bishop's orders, jurisdiction and temporalities. Hooker would have it that it is only in the last of
these that the king's power is involved.

> In a bishop there are these three things to be considered:
> the power whereby he is distinguished from other pastors;
> the special portion of the clergy and people over whom he
> is to exercise that bishoply power; and the place of his seat
> or throne, together with the profits, preeminences, honours
> thereunto belonging. The first every bishop hath by
> consecration; the second his election investeth him with;
> the third he receiveth of the king alone (HW 3. 419).

Hooker is here trying to minimise the role of the sovereign
in the making of bishops, but there are two qualifications that
should be added. Firstly, by his nomination of bishops for
election by cathedral chapters on pain of judicial penalties,
the king had unequivocally the sole right to actually appoint
bishops, to say who should be a bishop. Nomination is thus a
fourth point to be added to Hooker's three: orders, jurisdiction and temporalities. Secondly, Hooker holds that
episcopal power could only be exercised on the king's subjects
with the king's permission. In a fragment, Hooker states his
view that the bishop's authority

> resteth nevertheless unexercised except some part of the
> people of God be permitted them to work upon ... A
> bishop, whose calling is authorised wholly from God and
> received by imposition of sacred hands, can execute safely
> no act of episcopal authority on any one of the king's liege
> people otherwise than under him who hath sovereignty
> over them all (HW 3. 467).

So although the king cannot create bishops—only God
through other bishops can do that—in every other respect
bishops are wholly dependent on the king. The relation of the
episcopate to the Royal Supremacy perhaps illustrates that
the king had more real power in practice than seemed to have
been conceded, in theological terms, on paper. As Christopher
Morris aptly comments:

In a sense the king got the substance while graciously foregoing the shadow. So long as he could say who should be bishops, the king did not mind who consecrated bishops. If he was free to reduce the seven sacraments to three (as he did in effect by the *Ten Articles* of 1536), he had no wish to administer a sacrament in person.[11]

A definite shift of emphasis away from caesaro-papism is discernible in the latter part of the century. Cranmer and the civil lawyers had been prepared to grant the king almost unlimited powers as their deliverer from papal oppression. After the initial crisis, the Anglican divines supported the Royal Supremacy as the protector of episcopacy against the threat of more radical reform in a presbyterian direction; they were prepared to pay the price of some curtailment of the power of the bishops. When, at about the turn of the century, the *jure divino* claim for episcopacy began to be heard in Anglican apologetic, the puritan wing began to rally to the crown as a counterbalance to the overweening claims of the bishops.[12] Throughout the sixteenth century, then, circumstances in England favoured the doctrine of the godly prince. But two developments had the effect both of reducing the claims of the Royal Supremacy and of limiting its power in practice.

Firstly, Anglican writers under Elizabeth tended to stress the king's responsibility for merely the outward regiment of the Church and to play down his authority in doctrine by setting it in the context of the role of parliament as the lay synod of the Church. Thus Jewel disclaims: 'Concerning the title of "supreme head of the Church" ... first, we devised it not; secondly, we use it not; thirdly, our princes at this present use it not.' (Elizabeth was merely 'supreme governor'.) For Jewel, the prince was simply 'the highest judge and governor over all his subjects whatsoever, as well priests as laymen' (PS 4. 974). According to Fulke, the duty of the prince is not to perform any ecclesiastical function but 'to provide and command that they may be done as they ought to be.'

Neither do we call any king head of the Church, but only Christ: but in every particular Church the Scripture alloweth the king to be the chief magistrate, not only in governing the commonwealth but also in making godly laws for the furtherance of religion; having all sorts of men, as well ecclesiastical as civil, subject unto him, to be governed by him and punished also, not only for civil offences but also for heresy and neglect of their duties pertaining to the religion of God (PS 2. 261ff.).

Similarly, Hooker gives the magistrate 'supreme authority in the outward government which disposeth the affairs of religion so far forth as the same are disposable by human authority' (HW 3. 363).

Secondly, whereas Henry's supremacy had been a largely personal attribute, that of Elizabeth was increasingly regarded as shared with parliament: it was the supremacy of queen-in-parliament. Even under Henry, in spite of some unguarded remarks by civil lawyers and theologians (Tyndale, for example, had once claimed: 'The king is, in this world, without law and may at his lust do right or wrong and shall give accounts but to God only'), it had never been forgotten that the king was subject to, and the executive of natural and divine law; 'neither in his capacity as legislator by prerogative, nor as legislator with parliament, was he held to be above that eternal law'.[13] Moreover, it was affirmed with growing confidence as the century progressed that the king was subject also to positive law, both statute and custom, and to the laws of the Church. In his coronation oath, the king pledged himself 'to hold and keep the laws and rightful customs of this realm'. The supremacy of law even over the king is strongly asserted by Hooker, though he notes that the necessary restrictions on the king's power 'hath not hitherto been agreed upon with so uniform consent and certainty as might be wished'. Hooker lays it down as a self-evident truth that 'where the law doth give him dominion, who doubteth but that the king who receiveth it must hold it of and under the law'—and explicitly adds that this includes the positive laws of the Church (HW 3. 342, 357f.).

The grandiose pretensions of Henry and Elizabeth did not always accord with what parliament and the Church were prepared to concede. As J. J. Scarisbrick has shown, Henry himself thought of the supremacy in simple terms and of ecclesiastical authority descending from God to himself and as mediated through him to the body spiritual. But this was not the view that was sanctioned by parliament and supported by the Anglican Reformers.

Two views of the supremacy contended for dominance in sixteenth-century England: one claiming the supremacy as a personal attribute of the king received directly from God; the other seeing it as derived from the whole body politic and exercised by the king-in-parliament. While the former view seemed to prevail for the duration of Henry's reign—not only because of the king's overbearing personality and unrestrained ruthlessness, but also because parliament was united behind him in opposition to papal and clerical power—it was the latter view that ultimately triumphed in the Elizabethan age, notably in Hooker's definitive statement of the Anglican settlement. For although Elizabeth tried to repulse parliamentary attacks on her ecclesiastical policy with the claim that religion as a matter of state was her personal prerogative on which she would brook no criticism, she was, as Scarisbrick points out, standing on questionable ground constitutionally and, furthermore, she was out of tune with the thought of the great divines who adorned her Church for whom the protestant doctrine of the godly prince was not an excuse for caesaro-papism but a vindication of the rights of the laity in the Church of Christ.[14]

Thus Reformation ecclesiology ultimately—if not always very decisively—asserted the determinative significance of the gospel, the Church's christological centre, for its doctrine of the Christian ministry in all its forms, however historically conditioned. But that gospel, as the Reformers understood it, constituted a dynamic force, not a static state of affairs, at the heart of the Church's life. For, as Karl Barth once remarked, the Church is the crater formed by the explosion of the gospel. That explosion carried the protestant Churches forward in the mission of the true Church that forms the subject of Part III.

THE MISSION OF THE TRUE CHURCH

CHAPTER ELEVEN

THE REFORMERS AND MISSION

It is widely assumed that the protestant Reformers had no interest in foreign missions: though they believed that they had rediscovered the apostolic gospel, they had no apostolic vision of its spread to the uttermost parts of the earth. This is a view that modern historians seem to share with Counter-Reformation Roman Catholic polemicists. Cardinal Robert Bellarmine (1524-1621) listed among the numerous marks of the true Church its missionary activity and compared the strenuous efforts of Roman missionaries with the total failure of the protestants:

> Heretics are never said to have converted either pagans or Jews to the faith but only to have perverted Christians. But in this one century, the catholics have converted many thousands of heathens in the new world. Every year a certain number of Jews are coverted and baptised at Rome by catholics who adhere in loyalty to the Bishop of Rome; and there are also some Turks who are converted by the catholics both at Rome and elsewhere. The Lutherans compare themselves to the apostles and the evangelists; yet though they have among them a very large number of Jews and in Poland and Hungary the Turks as their near neighbours, they have hardly converted even so much as a handful.[1]

Modern historians of missions have seen no reason to dissent from Bellarmine's view. Stephen Neill, in his *History of Christian Missions*, seeks a balanced judgment and writes: 'It is clear that the idea of the steady progress of the preaching of the gospel throughout the world is not foreign to [Luther's] thought. Yet when everything favourable has been said that can be said and when all possible evidences from the writings of the Reformers have been collected, it all amounts to exceedingly little.'[2] K. S. Latourette's *History of* the *Expansion of Christianity* reveals once again the dismal record of the evangelical Churches compared to the Church of Rome: 'In the sixteenth century, the heyday of Roman Catholic missionary activity, protestants made almost no attempt to propagate the faith outside Europe.'[3] An even more severe judgment is expressed by W. R. Hogg who goes as far as to accuse the Reformers of lacking any perception of 'the missionary dimension of the Church':

> The Reformers evidenced no concern for overseas missions to non-Christians ... To document in detail [Luther's] lack of a theology of missions would require a small book ... Similarly, one searches John Calvin's *Institutes* and commentaries without finding any positive recognition of a theology of missions. Examination of Zwingli, Bucer, John Knox and Melanchthon produces the same negative report ... the overwhelming and well-nigh unanimous evidence points in the Reformers to no recognition of the missionary dimension of the Church.[4]

It is the aim of the third part of this book to present a rather different picture of the Reformers: to assess their concern for evangelisation and to examine their concept of mission.

It is, however, justified to speak in general terms of the strange silence of the Reformers on missions. When both Luther and Calvin comment on the Great Commission (Matt. 28), they remain bafflingly silent on the duty of present-day Christians to carry on the work of the apostles in bringing the gospel to 'every creature'. 'How are we to understand and hold this text ["Go ye into all the world"],' asks Luther, 'since the apostles have not really come into all the world?'

> For no apostle has ever come to us and many islands have been discovered even in our own times which are still heathen and no one has preached to them; yet the Scripture says that their doctrine has sounded in all lands and their line into all the world. Answer: their preaching has gone out into all the world although they [personally] have not come into all the world. This outgoing is begun and set

going, although it is not yet completed and accomplished; but it shall be preached wider and further until the last day. When this preaching is heard in all the world, then is the embassy fulfilled and completed in every respect; then also the last day shall come. It is with this embassy of preaching as when a stone is thrown into the water. It makes bubbles and circles and waves around it and the bubbles extend ever further and further, one chasing the other until they reach the bank. Thus it is also with preaching. It was begun by the apostles and it continually spreads and is pushed further and further by the preachers, though persecuted and driven here and there in the world and it is more and more widely proclaimed to those who have not heard it before, although it is quenched on the way and is declared heresy (WA 10 III. 140).

Here we wait in vain for the application that would follow naturally: we too must carry forward the message of the gospel throughout the world.

Calvin's treatment of the Great Commission is framed in similar terms to Luther's. His comment is polemical, against Rome, and historical: the exhortation one would expect never comes (CC *Harmony of the Gospels* 3. 250ff.). This strange silence constitutes the enigma of the Reformers and mission. Gustav Warneck points to the unexplained fact that no lament was raised over the practical difficulties of discharging the missionary obligation and claims that this was due to the fact that 'recognition of the missionary obligation was itself absent'. Warneck argues that the Reformers were prevented by theological prejudice from even thinking in missionary terms, let alone actually carrying out any missionary work. He concludes that 'insight into the permanent missionary task of the Church was really darkened in the case of the Reformers'.

THE BACKGROUND

In 1492 Columbus had stumbled upon the new world and five years later Vasco da Gama had become the first European to reach the west coast of India by sea. Boundless opportunities for the Christian Church were being opened up. As Latourette remarks, 'Discovery and conquest were opening the greatest door for expansion which any religion ever had.'[5] But on the world scene, Islam now held broader sway and exercised greater power than Christianity and was increasing it. The pre-Reformation Church was in decline. In addition, certain aspects of the Renaissance—a journey of discovery in another sense which had revived the learning of antiquity—were proving hostile to the Christian faith. A moribund, corrupt and intellectually discredited Church was hardly in a position to take advantage of the situation to propagate the faith. As Latourette suggests, it seemed that Christianity, its original impulse spent, had entered upon a tragic decline just when it faced the greatest challenge in its history.

When Calvin returned to Geneva in 1541 to attempt his programme of reform for the second time, the Jesuit Francis Xavier was on his way to India. In 1549, three years after the death of Luther, Xavier was preaching in Japan. His prayer for missions is sufficient comment on the spirit of his work: 'O God of all the nations of the earth, remember the multitudes of the heathen who, though created in thine image, have not known thee nor the dying of thy Son their saviour Jesus Christ; and grant that by the prayers and labours of thy holy Church they may be delivered from all ignorance and unbelief and brought to worship thee ...' As for the west, the first bishopric in the new world was established in 1511, the year that Luther entered Wittenberg.

The great voyages of discovery were motivated by the need for trade, the lust for gold, the desire for fame and sheer restless curiosity. But they were also linked to the missionary thrust of the Roman Church which had been more or less continuous for a thousand years. During that period the history of the Christian mission was of necessity the history of monasticism. It was a matter of course that the Christian faith should be taken to those parts of the world, hitherto unknown, except to legend, that were now made subject to Christian kings.

The year following Columbus' discovery, Pope Alexander VI divided the world into Spanish and Portugese spheres of operation and at the same time urged the Spaniards to seek to convert the peoples of the new world and 'to send to the said islands and to the mainland wise, upright, god-fearing and virtuous men who will be capable of instructing the indigenous peoples in good morals and in the catholic faith.'[6]

As well as the desire to bring the light of the gospel to those who lived in heathen darkness, the explorers, often commissioned by their sovereigns, aimed to enter into contact with the great Christian Churches, such as that of Prester John, which were believed to exist in unexplored parts of the world, with the ultimate purpose of constructing a great world alliance of the true faith which would be more than a match for the Turk. Motives were often very mixed. Vasco da Gama explained to the Indians that he was in search of Christians and spices. Bernal Diaz confessed that he and his fellows went to the Indies 'to serve God and his majesty, to give light to those who were in darkness and to grow rich, as all men desire to do'.[7]

OBSTACLES TO PROTESTANT MISSIONS

Both practical and theological obstacles had to be overcome before protestant missions could begin in earnest. There were in the first place serious practical difficulties. Until 1648 when the Peace of Westphalia brought to an end the religious struggle of the Thirty Years' War which devastated Germany, the protestants were fighting for mere survival and had neither the leisure nor the inclination to look to more distant horizons. Furthermore, when they were not fighting the catholics, protestants were arguing among themselves. As Stephen Neill aptly puts it:

> Instead of standing together and waiting for better times to clear their theological differences, protestants everywhere wasted their strength with honourable but blind and reckless zeal in endless divisions and controversies—strict Lutherans against Philippists, Lutherans against Reformed, Calvinist predestinarians against Arminians, Anglicans against puritans and independents.[8]

Internecine strife and theological controversy sapped the energy that might have gone into fulfilment of the Great Commission.

Besides this, opportunity for missions to the heathen was lacking to the protestants since they had no direct contact with heathen peoples; the sea lanes were dominated at that time by the navies of catholic countries; Switzerland for one had no outlet to the sea. While England was indeed a maritime nation, her explorers seemed to lack religious motivation. Cabot's *Ordinances* of 1553 advised explorers and settlers to be discreet about their beliefs; they should 'bear with such laws and rites as the place hath, where you shall arrive'.

Another important factor is that while a number of Reformers, such as Luther and Bucer, had been monks, the Reformation had rejected the entire monastic system and concept which for nearly a thousand years had provided the tradition, expertise and machinery of missions. Together with the new seminaries for secular priests, the religious orders continued to send out their highly trained and rigidly disciplined missionaries. The evangelical Churches could provide no structure to take the place of the monastic structure of Roman Catholic missions.

In the sixteenth century it was widely believed that there were lost Christian Churches in unexplored parts of the world, established by the preaching of the apostles. Pure legend attained almost dogmatic status in the belief that the Christian king Prester John ruled forty kingdoms in Africa. The Church of Prester John was appealed to in argument by both catholics and protestants, the catholics claiming that he acknowledged the authority of the pope. Among the Anglican Reformers, Becon asserted that Prester John practised communion in both kinds and Jewel that he had prayers in the vernacular (PS 1. 334) while Bale confused the issue by asserting that Prester John had merely founded a detestable and corrupt sect (PS 320). Similarly, protestants were aware of the existence of the Eastern Churches and Luther claimed—implausibly—that they believed in essentials the same as the evangelicals. In the seventeenth century John Gerhard alleged that there were more Christians in Great Tartary than in Europe. These points were deployed against Roman claims of catholicity but they also had the effect of inducing complacency about missions.

Secondly, there were, as Warneck particularly has stressed,

definite theological factors inhibiting protestant missions. The Reformers were disposed to think that the work of missions required a special office—one that either had already been fulfilled by the preaching of the apostles or rested solely with the sovereignty of God at the present time. For example, Calvin held that the offices of apostle, prophet and evangelist were extraordinary: 'they were not instituted in the Church to be perpetual but only to endure so long as Churches were to be formed where none previously existed'. But Calvin does not deny that God can raise up from time to time 'apostles—or at least evangelists' and looks upon the mission of Luther in this light: 'for such were needed to bring back the Church from the revolt of antichrist'. Calvin does not, however, regard the sending forth of missionaries or evangelists as a normal part of the Church's function, for he adds: 'The office I nevertheless call extraordinary because it has no place in Churches duly constituted' (Inst. IV. iii. 4). Alongside this, the evangelical doctrine of calling also hindered missions. 'Let everyone occupy his station for the gospel,' said Bucer, 'and the Church will grow.'

Moreover, the view gained ground that all nations had once—and once for all, apparently—been offered the true knowledge of God through the preaching of the patriarchs, especially Enoch and Noah. Even in cases where this preaching was not now effective the heathen still had the light of nature: natural religion was a *preparatio evangelica*. Luther himself rejected the notion that the heathen could be saved by the natural light and accused Zwingli of being 'a full-blown heathen' himself for suggesting that Hercules (!), Socrates, Numa, Cato, Scipio and others had been saved (LW 38. 290). But in the seventeenth century, the age of reformed scholasticism, Ursinus, Lutheran superintendent of Ratisbon, could say:

With respect to the heathen who are to be converted, they must not be barbarians who have hardly anything of humanity but the outward form, such as Greenlanders, Lapps, Samoyedes, cannibals; they must not be fierce and tyrannical, allowing no strangers to associate with them, like the remote Tartars beyond the Caspian Sea, the Japanese of the present day and whole nations in the northern regions of America. In short, they must not be headstrong blasphemers, persecutors of the Christian religion. The holy things of God are not be cast before such swine.[9]

Here Ursinus evinces an attitude usually associated with extreme hyper-calvinism. In the same vein, the *First Admonition to Parliament* criticised those prayers in the Book of Common Prayer which 'pray that all men may be saved without exception and that travelling by sea and land may be preserved, Turks and traitors not excepted ... In all their service there is no edification: they pray that all men may be saved.' In striking contrast, the Counter-Reformation pope, Paul III, declared in 1537: 'All are capable of receiving the doctrines of faith.'

A further factor in inhibiting missionary effort is the dominance of eschatology in the sixteenth-century mind. Luther's world of thought was incorrigibly apocalyptic: both he and Melanchthon believed the end of the world to be imminent. The darkness was already passing away; the night was far spent; the day was at hand. There could be no question of long-term missions to remote and inaccessible lands. Karl Holl has rejected this interpretation of the failure of the evangelicals in missionary work, arguing that if the end of all things prevented missions, it would equally well prevent the reform of the Church. But the point is precisely that Luther's belief in the imminent end was founded on the success of the evangelical reform—the gospel had at last revived—and the gathering opposition it faced from both pope and Turk, the forces of antichrist.

PROTESTANT MISSIONARY CONCERN

There were, however, several points of unquestionably genuine missionary concern in the protestant Churches of the Refomation. Erasmus had already boldly criticised the unspiritual methods often employed by Roman missions and with forceful eloquence had sought to lay the duty of true mission on the hearts of his contemporaries. Several of the Reformers—Melanchthon and Zwingli, for example—were deeply influenced by the Christian humanism of Erasmus and in certain respects never ceased to be his disciples, but they did not follow him here.

It is in the thought of Martin Bucer that more than one scholar has detected a true missionary vision. Henri Strohl, for example, has asserted that Bucer alone among the Reformers insists on the missionary task of the Church. Commenting on the injunction in Ezekiel 34.16 to seek the lost and bring back the strayed, Bucer remarks that the Church must bring to Christ those who know him not, sending forth the gospel from home territory even as far as heathen lands. As Bucer sees the matter, while God alone knows his elect, he has commanded us to go forth and call all creatures to eternal life. The Church is the city of God 'where God will rule by his word and Spirit more than anywhere else in the world, and from whence he will spread his saving doctrine into all the earth'.[10] Similarly, Knox's *Scots Confession* of 1560 proclaimed on the title page: 'And this glaid tydinges of the kingdom shal be preached throught the hole world for a witness to all nations and then shall the end cum.' Hadrian Saravia, who had now made his home in England and had been befriended by Richard Hooker, asserted in his treatise on the ministry in 1590: 'The command to preach the gospel to all nations binds the Church since the apostles have been taken up into heaven'—and was rebuked by Beza for it. It is, however, among the anabaptists and spiritualists that the missionary vision shines most brightly.

Among the radicals a distinctive concept of mission followed from a distinctive concept of the Church and of what it meant to be a Christian. Developing reformed principles to their logical conclusion, they stressed personal commitment and explicit faith, so pushing Luther's doctrine of the priesthood of all believers in the direction of a 'universal lay apostolate' (G. H. Williams). Individual anabaptists were evangelists rather than ecclesiastical reformers, sojourners rather than parishioners. Their sense of self-identity reflected aspects of the pilgrim, the mystic and the martyr. They saw the path of God's people in history as a path of suffering leading to its apocalyptic climax in the present age. The martyr theme, as Ethelbert Stauffer has shown, underlies the distinctive anabaptist concepts of baptism (into Christ's death), confession of faith ('faithful unto death'), and passive resistance ('like a lamb led to the slaughter'). As Conrad Grebel exhorted Müntzer in 1524: 'True Christian believers are sheep among wolves ... and must be baptised in anguish and affliction, tribulation, persecution, suffering and death.'[11]

The anabaptists seemed to prove in the crucible of suffering that theirs was the irresistible mission of the true Church. As F. H. Littell makes clear, the anabaptists did not regard themselves as a minority witness, temporarily withdrawn until the great Church should mend its ways. Neither did they accept the status of conventicles, little cells of piety, acting as a leaven within the great mass of baptised Christians in the territorial Churches. 'They believed that the true Church with its disciplined laymen carried history.' The Great Commission of Matthew 28 provided them both with their manifesto and their marching orders. 'Our faith stands on nothing other than the command of Christ,' they affirmed, 'for Christ did not say to his disciples, "Go forth and celebrate the mass," but, "Go forth and preach the gospel." ' They saw the apostolic mission being revived among them: Christ, declared Menno Simons, 'sent out his messengers preaching this peace, his apostles who spread this grace abroad through the whole world, who shone as bright, burning torches before all men, so that they might lead me and all erring sinners into the right way.'[12]

G. H. Williams' description captures the atmosphere of visionary ferment and expectation in which the anabaptist mission was born:

> Separated from the territorial Churches and on principle repudiating the whole conception of God's renewed people being controlled by magistrates, however benevolent, the radical sectarians fanned out in utter disregard of territorial boundaries and local laws, emissaries and exemplars that they were of a gospel at once new and old, to be shared by the whole world. With imaginations excited by the vistas opened before them in Bible study, from apocalyptic rumour and through wide travel, the radicals pondered what might be the providential and redemptive significance of the persistence of the Jews, the military successes of the Turks and the opening up of whole continents of aborigines who had never heard either

of Adam and his fall or of the second Adam and a providential redemption.[13]

The magisterial Reformers assumed that peripatetic evangelism had been completed in the early centuries; now each Christian has his own parish and each bishop his diocese and no one ought to claim a roving commission. They saw the anabaptist programme—namely, that every believer must 'go forth'—as subversive of the social order. The Lutheran Justus Menius, writing in 1544, complained that the anabaptists asserted that 'we are not true servants of the gospel ... because we do not wander around in the world like the apostles but stay put and have our definite residence and our appointed pay'. God sent only the apostles into the world and they, for their part, had ordained that 'the servant of the gospel does not travel here and there about the land' like 'strange, unappointed, spiritual gypsies'.

The restlessness of the anabaptists conflicted sharply with the Reformers' stress on following one's vocation and their view of the Christian family as a sort of Church in miniature. They took every opportunity to castigate the anabaptists. Luther, for example, remarked that, after their visit to the infant Christ in the manger, the shepherds went straight back to their flocks and did not wander in the woods like the anabaptists![14]

LUTHER ON THE MISSION OF THE CHURCH

Martin Luther's view of the mission of the Church now requires further consideration. Gustav Warneck, the father of missionary studies, claimed that missions were not an object of conscious concern for Luther. Warneck's views have, however, been subjected to devastating criticism by Karl Holl and Werner Elert and cannot now be allowed to stand. In favour of Warneck's case, it is true that Luther is aware of the existence of foreign Churches: 'In Armenia, Ethiopia, Mauritania, India and the lands toward the East there are still many Christians' (WA 12. 540). And Luther sometimes speaks as though the gospel has virtually completed its mission to all nations; it has been preached in Egypt, Greece, Italy, Spain and France; now it has come to Germany—'but who knows for how long?' (WA 23. 533). It is also interesting that Luther cannot believe that the heathen are longing to receive the gospel (WA 13. 541).

While he disagrees vehemently with Zwingli and the Socinians that the natural religion of the heathen could lead some of them to salvation, Luther accepts that the ancients may have been saved—but only through the preaching of the patriarchs, for salvation is of the Jews (LW 8. 133ff.; cf. 2. 42f.). Luther has of course heard of the newly-discovered 'islands', but he believes that no one—neither patriarchs nor apostles—has ever preached in these heathen places (WA 47. 565; 20. 526; 5. 547, etc.). He thinks that the story of the apostles dividing up the world between them for preaching the gospel is pure legend and he holds that Germany at least was never visited by an apostle. As Elert states: 'The idea of many later theologians—that the Church of the present time is no longer obligated to preach among the heathen because the apostles have already reached all—is totally foreign to him, just as it is to Melanchthon.'[15] The spread of the gospel throughout the world, begun by the apostles, is not yet complete: the servants are still going out into the highways and byeways to invite us to the feast (WA 17 I. 442).

In connection with the doctrine of the universal priesthood, Luther stresses the right and duty of every Christian to spread the gospel; he is obliged to do so on pain of losing his soul and incurring the grave displeasure of the Lord. 'If he is in a place where there are no Christians, he needs no other call than to be a Christian, called and anointed by God from within. Here it is his duty to preach and teach the gospel to erring heathen or non-Christians because of the duty of brotherly love, even though no man calls him to do so' (LW 39. 310).

It would be anachronistic to expect Luther to speak in terms of the missionary movement of the nineteenth century: he certainly had no clearly defined concept of the *structure* of missionary work. The key to Luther's thinking on this matter is his unequivocal grasp of mission as *the mission of the word of God*. The course of the gospel throughout the world is in progress and moving ever outward like the ripples on a pond. 'The gospel and baptism must come through the whole world' (*Das Evangelium und die Tauffe müssen durch die ganze Wellt komen:* WA 31. 339). 'Christ's kingdom is penetrating the whole world' (*Christi regnum per totum mundum transit:* WA 41. 594). Men are the weak and dispensable instruments of the irresistible power of the word of God. 'Though pastors may be weak and the world powerful, the holy gospel is still mightier and no obstacles can impede its progress. Even if all pastors were to be devoured, the gospel will make its way into the world all the better and transform the world' (LW 19. 98). As Elert puts it: 'The gospel always appears above the horizon, is always under way, is always on the attack.'[16]

CHAPTER TWELVE

THE SPREAD OF THE REFORM IN CHRISTENDOM

Mission is the Church going out into the world, but the Reformers saw that in their day the world had come into the Church. Both Luther and Calvin believed that their mission was primarily within the bounds of Christendom itself. In the preface to his *German Mass* (1526), Luther remarks that in the Churches there are 'many who have not yet believed or become Christians and the majority stand there and gaze to see something new, just as if we were holding divine services among the Turks or heathen'. When we consider the spread of the reform movement, we must reckon first of all with the personal mission of the individual Reformers—both their own sense of destiny and the impression that they made on contemporaries.

LUTHER'S PERSONAL IMPACT

Luther's closest followers—who, as A. G. Dickens reminds us, were not impressionable burghers but eminent and sophisticated humanists, brought up in the highly critical world of Erasmus, Reuchlin and Lefevre—came to regard Luther's mission as unique, original and divinely ordained. 'The chariots of Israel and the horsemen thereof!' was the lament raised by Melanchthon at Luther's death. No amount of discussion of predisposing social factors and intellectual tendencies can eclipse the overriding personal dominance of Luther himself. As the Roman Catholic scholar Imbart de la Tour has romantically described, Luther owed the success of his movement 'in the first place to himself, to his extraordinary personal powers which gave him mastery over men's souls and the ear of the multitudes'.

How we love to catch sight of him, not with the thickening and already tired features of the famous Cranach portrait, but still young and in monk's habit, as he appears in the little engraving which hangs in his chamber in the Wartburg. The body leans forward, poised to pounce upon the enemy, the bony fingers grip the Bible, the face is emaciated, with hard lines, piercing eyes almost burning with fever and strong taut lips, distended as if ready to sound to the multitudes the reveille of the new faith; he is all passion, movement, restless energy, indomitable will.

As A. G. Dickens justly states: 'Whatever values may now be placed upon Luther's attempt to reinterpret Christianity, one must at least credit him with a charisma and a communicative power almost unique in the history of modern western religion.'[1]

The reform spread through Christendom in two clearly distinguishable though not necessarily unconnected ways: by mass acceptance imposed by authority from above, and by personal choice and decision. It was by the method of mass diffusion that the crucial gains were made in the early years of the Reformation and reformed Churches established in Germany, England and Switzerland. But it is important to note that in many cases the imposition of the reformed religion followed close upon an initial upsurge of individual feeling. And, as Léonard has pointed out, it is necessary to distinguish between motives and methods: political methods were often followed at the behest of genuinely religious motives. Outside Switzerland (namely, in France, Scotland and the Netherlands) Calvinism spread chiefly by individual conversion.

This was the method originally envisaged by Luther; but, as we have seen, hard pressed by the excesses of the radicals, Luther eventually settled for a territorial Church; and the Lutheran mission was further hampered after Luther's death by the Peace of Augsburg of 1555 which, following the principle Cuius regio, eius religio, ordained that people in every kingdom should accept the religion of their ruler. , Protestant territory was extended by absorbing the bishoprics with their lands, protestant bishops often being elected by methods of naked political intrigue. In England parliamentary measures secured the establishment of the reformed religion; the legal enforcement of political decisions went on side by side with efforts to persuade individual consciences. Even the Elizabethan puritans believed in the state establishment of religion (though to put it like that is actually anachronistic) and that reform must come through the magistrate.

In Germany a wave of propaganda, unprecedented in volume and intensity, soon won the north of the country for the reform. The mass media of the time were fully exploited: crudely effective cartoons comparing the pomp and luxury of the papal court with the humility and simplicity of Christ; popular drama depicting the evangelical message; and the memorable if uninspiring verses of Hans Sachs in *The Wittenberg Nightingale* which could be sung by peasants at work:

> Luther teaches that we all
> Are involved in Adam's fall ...
>
> Christ the Lamb removes all sin;
> By faith alone in Christ we win.

But most powerful of all were the tracts of Luther himself, devastating, annihilating in their effectiveness. It is estimated that, even before Luther's decisive appearance at Worms, there were a third of a million pamphlets in circulation, either by Luther or in support of him. Between 1518 and 1523 the output of German printing presses multiplied sixfold and the number of German books printed went up from 150 in 1518 to 990 in 1524. As A. G. Dickens has pointed out, there thus occurred

> the first mass movement of religious change backed by a new technology, by the factor most clearly differentiating Luther's enterprise from its predecessors. Waldensianism, Wycliffism, Hussitism had made or failed to make, their several ways without the mechanical standardisation and reproduction of their manifestos.

It can plausibly be claimed that the Hussite movement failed through lack of propaganda. As Louise Holborn has commented, at the Reformation 'for the first time a religious and intellectual movement was not restricted to learned groups but had an immediate impact upon the people at large. This ... was one of the major factors in transforming a complicated theological debate into a great popular movement.'

It is interesting that Macaulay, writing in the 1840s from the point of view of 'the Whig interpretation of history', also saw the advent of printing 'in the fullness of time' as the decisive factor in securing the success of the Reformation. Before then, knowledge was largely confined to the clergy; 'not one man in five hundred could have spelled his way through a psalm; books were few and costly ...' Copies of the Bible, as Macaulay quaintly puts it, 'inferior in beauty and clearness to those which every cottager may now command', sold for prices which many priests could not afford. It was obviously impossible for the laity to search the Scriptures for themselves. But by the early sixteenth century, the availability of the printing press conspired with other factors to produce a situation that was ripe for the Reformation:

> The fullness of time was now come. The clergy were no longer the sole or the chief depositories of knowledge. The invention of printing had furnished the assailants of the Church with a mighty weapon which had been wanting to their predecessors. The study of the ancient writers, the rapid development of the powers of the modern languages, the unprecedented activity which was displayed in every department of literature, the political state of Europe, the vices of the Roman court, the exactions of the Roman chancery, the jealousy with which the wealth and privileges of the clergy were naturally regarded by lay-men ... all these things gave to the teachers of the new theology an advantage which they perfectly understood how to use.

A. G. Dickens has singled out two definite advantages that Luther enjoyed over his opponents in the pamphlet war. Firstly, he possessed a positive biblical message of good news and this 'lifted him above the cold tide of anticlericalism threatening to engulf German society'. Secondly, Luther had a flair for the simple, direct, concrete statement of profound religious truth, making it possible for the uneducated layman to grasp some essentials of his message.

Luther thus gave printed literature a new language (the vernacular), a new form (the pamphlet) and a new content (his own distinctive message). He described the art of printing as 'an unquenchable flame' and 'God's highest and extremest act of grace whereby the business of the gospel is driven forward'. His own influence was decisive in transforming printing from a somewhat esoteric art into an instrument for moulding public opinion. The ferment thus created came at a critical time for the Reformation and succeeded in establishing it as an unstoppable movement; but it did not last. After 1524 the output of the presses began to ebb, 'a clear indication', remarks Louise Holborn, 'of the break between the religious reformers and the common man. The protestant Churches in Germany were henceforth built up by the princes and theologians and popular response was no longer the determining factor.'

The modern reader of Luther is inevitably struck by what Dickens aptly describes as 'the antinomies between Luther's massive commonsense and his hasty injustices, between his brutal invective and his delicate spiritual perceptions'. But the impression made on contemporaries was rather different. 'Instead of an exhausted, bloodless, hairsplitting and sometimes nonsensical theology, lost in the subtleties of logic or the cloudy abstraction of systems, instead of coarse or frivolous sermons,' writes Imbart de la Tour, 'here was a simple, practical message, human even in its contempt for man, so impregnated with the Bible that it almost reproduced its cadences, sometimes so close to Christ that it seemed like an echo of the gospel. How could Christian Europe fail to be moved?'[2]

Though dwarfed by the enormous significance of the printing press, the role of students and itinerant scholars in spreading Reformation theology should not be underestimated. The fact that the number of students in the university of Wittenberg increased from 162 in 1516 to 579 in 1520 speaks for itself. The spectacular notoriety of Luther himself would undoubtedly have helped to attract them. Outside of Germany the spread of Reformation ideas depended even more directly on the world of scholarship. Where German was not spoken, Luther could not appeal directly to the masses; he could only reach them through the mediation of scholars who would read his Latin works. These men (Tyndale, Bilney, Frith, Cranmer and Barnes in England; Olavus Petri in Sweden; Lambert, Zwingli, Oecolampadius) were all, as H. J. Hillerbrand has pointed out, young and unknown men, not holding prestigious appointments in the academic or ecclesiastical establishments and with pronounced humanist sympathies. Luther of course appealed at first to a wider humanist circle and his ideas were given currency by it, but this temporary state of affairs was due to a misunderstanding of what was at the heart of Luther's message—as the rift with Erasmus over *The Bondage of the Will* shows.[3]

THE ANABAPTIST MISSION

While the magisterial Reformers believed that their mission was to reform Christendom, the anabaptists were convinced that the Reformers and their followers were themselves in need of conversion. Attempts to repress the radicals only served to further their mission as, driven from their homes, they went forth preaching their message at every opportunity. In this way the radical gospel not only pervaded protestant countries but also entered many areas closed to the protestant movement by its acceptance of the territorial principle. When in 1525 the first anabaptist congregation at Zollikon near Zurich was scattered, the members went forth in the belief that they were being called to fulfil the great commission. They would do so, G. H. Williams remarks, 'in programmatic heedlessness of the territorial and prudential limitations imposed by the magisterial Reformers'. They thus represent, in the view of F. H. Littell, 'an early protestant vision of a world mission unrestricted by territorial limitations and in a unique fashion foreshadow the later concept of the Church as a band of missionary people'.[4]

True to their principle of restitutionalism—a programme to restore the New Testament community—the radicals sought to follow apostolic methods: open-air preaching and letter-writing were thus the two divinely sanctioned forms of evangelism. While the radicals were indeed assiduous letter-writers, it was obviously the former method that could reach the masses. G. H. Williams has described a not uncharacteristic scene near St Gall in 1525:

> The exhortations of the anabaptist revivalists every evening and on holidays in the mountains, woods, fields and at the gates of the city had become so frequent and exciting that the town churches were drained of their attendants, divided in their counsel and deprived of alms for the sustenance of the poor.

As a result, the town council put a stop to all gatherings outside the churches.[5]

Hans Hut was one of the greatest anabaptist missionary preachers, baptising thousands and citing Matthew 28 as his warrant to both preach and baptise. But the anabaptist missionary impulse was eventually crippled by persecution among the South Germans and Swiss and by peace and prosperity among the Dutch Mennonites.

CALVIN AND THE CONVERSION OF FRANCE

From his point of vantage in Geneva Calvin could overlook the frontiers of his native land; the conversion of France to the reformed religion lay closest to Calvin's heart. Like Luther, he thought of himself as merely an instrument of the mission of the word of God.

> Seeing God hath given us such a treasure and so inestimable a thing as his word is, we must employ ourselves as much as we can that it may be kept safe and sound and not perish ... First of all, let every man see he lock it up fast in his own heart. But yet it is not enough for us to have an eye to our own salvation, but the knowledge of God must shine generally throughout all the world and everyone must be partaker of it; we must take pains to bring all them that wander out of the way to the way of salvation; and we must not only think upon it for our lifetime but for after our death.[6]

In France the work of Lefevre d'Etaples, the Christian

humanist who had taught justification by faith in his commentary on the epistles of St Paul some years before Luther, had prepared the way for a massive invasion of reformed propaganda. Calvin's own influence can be traced back to 1536 and the first edition of the *Institutes of the Christian Religion* with its 'Prefatory Address to His Most Christian Majesty, The Most Mighty and Illustrious Monarch, Francis, King of the French'. In 1541 the work appeared in a French translation and was followed ten years later by Calvin's French Bible. Preachers from Geneva began to arrive in 1553, reinforced by a constant stream of letters from Calvin himself containing encouragement and advice. In 1555 Jacques L'Anglois was sent to the congregation at Poitiers, which perhaps Calvin himself may have helped to organise. The Genevan Company of Pastors recorded that 'the brothers of Poitiers required this church to send them an upright man to minister to them the word of God'. Thereafter the principle was followed that missionaries were only sent from Geneva upon request.

The evangelisation of France by Genevan missionaries was undertaken almost entirely by Frenchmen returning to the land they had left either to avoid persecution or to seek a protestant education. Many of the young men lodged with professors of the Genevan Academy. They listened to Calvin's daily sermons and received as lectures much of the material now preserved in the commentaries. Students had to undergo rigorous examination as to their theological orthodoxy, preaching ability and private morality. Production of evangelical literature kept pace with the training of missionaries. By 1564 there were more than thirty-four printing presses operating in Geneva. In 1561 forty-eight titles were published. In the same year the peak of missionary activity was reached with more than 151 separate missions being undertaken, involving 142 men. Books and missionaries were together organising the restive French public for the religious revolution that eventually broke out in 1562.

In 1558 there were reckoned to be about thirty-four reformed churches with ministers in France. In the following year the first national synod assembled in Paris and, two years after that, Admiral Coligny claimed 2,150 congregations. Calvin, astonished by this rapidity of growth, wrote advising restraint and consolidation. But the rigours of holding services in woods and fields in all weathers took its toll of health and, besides this, an uncertain number of pastors, perhaps ten or a dozen, were martyred before the Wars of Religion began—some murdered by thugs, others executed for sedition, but none for heresy. The Calvinist Church organisation in France has been described by R. M. Kingdon as like a living spider's web with gossamer strands reaching into nearly every corner of the country, intersecting at urban commercial centres, converging on the royal court, while the Genevan Company of Pastors kept vigilant watch to detect instantly the breaking of any strand. G. R. Elton has remarked that French Calvinism 'had all the advantages of a subversive movement organised in cells and filled with a total faith in the future'. And another writer concludes: 'Thus a force from beyond the frontiers gave to the groups of Calvinists in France a supra-national character, a position of *imperium in imperio.*'[7]

The period of Calvin's illness and death saw a drastic decline in the scale of Genevan missionary effort with only a partial recovery under Beza (though some of the gaps were filled by pastors sent out by Guillaume Farel from Neuchâtel[8]). During the period 1563 to 1572 only thirty-one missionaries are mentioned, of whom twenty-eight went to France (and one, Thomas Cartwright, to England!). This compares with the figure of eighty-eight sent to France alone during the previous seven years. What were the reasons behind what R. M. Kingdon describes as 'this curious collapse'?

First of all, the death of Calvin had in itself robbed Geneva of its greatest single attraction to the idealistic French intellectuals who made the most likely missionary candidates. Secondly, the state of war in France and the outbreak of plague in Geneva constituted serious practical difficulties. Thirdly, the Genevan Company of Pastors was itself torn by dissension after Calvin's death. One half of all French protestant ministers had been students at the Genevan Academy and half of these had then served as pastors in Geneva: so, as Kingdon suggests, a greater proportion of French ministers than in the peak period of missionary endeavour had been moulded by 'the increasingly rigid matrix of Geneva' and, rather than strengthening the movement, this fact may have contributed to the existing tensions within the French congregrations caused by Genevan inflexibility.[9]

A further factor is the increasing importance of military protection for the pastors. Attached to Huguenot noblemen as domestic chaplains, they sometimes enjoyed an armed escort for itinerant preaching. In Holland too, where the protestants had emerged into the open in 1566 and begun to worship in the fields, members of the huge congregations would often be armed and the preacher sometimes be escorted to his pulpit by a body of mounted troops.

The mention of military force leads naturally to some reference to Zwingli, who died, sword and battleaxe in hand, on the field of Cappel in 1531 in the war between Zurich and the catholic cantons. For those who believed—as some of the Reformers, including Zwingli, certainly did—that the judicial laws of Moses were still binding, the idea of a holy war, like that of Israel against the Canaanites, was simply the logical conclusion. In such dramatic and sometimes bizarre ways did the Reformation spread through Christendom.[10]

CHAPTER THIRTEEN

THE CONVERSION OF THE JEWS

The ferment of the Reformation in western Christendom was paralleled by a comparable movement within the Jewish communities. The sixteenth century was an age of messianic expectation and speculation. The discovery of new lands signified to many Jews the imminent recovery of the lost tribes of Israel—a necessary prerequisite to the day of redemption. The triumph of humanist scholarship with its revival of Hebrew, followed by Luther's challenge to Rome, seemed to signal an era of greater freedom for the Jews whose existence had been rendered almost impossible during the later middle ages.

A cross-fertilization of ideas took place between Jews and protestants: the Jews were attracted by the liberty which Luther's message seemed to promise and by the Old Testament orientation of much protestant theology (Luther lectured on the Old Testament for twenty-eight out of a total of thirty-two years); the Reformers, humanists that they were, patronised Hebrew teachers and often engaged in friendly dialogue with Jewish rabbis.

The Reformers had in fact a love-hate relationship with the Jews: while they saw them as allies and potential converts, they remained implacably opposed to Jewish antitrinitarianism, millennialism, salvation by works and legalism. The term 'Judaizer' was a theological insult hurled by protestants not only at radicals and papists but at each other. For the Jews of Europe, the Reformation proved to be a false dawn and at times threatened to subject them to greater oppression than they had suffered in the Middle Ages.

THE POSITION OF THE JEWS

In the early sixteenth century, Jewish enclaves were menaced by the rise of nationalist feeling, the strengthening of state power, and the reception of Roman law with its centralising and totalitarian tendency. The Jews had suffered a series of expulsions from the countries of Europe, having been expelled from England in 1290, from France in 1394, and from Spain, Portugal and Sicily in 1492. During the late fifteenth century the Jews had been ejected from many German states and the process went on uninterrupted by the Reformation, with Hesse expelling them in 1524 and Saxony in the 1530s.

The Lateran Council of 1215 had decreed that Jews must wear a badge of identification. The Council of Basle (1431-43) announced repressive measures against them, to be accompanied by a campaign of conversion: the first step was to add the study of Hebrew and Aramaic to the curricula of the theological schools. Papal efforts to control the Jews were intensified by the Counter Reformation: Pope Paul IV (1555) reintroduced ghettos, badges and restrictions on trade, prohibited the Jews from owning property, demolished synagogues and burned copies of the Talmud. Twenty-four Jewish residents of the papal states were burned at the stake for refusing baptism. A contemporary remarked: 'They preferred to do away with their bodies through fire than their souls through water.'

The Jews were also suspected of favouring the victory of the Turks—a plausible supposition since in the Turkish empire Jews were not only permitted to practise their faith freely but also enjoyed special privileges; some had emigrated from Christian lands for that reason. Jews and Turks were lumped together, not only in theological polemic (Luther said of the Roman doctrine of penance: 'How does this faith differ from the faith of Turks and heathen and Jews? All of them too would make satisfaction by their works.') but also in popular suspicion. As the Turks advanced, Jews were expelled from Bohemia and parts of Austria in the mid-sixteenth century.

On the other hand, both popes and princes found the Jews indispensable when they needed to raise money for their pet projects—an expanding mercenary army or a new palace. A tradition had arisen than Jews were regarded as the prerogative, if not the actual possession of the emperor (*Judenregal*). In return for imperial protection, they performed a necessary financial service. This arrangement seemed to be in danger of lapsing when Charles V began his reign in 1519. Frederick III (d. 1493) had favoured the Jews, but Charles' immediate predecessor Maximilian I had proved unpredictable and weak. Jewish anxieties were aroused when Charles proceeded to grant the *Judenfreiheit* (freedom to expel or refuse admittance to Jews) to various towns. The Diet of Worms (1520), at which Luther had made his decisive stand, ordered that 'Jews who commit usury or make loans on stolen goods shall be given neither abode nor shelter and shall have neither peace nor safe-conduct within 'the Reich.' The Jews of the empire had, however, found a timely and effective champion in Josel of Rosheim (1478-1554) whose voice was to carry weight with emperor, prince and reformer throughout the first half of the sixteenth century.[1]

JOSEL OF ROSHEIM

Josel was a combination of the cultured man of affairs of the Renaissance and the ascetic contemplative of the German-Jewish mystical tradition. In all probability largely self-educated, Josel had familiarised himself with the legal concepts and intellectual trends of the time. As Selma Stern describes:

> He was amazingly conversant in biblical, talmudic, philosophical and cabbalist literature; he had a good knowledge of medieval Jewish history and literature, and perfect mastery of Hebrew. He was skilled in the detailed interpretation of customs, rituals and ceremonies and well-versed even in the most complex regulations of Mosaic and talmudic law. He had a sharp legal mind and he was a master in the art of debating.

Josel's inner life was characterised by the pursuit of resignation, love, gentleness, the vision of God and the acceptance of suffering. He had first come forward as the defender of the rights of his people as early as 1507 and soon established himself as secular leader of the Jews of Germany, being known as Commander of all Jewry. Josel was appointed to this office not by the emperor himself (this was not without precedent) but by the popular acclaim of the Jewish people over whom he exercised a purely moral authority. Just as the various social groups fashioned by the upheavals of the sixteenth century—the peasants, knights, protestants and anabaptists—had chosen their own leaders, so too, as Stern points out, the office held by Josel of Rosheim was created by the unprecedented demands of the century in which he lived.

At the time of the Diet of Augsburg of 1530, rumours were rife of the Jews being in league with the Turks: Gog and Magog, they together heralded the coming of antichrist. At the Diet the Jews were also blamed for the Reformation, 'because they had taught their faith to Lutherans'. Luther was accused of being a 'patron of the Jews' and a 'half-Jew', Zwingli of having obtained his knowledge of the Bible from a Jew and Bucer of being of Jewish descent. A bond of personal respect and sympathy seems to have been established between Josel and the emperor and the charges against the Jews were dismissed.

But Josel was under no illusion about his own people. He knew, says Stern, that such was the greed of the Jews that only a moral and spiritual rebirth would alter their attitude and thus their relation to the Christian society in which they lived. Josel was not a politician: he was a visionary and a reformer with a flair for public affairs. While he sought the regeneration of the Jewish people, he took the precaution while at Augsburg of drawing up regulations concerning money-lending to which he obtained the agreement of Jewish representatives. The document ended with an appeal to all estates to follow the lead of Charles V and to permit the Jews to work unmolested—'For we too are men, created by Almighty God to dwell on earth and to live and work together with you and in your midst.'

Like his Jewish contemporaries, Josel was fascinated by the phenomenon of the Reformation; he warmed to the Reformers both as humanist scholars and as—supposedly— heralds of a new liberty, for until the Reformation, the Jews had been the only island of dissent in the *Corpus Christianum*. Jewish-Christian dialogue was fostered by the humanist assumptions held in common. Luther's writings were eagerly read by Jews far and wide—even in Jerusalem.

Josel used to attend the sermons and lectures of his friend, the Reformer and Hebraist Wolfgang Capito of Strasbourg— slipping out, however, as soon as the preacher became evangelistic. Combined with the voyages of discovery and the comparative security achieved by the mediation of Josel, the Reformation emboldened the Jews and they began to prosely- tise among Christians. Study of the interaction of Christian and Jew in the sixteenth century is still rudimentary and the situation has changed little since S. W. Baron complained in 1932 that 'no comprehensive study has thus far been published about the relationship between protestantism and Judaism or about the former's impact upon Jewish history'.[2]

A certain David Reubeni appeared in the courts of Europe claiming to be king of the lost tribes of Israel and to reign over 300,000 subjects in the Arabian desert. He sought the support of the pope and Christian kings for a crusade to deliver the holy land from the Turk. For his part, he would mobilise European Jews in the sacred cause. Diogo Pires, a young Portugese nobleman, was captivated by Reubeni's campaign and, calling himself Solomon Moicho, he announ- ced that the Messiah would appear in 1540 (the sack of Rome by German mercenaries in 1527 seemed to him to signify the fall of Edom and the hour of deliverance for the Jews).

Josel of Rosheim saw the wider implications of the movement and warned Molcho not to alarm the emperor. He realised that a joint Jewish-Christian crusade against the Turk would spell grave danger for Jews everywhere. Since the Turks had given refuge to the Jews, the emperor would not be able to take their loyalty for granted. The sultan for his part would certainly expel all Jews from his territories. Josel was also fearful lest ferment among the Jews be met by the authorities in the same way as the agitation of anabap- tists. His fears were justified: Reubeni was unmasked as a fraud and Molcho burned at the stake.

Sometimes there was a link between messianic Jewish movements and millenarian anabaptist communities. The anabaptist Augustin Weber set out to create the new Jerusalem over which he would rule as king; Jews would be especially welcome there and he sent out messengers to invite them to enter the kingdom. (Such phenomena as these foreshadowed the philo-semitic lunatic fringe in Cromwell's Commonwealth when John Robbins the Ranter planned to lead an expedition of 144,000 to reconquer the Holy Land, and trained them on dry bread, vegetables and water.)[3]

LUTHER AND THE JEWS

Luther's view of the Jews has been the subject of extensive research.[4] The strange metamorphosis in his attitude—from the warm and encouraging approach of his early writings to the bitter and brutal rejection of his later years—remains a puzzle. But the whole matter becomes a little less perplexing when we bear in mind two qualifying factors. Firstly, Luther's early openness was dictated purely by considerations of missionary tactics rather than by any anachronistic principles of toleration or of a pluralist society. Secondly, his later onslaught was part and parcel of the last-ditch mentality of Luther's old age. He felt betrayed by all the many groups who had initially welcomed the reform—humanists such as Erasmus, sacramentarians such as Zwingli, radicals such as Karlstadt, demagogues such as Müntzer—only, in Luther's view, to twist its message to suit their own ends. The Jews too, who had misunderstood Luther, fell into this category. It was Luther *contra mundum.*

In 1523 Luther wrote to Bernhardt, a baptised Jew whom he hoped to involve in preaching to the Jews: 'When the golden light of the gospel really arises to shine, it is to be hoped that many Jews will become seriously and truly converted, so being snatched into the presence of Christ.' In the same year Luther expressed the hope that 'many Jews may become ardent Christians when they are treated kindly and are guided gently on the basis of holy Scripture'.[5]

Luther put this programme of gentle guidance into effect in his tract of 1523 *That Jesus Christ was born a Jew* (LW 45), praised by Justus Jonas as the best missionary tract ever written. The papists have behaved towards the Jews in such a way, Luther wrote, that 'a good Christian was bound to become a Jew. They were treated as though they were dogs. ... Yet Jews are our kinsmen and brethren of our Lord and God granted the holy scriptures only to these people.' Luther thought that they could not be expected to swallow

Christian dogma whole: let them be led to faith by gradual stages:

> Let them first be suckled with milk and begin by recognising this man Jesus as the Messiah; after that they may drink wine and learn also that he is true God. For they have been led astray so long and so far that one must deal gently with them as people who have been all too strongly indoctrinated to believe that God cannot be man (LW 45. 229).

The Jews should not be driven to usury by exclusion from society but accepted 'so that they could convince themselves of the teaching and the good life of Christians'.

> If we really want to help them, we must be guided in our dealings with them not by papal law but by the law of Christian love. We must receive them cordially and permit them to trade and work with us, that they may have occasion and opportunity to associate with us, hear our Christian teaching and witness our Christian life. If some of them should prove stiff-necked, what of it? After all, we ourselves are not all good Christians either (ibid.).

In much the same vein, Luther commented on Psalm 22: 'Who would adopt our religion, even if he were a most humble and patient person, when he sees how cruelly, hatefully and in a cattle-like rather than Christian-like fashion [the Jews] are treated by us?' (WA 5.7III. 168).

In 1535-36 the elector John Frederick of Saxony began to take repressive measures against the Jews in his domain, forbidding them to settle, sojourn or do business in Saxony, or even to travel through the land. Josel of Rosheim lobbied Capito and Bucer to approach Luther and, through him, the elector; he then tried to see Luther in person. Luther wrote to Josel, addressing him as his dear friend but refusing an interview. 'This letter,' writes Selma Stern,

> which is couched in friendly and serious terms, reflects the ambivalent attitude of the Reformer to the Jewish problem. It mirrors the tragic inner conflict which tortured

him as long as he lived: his love for 'ancient pious Israel to whom the mystery of God has been revealed' on the one hand and his aversion to this self-righteous and obdurate people who did not understand God's promise and his revelation, on the other.[6]

The letter also reflected a significant change in Luther's approach to the conversion of the Jews. No longer was he content to win them to Jesus the man first and then by gradual stages to full Christian belief: here he sets before them the divine Christ whom to reject is to incur the terrible wrath of God. Shortly after this incident Luther remarked: 'What should one grant to the Jews who harm the people with regard to life and property and entice so many Christians away with their false beliefs and superstitions?' (WA Tischreden 3. 141). He also declared that, were he to baptise a Jew, he would take him to the Elbe, hang a stone round his neck and drop him in the river with the words: 'I baptise you in the name of Abraham.'[7]

Luther's growing obsession with the Jews was compounded of exasperation at the exegesis of rabbinic scholars who could not see Jesus Christ in the Old Testament and alarm at reports of a sabbatarian sect which had converted from the evangelical faith to Judaism, practised circumcision and awaited the Messiah. Luther responded with his tract *Against the Sabbatarians* (1538 LW 47). At the end of his life Luther produced three consecutive polemics against the Jews: *On the Jews and their Lies* (1542-43 LW 47). *Vom Shem Hamphoras* (on the divine name, 1543 WA 53) and *On the Last Words of David* (1543 LW 15). In these works Luther gave credence to all the medieval superstitions about the mischief-making of the Jews, including ritual murder, poisoning of wells and sorcery. He advocated a programme of burning the synagogues, confiscating Jewish books, prohibiting rabbis from giving instruction and restricting the Jews to menial tasks. If all this failed to control them, they should be expelled like mad dogs. Luther's sermon, 'Admonition against the Jews', preached only four days before his death, concluded: 'If the Jews wish to be converted, give up their usury and accept Christ, we shall readily pardon them

and treat them as our brothers ... If not, we shall not bear
and tolerate them among us' (WA 51. 187ff.).

Luther's outbursts met with an immediate response.
Bullinger wrote to Bucer that Luther's *impurissime* remarks
were better suited to have been written by a swineherd than
by a shepherd of souls.[8] Josel of Rosheim complained that no
other scholar (as opposed to rabble-rouser, etc.) had ever
suggested that the Jews be treated in the manner advocated
by Luther. But a Lutheran preacher of Strasbourg announced that it was now permissible to kill Jews; as Josel put it in
a petition to the magistracy: 'People at large speak openly
that any harm done to the Jews—whether in body or in
property—would be forgiven because Dr Martin Luther had
expressed such an opinion in print and urged that it be
preached.' Luther's advice prompted several states to expel
the Jews, though none followed his recommendations to the
letter. As late as 1558, twelve years after Luther's death, a
certain pastor Ehrhardt proclaimed: 'We ought not to allow
Jews to live among us, nor are we to eat and drink with
them.' Their synagogues should be burned and their
treasures appropriated according to the 'faithful advice and
regulations given us by our divinely enlightened Luther'.[9]
Had Luther's word been translated into deed, comments
Nijenhuis, 'the existence of the Jews in our hemisphere
would have been more menaced than at any time in the
Middle Ages'.[10]

The astounding thing to a modern reader is that even these
last paranoid effusions of Luther were intended to serve a
missionary purpose. 'May our dear Lord mercifully convert
them,' Luther prayed at the end of *On the Jews and their
Lies*; and *Vom Shem Hamphoras* concluded with the words:
'To those who want to be converted, may God grant his grace
so that at least a few of them together with us would
acknowledge and praise God our Father, our creator, and
Jesus Christ and the Holy Spirit in eternity, Amen.'

But Luther had become progressively less hopeful that
Jews in any significant numbers would be converted; at the
end of his life he complained that it was easier to convert the
devil than a Jew. He saw the doctrines of the Incarnation and
the Trinity as the great stumbling block to both Jews and
Moslems. Against rabbinic exegesis, he claimed that not only

the Trinity but also the two natures of Christ were taught by the Old Testament. Belief in one God will not save either Jews or Moslems unless they come to know him through Jesus Christ. As Luther declares in *On the Last Words of David*: the God who said in the first commandment, 'I am the Lord your God: you shall have no other gods before me', is none other than he who was born of a virgin and hung on a cross.

How the Jews and Mohammed would rant if they heard that! Nevertheless, it is true and will eternally remain true and he who disbelieves this will tremble before this truth and burn for ever ... Therefore it is of no avail to Jews, Turks and heretics to feign great religious zeal and to boast against us Christians of their belief in the one God, the creator of heaven and earth, and that they devoutly call him Father. These are nothing but inane and empty words with which they take the name of God in vain ...

By inventing a god for themselves, they end up by worshipping the devil (LW 15. 313ff.). The Jews are beyond redemption; their conversion is 'impossible' (LW 47. 137). Gordon Rupp has aptly summed up Luther's final position: 'As we follow Luther through the years, we find a signal instance of how we become like what we hate. We see a growing obstinacy, a hardening of heart, a withering of compassion, a proneness to contemptuous abuse—the very things he thought were the marks of judgment on the Jews.'[11]

OTHER REFORMERS AND THE JEWS

Those most influenced by humanism tended to be on better terms with the Jews, though sometimes a residual anti-semitism remained. 'Who among us does not heartily dislike this race of men?' asks Erasmus ironically. 'If it is a Christian matter to hate Jews, all of us are sufficiently Christian.' Reuchlin, on the other hand, expressed the hope that the Jews would be won by kindness and compassion and there were highly competent Hebraists among the Reformers. Conrad Pellican of Basel had taught himself Hebrew grammar without the help of teachers, purely by collating widely scattered Latin transliterations of Hebrew. Osiander, who had been reviled as a 'rabbi' because of his knowledge of Hebrew, criticised Luther's books on the Jews and pointed out so many inaccuracies that Melanchthon kept the letter from Luther. Osiander had long been a defender of the Jews. 'Is it true that Jews kill Christian children and use their blood?' he asked in 1541. Such charges were pure fabrication.

Though, like Capito and Osiander, Melanchthon befriended the Jews, he was delighted with *On the Last Words of David*, praising it as 'enjoyable reading'. Zwingli, influenced here by his belief in the binding authority of the Mosaic judicial law, asserted that 'no government should be so dishonest with its citizens that it tolerates Jews or other usurers.'[12]

Servetus, the heterodox radical, had suggested that Jews and Moslem would never be converted while Christians made acceptance of the trinitarian doctrine a condition of baptism. Servetus was deeply influenced himself by Jewish speculative writings and was accused by Calvin of 'judaizing'. But he was not a legalist and believed that the Old Testament law had been abrogated. He had more justification when in return he accused Calvin of 'judaizing' and of 'Jewish legalism'.[13]

Calvin himself had little contact with Jews. They were absent from the parts of France in which Calvin had lived and they had been expelled from Geneva in 1491. Though a Jewish quarter existed in the city in Calvin's time, he was not in favour of their official readmittance. Among Calvin's papers there is a document entitled 'An Answer to some Jews' questions and objections'. S. W. Baron has conjectured that this is the record of a dialogue between Calvin and Josel of Rosheim and may have taken place in Strasbourg in 1539.[14]

A programme for dealing with the Jews, in some respects similar to Luther's own proposals, was drawn up by Martin Bucer and his colleagues in response to Philip of Hesse's request for advice on how to treat the Jews.[15] In Bucer's view it was the responsibility of the state to maintain the true religion. The suppression of false religions was therefore required both by natural and divine law (though there were

precedents for the toleration of a false faith in the body politic
under strict conditions).

There were three further reasons for penalising the Jews.
Firstly, their vicious conduct in the past was sufficient
justification for exiling or punishing them. Secondly,
Christians need to be protected from false teaching. Thirdly,
it is revealed in Scripture that God has ordained punishment
for them and requires the secular ruler to carry it out. After
this, it is salutary (and surprising) to note Eells' comment
that Bucer was not obsessed, like Luther, with the Jews and
did not attack them in his writings. He did not pursue the
matter with Philip. 'His opinion was called for, he gave it
with candour and care and then let the matter drop.'[16]

But Philip did not intend to comply with the advice of the
theologians. He could not see why, he replied, the Jews
should be treated so harshly and kept within such narrow
confines as suggested in the counsel from the learned
gentlemen. He had been unable to find anything in either the
Old Testament or the New to suggest that it was mandatory
to deal cruelly and unkindly with the Jews. What he was
prepared to insist on, however, was that the Jews of Hesse
should be compelled to listen to sermons from protestant
missionaries. Philip was more inclined than Bucer to favour
theological arguments about the Jews' place in the scheme of
salvation and to hope for an eventual turning of the Jewish
people to Christ.

The *locus classicus* for this view is of course Romans
11.25ff.: 'and so all Israel shall be saved'. When Luther gave
his lectures on Romans in 1515-16 he was convinced that
Scripture as a whole taught a future turning of the Jewish
people, but not that Romans 11.25 was decisive on this point.
St Paul's statement is obscure, he says, but the fathers are
agreed that this is its meaning (LW 25. 429). Calvin, when
he comes to comment on this text, tries to retain both the
literal and the spiritual meaning of 'all Israel', while making
clear his belief that the Jews would one day be converted to
Christ.

Many understand this of the Jewish people, as if Paul
were saying that religion was to be restored to them again
as before. But I extend the word Israel to include all the

people of God, in this sense: when the Gentiles have come in, the Jews will at the same time return from their defection to the obedience of faith. The salvation of the whole Israel of God, which must be drawn from both, will thus be completed and yet in such a way that the Jews, as the first born in the family of God, may obtain the first place (CC Romans, 255).

Bucer's view seems to have contained an element of inconsistency. His commentary on Romans of 1536 is marked, according to Nijenhuis, by an 'unresolved tension between an individualistic and therefore exclusivist view of election which could do little justice to the idea of a permanent place for Israel as a nation in God's plan of salvation, and a more universalistic one which took into consideration the idea that the whole of Israel might be saved'.[17] The literal interpretation of the text, namely, that the Jewish nation would one day corporately accept Christ, became dominant in puritan theology, being favoured by Peter Martyr, Theodore Beza, William Perkins, William Gouge, John Cotton, John Owen, Samuel Rutherford, Joseph Mede and the editors of the Geneva Bible—among others.[18]

Meanwhile, actual attempts to convert the Jews were not entirely lacking. Sebastian Münster, a former Franciscan monk who became one of the most eminent Hebraists of the sixteenth century, did his best to promote Jewish missions. He published a parallel text of the Old Testament in Hebrew and German in 1534-35, translated Matthew and Hebrews into Hebrew and produced two tracts, 'Dialogue of a Christian with a Jew' and 'The Christian and Jewish Messiah' in Hebrew and Latin. Elias Schaddaus, a Jewish convert to protestantism, was for many years pastor in Strasbourg and professor of theology. He addressed sermons and pamphlets to the Jews and planned a Hebrew and Yiddish translation of the New Testament. In 1533 Urban Regius directed a Hebrew epistle to the Jews of Braunschweig in which he drew on Luther's writings to convince them of the truth of Christianity. Immanuel Tremellius of Ferrara, a converted Jew, helped to compile the Heidelberg Catechism and became Regius Professor of Hebrew at Cambridge. Also in Cambridge, Hugh Broughton (d. 1612) proposed a translation of the New Testament into Hebrew and was only prevented from going himself as a missionary to the Jews of the Near East by the weight of ecclesiastical authority. A student of prophecy, he too was convinced of a future turning of the Jews.

While Luther's attacks on the Jews were going into circulation, the emperor Charles V was reaffirming the privileges of the Jews and their imperial protection (1544). In 1546 the protestant alliance was defeated by the emperor's armies. Josel of Rosheim, who had initially looked to the Reformers as the harbingers of a new liberty, now prayed for the success of the emperor. This change of heart and of sympathy on the part of the veteran defender of Jewish interests, scholar and contemplative, is a vivid commentary on the failure of the Reformation where the Jews were concerned. As Selma Stern justly remarks in her biography of Josel: 'He could not forget that Luther had threatened his brethren with death and destruction, that John Frederick had expelled them from his country, that Bucer had spoken out against them in his "Advice" and that the city of Strasbourg had closed its gates to them.'[19]

CHAPTER FOURTEEN

MISSIONS TO THE HEATHEN

THE PARADOX OF EVANGELISING ANTICHRIST

To speak of the heathen in the sixteenth century meant first and foremost to speak of the Turk, that is to say, antichrist. The Turkish threat loomed like a dark cloud over Christendom, menacing the existence of catholic and protestant Churches alike. In 1453 Constantinople had finally fallen. In 1521 Belgrade and in the following year the strategic Christian city of Rhodes were taken by Suleiman the Magnificent at the head of an army of nearly a third of a million men. Vienna stood next in line. The pope responded with a call to a holy war, a crusade.

Luther's first reaction was to warn against seeking to resist the judgment of God. He regarded the pope and the Turk as twin manifestations of antichrist—they were both worldly princes who corrupted the gospel, lived by the sword, exhorted men to war, violence and crusades, degraded the holy estate of matrimony (the Turk by polygamy, the pope by clerical celibacy), and taught salvation by works.

Thus the Turk was thoroughly popish and the pope altogether Turkish; Turk and pope were Gog and Magog, the political and the spiritual enemies of Christ. The Turk was the body and the pope the soul of antichrist. For good measure, Luther threw in the radical protestants, the sacramentarians, because of their legalism and iconoclasm. 'Mohammedans, papists, sacramentarians ... do not hold to the word of God but to their own self-righteousness ... they perform many things, make sacrifices, but they are still always in doubt,' remarks Luther in the *Table Talk*. When the question is asked, Why were the Reformers so slow to undertake missions to the heathen?, one ought to bear in mind the paradoxical aspect of the proposal to evangelise antichrist.[1]

It would also be as well to note at this stage the *prima facie* implausibility of trying to convert strict Moslems. It is true that Cranmer, at least, did not regard this as beyond the bounds of possibility but he did feel that a united protestant front was an essential prerequisite. He wrote to Vadian in 1537 urging concord and arguing that 'we should easily convert even the Turks to the obedience of our gospel if only we could agree among ourselves and unite together in some holy confederacy' (PS *Original Letters*, 14).

Others were less confident. Acontius, the advocate of religious toleration, pointed out with patent reasonableness in his book *Satanae Stratagemata* in 1565 that it was useless to quote the Bible to a Turk who did not accept its authority. Erasmus, who expressed the wish that not only 'the lowliest women' but even Turks and Saracens should have the gospels and epistles available in their own language, felt the absurdity of presenting scholastic theology to the Turks:

> But what do you think would happen if we set before the vanquished—since I don't believe we shall kill them all—in order to win them to Christ, the works of Occam or Durandus or Scotus or Gabriel [Biel] ...? What will they think, what impression will they get, since they are surely men if nothing else, when they hear those thorny and intricate arguments about instances, quiddities and relationships—especially when they see those great professors of religion disagreeing about these matters among themselves ...? What indeed will they think when they see the question is so difficult that it has never adequately been settled what words should be used in speaking of Christ?[2]

The matter would hardly have been improved, we might think, by substituting protestant wrangling over the eucharistic presence or predestination for the scholastic subtleties of catholic theology. The Turks were assumed to be virtually impervious to the Christian gospel. As J. H. Parry has pointed out with reference to catholic missions:

> Nobody supposed that any serious impression could be made upon Islam by preaching or by rational disputation. Muslims were not only powerful and well organised; they were also—though diabolically misguided—clever, con-

fident and civilised. A missionary friar would have had no
more chance of making converts in Granada or Damascus
than would a mullah in Rome or Burgos. He would have
been considered at best an interesting curiosity, at worst a
spy or a dangerous lunatic ... Genuine conversion on a
wide scale was generally assumed to be an impracticable
ideal.[3]

THE RADICALS

The radicals, however, present a notable exception; the wide
range of views within radical thought on the Turkish
challenge constitute various facets of a distinctly positive
approach. Lacking the predestinarian inhibitions of the
magisterial Reformers, the missionary outlook of the radicals
was strengthened by the belief that Christ had died for the
salvation of all mankind. In 'various theological adjustments',
as G. H. Williams put it, they had taken account not only of
the pagan races beyond Islam in Africa, India, Cathay and
the Americas but even of pagans who had lived before
Christ—hence their wish to retain the credal clause concerning the descent into hell.

Among radical Reformers, the Moslems were regarded
variously as the instrument of God's wrath or, alternatively,
of God's redemption (Suleiman being a new Cyrus); the
objects, together with the Jews, of missionary endeavour in
the last days; or, finally, as already members of the true,
spiritual, interfaith Church by virtue of their supposed
conformity to the inner word. The straightforward missionary approach is represented by the little group of
anabaptists at Zurich who announced that they were going
'to the Red Indians over the sea' because their gospel had
been rejected by civilised Europeans. The concept of the
ecclesia spiritualis, on the other hand, requires further
elucidation.

The spiritualist Sebastian Franck wrote in his *Letter to
John Campanus:* 'Consider as thy brothers all Turks and
heathen, wherever they be, who fear God and work
righteousness, instructed by God and inwardly drawn by
him, even though they have never heard of baptism, indeed,
of Christ himself, neither of his story or scripture, but only of

his power through the inner word perceived within and made fruitful ... There are many Christians who have never heard Christ's name.' Franck shared this view with Castellio, the advocate of toleration, Coornhert, the Dutch mystical human- ist and disciple of Franck and, to an extent, Denck. Dietrich Philips too can write in his treatise *The Church of God:*

> The Jews and Israelites cannot be counted alone as the congregation of God, but all who truly confessed, feared, honoured God and lived according to his will by the law of nature inscribed by God in their hearts. And all among the heathen who have believed in Jesus Christ are, in their uncircumcision of the flesh and in their heathendom, counted as a spiritual seed of Abraham and of the promise. Hence it follows that they have been of God and of Christ.[4]

The radicals, with their detachment from the magisterial structure of society, were able to consider the Turkish phenomenon in more purely theological, rather than political, terms. As G. H. Williams puts it:

> Whatever the stress, whether tutelary chastisement or missionary conversion or interfaith concord, the radical Reformation as a whole differed from the magisterial Reformation in breaking away from the territorial or political aspects of the Moslem challenge in an effort to make a religious or specifically theological adjustment to the new world-situation characterised by the Turkish military advances on Christendom.[5]

LUTHER

Luther himself had the typically Renaissance interest in discovering facts about the life of other peoples and lands. He deplored it that the authorities had suppressed information on Moslem and other cultures but was himself well informed. In 1530 Luther wrote a preface to a work by a Dominican monk who had spent more than twenty years in a Turkish prison, describing Moslem religion and customs *(De ritu et moribus Turkorum)*. In 1542 he edited and translated the

Verlegung des Alcoran Bruder Richardi, a refutation of the Koran, supplying an introduction and conclusion (WA 53).

Luther was also closely involved in the project to produce a reliable Latin translation of the Koran. (It is indicative of the small world of Reformation Europe that so many of the Reformers were to some extent involved: Luther, Melanchthon, Calvin, Bucer, Pellican and Amerbach.) An Arabic text had appeared for the first time in Europe in 1530, edited by Paganini. A professor of oriental languages in Zurich, Buchmann (known as Bibliander), had obtained the Arabic text and a couple of Latin translations and with the support of Melanchthon (who eventually contributed a preface), Bibliander proposed to publish a Latin text in Basel. When the plan met with opposition from the local magistrates on the grounds that the matter was heretical, appeal was made to both Calvin and Luther. Calvin's reply is not known—he never in fact read the Koran, it seems—but Luther did intervene, expressing his strong desire to read the famous Koran. As a result of Luther's support, the text finally appeared in 1543.

While Luther welcomed the project as a contribution to knowledge of Moslem religion—an essential prerequisite in his view to evangelising the Turk—others, notably Melanchthon and Bucer, hoped that the Latin text would provide polemical material for the refutation of Moslem and Jewish errors. Luther recognised that the Koran included Jewish, Christian and pagan elements and he described it as 'utterly uncouth, with fabricated, deliberate, shameful lies, openly permitting murder, adultery, unchastity, the destruction of marriage and other shameful abominations and deceptions' (WA 22. 150).

Melanchthon, while characterising the Koran as *deliria abominanda*, thought that it contained elements of the original revelation made to 'Noah and his sons' and corrupted in the transmission (CR 5. 11). For Melanchthon, there is no salvation outside the Church (*extra ecclesiam non est salus*) but in the case of a Christian languishing in a Turkish prison who, by confession and intention, binds himself to belong to the Christian Church, the true Church is concealed not destroyed (*quod velit veram ecclesiam non deleri*: CR 14. 891). The prisoner of the Turks, remarks Luther, should 'adorn and praise the gospel and the name of Christ' and so 'disgrace the faith of the Turks—and perhaps you would convert many' (WA 30 II. 194).

Luther was prepared to recognise the good points of Moslem culture and religion. While he criticised salvation by works, religious wars, polygamy and iconoclasm, he praised the seriousness of Moslem services, the strict life of the mullahs, their love of the truth as they saw it and the discipline of the Turkish army. The task of missionaries would be to purify and deepen the existing moral code and to embrace with a clear conscience harmless laws and customs. Until laws could be superseded by the full liberty of a Christian man, it was above all essential that Moslem legalism should not be replaced by a new Christian legalism.[6]

Luther's attitude to the Turkish war seems riddled with inconsistency and opportunism until we realise that it was fundamentally dictated by his doctrine of the Two Kingdoms. This doctrine—pivotal in Luther's thought—enabled him to make a clear distinction between a holy war or crusade, as proposed by the pope, and a just war or war of self-defence.

As early as the *Ninety-five Theses* Luther had claimed that the pope could only remit penalties that he had himself imposed, i.e., earthly penalties, and had no power over heavenly chastisements. But the Turkish invasion was, in Luther's eyes, precisely such a judgment sent from God. The appropriate attitude was not, therefore, to take up arms for a holy war—this would be tantamount to resisting the hand of God—but rather repentance and submission to the chastisement. 'To make war against the Turks is nothing else than to strive against God,' Luther held. Melanchthon thought that the steady advance of the Turks could be paralleled chronologically by the definition of the doctrine of the mass in the thirteenth century: the one was a judgment following hard on the heels of the other. So to propose, as the pope was doing, to meet a spiritual crisis with political and military weapons was a crass confusion of the Two Kingdoms.

This was the thinking behind Luther's consistent opposition to the war against the Turk until 1523: he was opposed on theological grounds to the whole concept of a holy war. A spiritual adversary must be met with the spiritual weapons of prayer and preaching. In his treatise on the Christian's relation to the magistrate *(Von weltlicher Obrigkeit)* of 1523 (LW 45), Luther looked at the problem not from the point of view of spiritual regiment but from that of worldly regiment. He argued that a Christian's duty was above all to obey the commands of the magistrate (save for conscience) and as far as the magistrate himself was concerned, it was his duty to protect the lives and property of his subjects. Luther concluded that there were therefore legitimate, just wars, characterised as such by, firstly, the command of the prince and, secondly, the need for self-defence. Considered as a military threat, the Turk could properly be combated with earthly weapons. In accordance with Luther's teaching, the Diet of Speyer of 1529 agreed to provide troops for defensive purposes only.

When one considers the circumstances, it is natural to assume that Luther's change of attitude was governed by purely opportunistic motives. By 1529, when the Turks were at the gates of Vienna, the pope, the emperor and the king of France were united against both the evangelicals and the Turks. The German protestants were in a dilemma: if they rallied to the holy war, they would be defending and perpetuating the detested papacy; if they stood aloof, they would be aiding and abetting antichrist in another form. It cannot be denied that the protestant leaders exploited the opportunities arising from the conflict between Hapsburg and Ottoman. As a scholar has reasonably concluded: 'The consolidation, expansion and legitimising of Lutheranism in Germany by 1555 should be attributed to Ottoman imperialism more than to any other single factor.'[7] It was a happy compromise, and one that accorded with the doctrine of the Two Kingdoms, for the evangelicals to contribute to the defence of Europe while not recognising the holy war.[8]

Luther and Melanchthon viewed the conflict in sombrely apocalyptic terms. 'After the Turks the last judgment follows quickly,' Luther commented at the end of his life. The cosmic drama in which Gog and Magog, Turk and pope, had their allotted roles to play, was fast approaching its close. Both Luther and Melanchthon were reassured by their reading of prophecy that the Turk (the little horn of Daniel 7) would not ultimately prevail. Of the four great horns of Daniel's vision, the fourth stood for the Roman empire and the Reformers drew the conclusion that the *Germanic* Holy Roman Empire—for that, astonishingly, is how men saw it— would not therefore be overcome by the little horn that had risen up against it. Calvin, as is well known, never ventured a commentary on the book of Revelation, though he did comment on Daniel. It is interesting that, having considered the interpretations of Luther and Melanchthon, Calvin concludes: 'Neither opinion seems probable to me.'[9]

After the death of Luther, a number of projects were advanced to attempt the evangelisation of the Turks. In the 1550s an effort was made to bring the evangelical message to the southern Slavs as a way of infiltrating Turkey and the New Testament was translated into Glagolitic. 'By this means,' it was said, 'so we hope, the right Christian religion and the true saving gospel will be promoted throughout Turkey, that the heart and disposition of the Turks will be renewed to the holy faith ... and that in time our Saviour Jesus Christ will be made known in Turkey.' There were also proposals to translate Luther's catechism and other works into Arabic. In 1583 Duke Ludwig of Wurtemberg sent a scholar 'to the kingdom of Fezzan beyond Spain to learn the Arabian language and what kind of teaching these nations have, in order that by this means our saving religion might be propagated among these barbarian people'.[10]

CALVIN

In 1555 Calvin was approached by a certain Durand de Villegaignon, who had the backing of Admiral Coligny, about the provision of pastors from Geneva to minister to a small Huguenot settlement in the bay of Rio de Janeiro. The whole episode is rather obscure since neither Villegaignon's letter nor Calvin's reply have survived. But the Genevan Company of Pastors did in fact commission two of their number to sail with several hundred Huguenots for Brazil. Hoping not only to minister to the protestant families but also to convert the natives, they were apparently dismayed by their savagery and stupidity. The story has a tragic sequel: Villegaignon had meanwhile reverted to Rome and the project collapsed. The Huguenots were forced to start on the long voyage back to Europe; but, the ship being too heavily laden, five of them tried to slip back to the coast of Brazil in a small boat. They were captured and made to sign a confession of faith (which survives today). One escaped and one was spared because he was a tailor but the other three were strangled and their bodies thrown into the sea. It is significant that this first protestant attempt to colonise the new world included a missionary purpose and ended in martyrdom.[11]

Enough has perhaps been said to show that, contrary to a widespread assumption, the Reformers and their followers were not bereft of missionary vision or totally uninvolved in missionary activity. Their chief concern was with the spread of the reformed faith in Christendom, conceived as the mission of the word of God, but, in spite of enormous practical and theological problems, they also looked beyond the immediate horizon to the diffusion of the gospel throughout the world. Although it takes us beyond the sixteenth century, it may be helpful to sketch one or two aspects of the beginning of protestant missionary effort in an organised form.

THE BEGINNINGS OF PROTESTANT MISSIONS

The first missionary martyr of the Lutheran Church was the Austrian baron, Justinian Ernest von Welz. In 1664 he began to issue a series of passionate appeals to his fellow Lutherans to face up to the challenge of world mission. One bears the title: *A Christian and true-hearted exhortation to all right-believing Christians of the Augsburg Confession respecting a special association by means of which, with God's help, our evangelical religion might be extended.* Finding his call ignored and his attempt to establish chairs of mission in the universities having failed, von Welz also suffered the sharp censures of Ursinus of Ratisbon for wanting to cast pearls before swine. Thus rejected, he abandoned his baronial title, got himself ordained and sailed to Dutch Guiana where he died shortly afterwards. In 1664, the year of von Welz's appeal, John Eliot, apostle to the Red Indians, issued his Indian Bible, and August Hermann Francke, future leader of the Lutheran renewal movement known as Pietism, was a babe in arms. Meanwhile, the Moravian Church, with its close communities of clergy and laity, was better organised to tackle the missionary task and began to take the lead in protestant missions.

Quite apart from their attitude to the Jews, which does not concern us here, the ideas and achievements of the puritans, notably Eliot and Baxter, figure significantly in the development of protestant missions—although we are told that 'the Great Commission does not occupy a large place in puritan thought'.[12] In the same writer's opinion, 'the monumental work of John Eliot towers above the low level of mission consciousness in seventeenth-century protestantism'. Richard Baxter corresponded with Eliot across the Atlantic for twenty-six years on the subject of missions. Apart from the cause of Christian unity, missions were Baxter's greatest concern. 'No part of my prayers are so deeply serious as that for the conversion of the infidel and ungodly world.' He urges men of influence and wealth to send out 'the choicest scholars' for translation work. He admires the courage and initiative of the Jesuits in the Far East: 'I take it to be my duty greatly to honour them … Yea I think them much more laudable that did those great things, though in a culpable manner, than those protestants that ever had opportunity and have done nothing themselves but find fault with them that did it.'[13]

The cause of missions was going forward in other ways. With the rise of Pietism in Germany went a concern for evangelism. Francke was able to supply the king of Denmark with two young men who eventually reached India in 1706, the first protestant missionaries to arrive there from Europe. The Swedes were attempting to preach the gospel both to the Lapps and the Delaware Indians. The Dutch were active in the East Indies and Brazil. In the East their methods left something to be desired: ministers were virtually civil servants and received a cash bonus for every native baptised; special privileges were granted to converts.

From the first, English activity in North America was closely linked to missions. The first charter of Virginia, awarded by James I in 1606, stated that the purpose of the enterprise was the propagation of 'the Christian religion to such people as yet live in darkness and miserable ignorance of the true knowledge and worship of God'. The emblem of the Massachusetts Bay Colony was 'Come Over and Help Us'. Perhaps the change of attitude was most clearly symbolised by the addition of a form of adult baptism to the Book of Common Prayer in 1662. This service for 'the ministration of baptism to such as are of riper years and able to answer for themselves' was primarily added to meet pastoral needs arising from neglect of religious observances during the English Civil War and the growth of baptist views, but it was also intended for use in the colonies where the natives were now able to answer for themselves in confessing their faith.

Whatever their limitations may have been in heeding the call to mission, the Reformers did recognise the power of the message itself, as distinct from the methods used to proclaim it. They revived the gospel and so made mission possible. They saw themselves as servants of the mission of the Word of God. They acknowledged the power of ideas to shape history and were willing that these ideas should be entrusted to the mass media of the time—the cartoon and the printed sheet—though they should become distorted in the process. Calvin training his young preachers, Baxter calling for the choicest scholars, were both recognising that mission, as one of the primary tasks of the Church, deserves the best resources it can offer.

CONCLUSION:
THE RELEVANCE OF
REFORMATION ECCLESIOLOGY

We began by trying to discover the central principle of the Reformers' doctrine of the Church, the heart of Reformation ecclesiology. This was not far to seek for it was enunciated by Martin Luther in the *Ninety-five Theses* of 1517: 'The true treasure of the Church is the holy gospel of the glory and the grace of God.' For Luther and all the Reformers, the gospel constituted the christological centre of the Church. This was the primary impulse of Reformation ecclesiology. All other issues, such as the question of the boundaries of the Church—what I have described as the problem of defining the circumference—were definitely secondary.

Once set the gospel at the centre and it must be allowed to exert an overriding influence on all other aspects of ecclesiology. It must be decisive for the doctrine of the *ministry:* if the gospel is constitutive of the Church, it follows that it is constitutive of the ministry too. It must be decisive for the concept of the Church's *mission:* for the Reformers, mission was simply the Church on the move, the Church getting under way; and once the Church is defined in terms of the gospel, mission will be understood as the mission of the Word of God.

In this final chapter, I want to take the opportunity to draw out some of the implications of this position and to suggest some of the ways in which Reformation ecclesiology may have a direct bearing on the problems of the Church today.

I. First of all, three points that emerge from our study deserve underlining.

(1) There is remarkable agreement among the mainstream Reformers on the essentials of the doctrine of the Church. Protestantism is often accused of being divisive, but the extent to which the Reformers stood together on this matter should not be underestimated. Agreement went much further than

this of course. Apart from the question of the exact nature of Christ's presence in the sacrament of holy communion, there is a genuine consensus of Reformation theology and it was believed by Bucer and Calvin that, had it not been for the intransigence of Luther and Zwingli, neither of whom was prepared to regard the other as an equal, agreement could have been reached on the question of the 'real presence' as well.

In *La Pensée de la Réforme* H. Strohl expresses his conviction that the Reformers had more in common than was sometimes supposed (even by themselves). He speaks of 'la concordance très grande des thèses de tous les Réformateurs', and traces this to their common attention to holy Scripture. Strohl's book is an attempt to show that it is possible to effect a 'synthèse des affirmations essentielles de la Réforme'. As far as our present purpose is concerned, we note that this consensus was particularly apparent in the doctrine of the Church.[1]

(2) Full weight should be given to the 'catholic intention' of the Reformers. Paradoxical as it may seem when we consider the sad divisions of the Church that stem from the Reformation, the fact is that the Reformers believed that their work was to save the catholic Church. But in order to save the Church they had first to save the gospel. As J. T. McNeill bluntly puts it, 'In repudiating Rome, Luther meant to indicate not his own but Rome's exclusion from the catholic Church.' By Rome, Luther did not, needless to say, mean the mass of the catholic faithful but the papacy and the papal court. Luther often complained that the Romanists were virtually demanding an alteration of the creed to 'I believe in the Church of Rome'. As Aulén has pointed out in his *Reformation and Catholicity*, catholicity is not a geographical but a qualitative conception.[2]

Another Lutheran scholar, Jaroslav Pelikan, borrowing from Tillich, employs the terms 'catholic substance' and 'protestant principle' and claims that Luther attempted to reform the catholic substance by means of the protestant principle in an attitude of 'critical reverence'. Even those who may not be able to accept that catholic substance was in fact preserved intact by the Reformers can at least respect their intention.[3]

(3) It follows immediately from this that the reluctance of the Reformers to accept the divisions between themselves and Rome and between one protestant Church and another should be acknowledged. Only slowly and reluctantly did they come to accept that division was inevitable. The Reformers were definitely not sectarian and ceaseless efforts were made to restore unity among themselves and with Rome. Great councils of the Church were a feature not only of the Middle Ages but also of the immediately post-Reformation period. As McNeill has pointed out in *Unitive Protestantism* and in his contribution to the *History of the Ecumenical Movement*, protestantism continued the well-established tradition of conciliar as opposed to monarchical catholicism.[4]

The dignified, sober, yet unrepentant language of Bishop Jewel may serve to sum up the Reformers' attitude on this point:

> As touching that we have now done, to depart from that Church whose errors were proved and made manifest to the world, which Church also had already evidently departed from God's word; and yet not to depart so much from itself as from the errors thereof, and not to do this disorderly or wickedly, but quietly and soberly—we have done nothing herein against the doctrine either of Christ or of his apostles (PS 3. 79).

To summarise these three points: there is a coherent body of Reformation theology; it is an integral part of the wider Christian tradition; its claim to preserve catholicity in essentials must be faced with all seriousness.

II. The Reformation concept of the Church has been vigorously reasserted in modern theology—sometimes in unexpected quarters. To illustrate this I shall call two protestant and two Roman Catholic witnesses.

(1) An English free church theologian who in a number of ways anticipated later developments in modern theology was P. T. Forsyth. He also called attention to the true essence of the Church. Forsyth's theology of the cross *(theologia crucis)* enabled him to grasp the Church's christological centre. In *The Church and the Sacraments* (1917) he asserted that 'the

Church's one foundation and the trust of its ministry is not simply Christ but Christ crucified'.

> The Church rests on the grace of God, the judging, atoning, regenerating grace of God which is his holy love in the form it must take with human sin. Wherever that is heartily confessed and goes on to rule we have the true Church. In so far as the Church is a creature, it is the creature of the preached gospel of God's grace, forgiving, redeeming and creating us anew by Christ's cross. The Church was created by the preaching of that solitary gospel and fortified by the sacraments of it which are, indeed, but other ways of receiving, confessing and preaching it. The Church is the social and practical response to that grace. Wherever that gospel is taken seriously ... there is the Church.

Here indeed is the authentic voice of Reformation theology.[5]

(2) At about the same time, the identical conviction was beginning to make itself powerfully felt in Karl Barth's early work. In the *Römerbrief* (2nd edn 1921) Barth describes the Church as 'no more than a crater formed by the explosion of a shell'—the gospel. It seeks to be no more than the 'void in which the gospel reveals itself'. In the later *Church Dogmatics* Barth allows formal aspects of ecclesiology a little more room. He affirms the visibility of the Church against any kind of 'ecclesiastical Docetism'. The Christian Church is 'a phenomenon of world history which can be grasped in historical and psychological and sociological terms like any other'. But it cannot be reduced to these—they do not tell us what the Church *is.* To discover this, faith is required. *Credo ecclesiam* involves a 'third dimension in which the Church is what it is'—the body of Christ. This third dimension points us to the christological reality at the centre of the Church's life.

> What is this being of the community, this spiritual character, this secret, which is hidden in its earthly and historical form and therefore invisible, or visible only to the special perception of faith? The answer—which does

indeed point to a third dimension—can only be this: The community is the earthly-historical form of existence of Jesus Christ himself ... The Church is his body, created and continually renewed by the awakening power of the Holy Spirit.

But it is not only in protestant theology that the Reformation concept of the Church has made itself heard.[6]

(3) The Roman Catholic theologian who has evidently made much of Luther's doctrine of the Church his own is Hans Küng of Tübingen—though his little book *Why Priests?* is more radical than Luther himself! In his major treatise on *The Church* Küng takes the basic principle of Reformation ecclesiology as his own starting point when he asserts: 'One can only know what the Church should be now if one also knows what the Church was originally. This means knowing what the Church of today should be in the light of the gospel.' Created by the gospel, the Church remains subject to the gospel as its permanent criterion. It 'must return to the place from which it proceeded; must return to its origins, to Jesus, to the gospel'.

The implications for Roman Catholic theology would be momentous. His evangelical principle leads Küng to affirm that the Church is an object of faith rather than an empirical reality (he claims to find this in the Tridentine Catechism) and to recognise other ecclesial bodies as valid Churches possessing valid ministries and valid sacraments. Küng is able to strengthen his claims by invoking the spirit and sometimes the actual decisions of the Second Vatican Council. The principle that the present life of the Church depends on its source in the holy gospel was accepted by the Council:

The mystery of the holy Church is manifest in her very foundation, for the Lord Jesus inaugurated her by preaching the good news, that is, the coming of God's kingdom ... By everywhere preaching the gospel ... the apostles gathered together the universal Church ... The gospel which was to be handed down by them is for all time the source of all life for the Church.[7]

(4) Another distinguished theologian in the catholic

tradition, but an Anglican this time, is Michael Ramsey, whose work in ecclesiology is marked by its determination to hold fast to the christological centre while at the same time doing full justice to the requirements of catholicity and apostolic order as he understands it. Michael Ramsey argues, therefore, for the coinherence of gospel and Church. The impressive and constructive way in which he develops his case in *The Gospel and the Catholic Church* (1936) and his fascinating attempt to ground a doctrine of order and ministry in the nature of the gospel itself need not detain us here. It is enough to note the unswerving adherence to the gospel of Christ as the true treasure of the Church that informs his work—Luther's declaration of 1517 provides both a text and a refrain for *The Gospel and the Catholic Church*.

Michael Ramsey asserts:

The full recovery of the doctrine of the Church is bound up with the return of the gospel of God. Catholicism, created by the gospel, finds its power in terms of the gospel alone. Neither the massive polity of the Church, nor its devotional life, nor its traditions in order and worship can in themselves serve to define catholicism; for all these things have their meaning in the gospel, wherein the true definition of catholicism is found.

In words that bring Luther's message to the centre of contemporary theological discussion, Michael Ramsey affirms: 'Catholicism always stands before the church door at Wittenberg to read the truth by which she is created and by which also she is judged.'[8]

III. Finally, I should like to indicate briefly several points at which I believe the account of Reformation ecclesiology attempted in this book has a direct bearing on current ecumenical issues.

(1) The witness of the Reformers in the matter of ecclesiology is primarily to the christological centre, the holy gospel of the glory and grace of God revealed in Jesus Christ. But they had also to face the question of the circumference: how do we identify the visible Church, where does it begin

and end, what are the lines of demarcation, if any? The development of the doctrine of the marks of the true Church, as we have traced it in the first part of our study, seems to reveal the failure of a rigid, purist approach to this question. Concern for discipline and doctrinal purity, when taken to an extreme, became self-defeating and an escalating process of separation tended to diminish the Church to a mathematical point. We recall that Robert Browne, the separatist, was expelled from his own congregation! The concept of the *notae ecclesiae* was not able to bear the weight laid upon it and the Anglican divines Hooker and Field broke with it altogether and accepted a more pragmatic view of the visible Church as consisting of all those who make the outward confession of faith in Christ by baptism.

In my opinion, this provides the only realistic platform for discussions between Churches today. The doctrinal basis of the World Council of Churches—confession of Christ as God and saviour—is obviously very close to this particular strand of Reformation theology and it is arguable that, far from being a reductionist version of the Christian faith, the WCC basis simply happens to reflect the final outcome of sixteenth-century debates on the nature of the visible Church. Hooker's own theology—in particular his view of justification—is a standing reminder that such a pragmatic view of the visible Church does not of itself entail any sacrifice of the christological and evangelical centre.

(2) The Reformers affirm that where the gospel is, Christ is; and where Christ is, there is the Church. All that is necessary to authentic 'Churchhood' is the possession of the gospel. Nothing else can be regarded as the *sine qua non*. This is not, however, to say that nothing else is necessary to the effective life and witness of the Church, only that nothing but the reception of the gospel is essential to make the Church the Church. If the gospel alone validates the Church, it validates the Church's ministry too. Only the preaching of the gospel is required to constitute a given ministry as the ministry of the Christian Church. Other considerations may have to be introduced to define a *regular* ministry and to safeguard good order in the Christian community, but that is a separate question over and above the primary question of

the validity of a ministry. That can only be determined by the gospel that is being preached.

Thus the theology of the Reformation brings a judgment to bear on all attempts to invalidate or withhold recognition from the ministries of Churches that lack the historic episcopate. To import an exclusive theory of apostolic succession to the central place in the doctrine of the ministry is to overthrow the christological foundation and to attempt to over-define the circumference at the expense of the centre.

Apostolicity is not to be achieved in such a way. The four credal dimensions of the Church—unity, holiness, catholicity and apostolicity—are eschatological not empirical—they cannot be secured with cast-iron guarantees. As Karl Barth has remarked, the exclusive doctrine of apostolic succession is an attempt to provide historico-critical proof of the fourth attribute of the Church! No, the gospel validates the ministry and sacraments of the Church, not *vice versa*. As Gustav Aulén has put it:

> The office of ministry is a divine institution and as such it is indispensable in the life of the Church. But it is not the order that guarantees the effectiveness of the means of grace. On the contrary, it is the means of grace, effective in themselves, or rather the means of grace made effective through the continuing work of Christ, which necessitate and define the order. If the office of the ministry were to guarantee the effectiveness of the means of grace, the relationship between the means of grace and order would be reversed.[9]

This is not, however, necessarily to do away with episcopacy altogether. Our study of the doctrine of the reformed episcopate in Part Two provides sufficient evidence that the fundamental principles of the Reformers—Luther and Calvin as well as the English divines—were not regarded as incompatible with episcopacy as such.

(3) If the gospel alone constitutes the Church, there can be no absolutising of traditional doctrinal formulas or liturgical forms. The holy gospel relativises all attempts to capture or embody it. This point can be put in terms of the relation between the Church and the kingdom or reign of God or,

alternatively, in terms of the 'protestant principle'. Here we seem to get to the root of the difference between Reformation ecclesiology and traditional 'catholic' ecclesiology—whether Roman, Orthodox or Anglo-Catholic.

Having said this, however, we have to recognise immediately that this statement can only be made in an archetypal sense. Churches of the Reformation can become more hidebound by tradition than the Church of Rome. Since the death of Barth, protestants have not been able to show any theological work remotely comparable to the massive evangelical theologies of Roman Catholic scholars like Küng and Schillebeeckx. Nor have they been able to undertake the energetic and radical reform of Church life that stemmed from Vatican II. Considered merely in an archetypal sense, however, the contrast between Reformation and Roman Catholic ecclesiologies is useful.

Archbishop William Temple once remarked: 'I believe that all the doctrinal errors of Rome come from the direct identification of the Church as an organised institution, taking its part in the process of history, with the kingdom of God.' If this identification is made it becomes patently impossible for the dynamic energy of the gospel at the Church's centre to exercise any reforming influence over the accumulating dead wood of tradition in the form of either dogma or Church law. The Church cannot say, We were wrong; we have taken a wrong turning; we must retrace our steps. It can only attempt the theologically dubious reinterpretation of dogmas which may once have meant something entirely different.

This kind of double-think cuts at the nerve of theological integrity, but it is virtually inevitable where Church and kingdom are identified as in traditional Roman Catholic theology influenced by Augustine. No theories of the development of doctrine, however subtle, can get catholic theology out of this cleft stick. The process has to be put into reverse; a sort of 'development by demolition', as Schillebeeckx calls it, has to begin.

There are signs that this is precisely what is beginning to happen. In post-conciliar Roman Catholic theology there has been a marked change of mood—indeed, a change of mind— on this question. The Second Vatican Council's *Dogmatic*

Constitution on the Church pointedly avoids making the identification of Church and kingdom. It asserts that the kingdom of God is primarily manifested in the person of Christ and in the preaching of the gospel. 'In Christ's word, in his works, and in his presence this kingdom reveals itself to men.' The Church experiences only a foretaste, as it were, of the kingdom:

> The Church, consequently, equipped with the gifts of her Founder and faithfully guarding his precepts of charity, humility and self-sacrifice, receives the mission to proclaim and to establish among all peoples the kingdom of Christ and of God. She becomes on earth the initial budding forth of that kingdom. While she slowly grows, the Church strains toward the consummation of the kingdom and, with all her strength, hopes and desires to be united in glory with her King.

Hans Küng has gone even further in stressing the actual discontinuity between Church and kingdom. 'The transcendental and eschatological character of the reign of God, as the reign of *God,* makes any identity or even continuity out of the question.' The truth is quite the other way:

> So far from stressing identity, we should be concerned to stress the basic difference between the Church and the reign of God ... The eschatological community of believers comes from the preaching of the reign of God— the reign of God is its goal, its limitation, its judgement. The Church is not the kingdom of God, but it looks towards the kingdom of God, waits for it, or rather makes a pilgrimage towards it and is its herald, proclaiming it to the world.

These two statements are not far from the spirit of Reformation theology.[10]

The concept of the protestant principle, enunciated by Tillich in *The Protestant Era* (1948) and further developed in his *Systematic Theology*, is an alternative way of expressing the critical, relativising function of the Christian gospel over against all human expressions of it. Tillich defined the principle as 'the theological expression of the true relation between the unconditional and the conditioned or, religiously speaking, between God and man'. It stands for the recognition of the claims of the infinite over the finite, the absolute over the relative, the eternal over the temporal, and exposes as idolatry all overt or covert attempts to reverse this relation. It may prove to be one of the more enduring features of Tillich's eclectic and fundamentally heterodox theology.

According to the protestant principle, the Church's christological centre must never be stifled by the accretion of unrevised traditional doctrines or ecclesiastical structures; rather it must be allowed to judge and reform them. As T. F. Torrance has put it, the Reformation stood for the supremacy of the word of God over all human tradition and for 'theological activity as the repentant rethinking of all tradition face to face with the revelation of God in Jesus Christ'.[11]

Reformation theology thus emphasises the inescapably theological nature of the ecumenical task and the radically self-searching, self-questioning method of theology in submission to the word of the gospel. It underlines the essentially progressive and revisionary character of Christian theology. In language strikingly and significantly echoed more than four hundred years later in the Barmen Declaration of the German Confessing Church, the Reformers gathered at Berne in 1528 expressed it like this:

The holy Christian Church, whose only head is Christ, is born from the word of God, abides in the word, and hears not the voice of strangers.

BIBLIOGRAPHICAL NOTES

Note   1. The titles of journals mentioned only once are given in full in the notes.

2. Titles enclosed in square brackets are of works I have been unable to obtain during the preparation of this book.

ABBREVIATIONS
used in the notes

JEH	*Journal of Ecclesiastical History*
CH	*Church History*
JTS	*Journal of Theological Studies*
SJT	*Scottish Journal of Theology*
ARG	*Archiv für Reformationsgeschichte*
MQR	*Mennonite Quarterly Review*

INTRODUCTION: THE REFORMATION CONCEPT OF THE CHURCH
(pp. 1-9)

1. E. G. Rupp, *The Righteousness of God* (London, 1953), p. 310.
Full bibliographies on the ecclesiology of the Reformers are to be found in
E. G. Léonard, *A History of Protestantism: Vol. 1, The Reformation*
(Edinburgh and London, 1965). General works which contain some
discussion of the *notae ecclesiae* are: Benno Gassman, *Ecclesia Reformata:
die Kirche in den reformierten Bekenntnisschriften* (Freiburg, 1968);
Henri Strohl, *La Pensée de la Réforme* (Neuchâtel, 1951); T. F.
Torrance, *Kingdom and Church* (Edinburgh, 1956); Henri Strohl,
'L'Église chez les Reformateurs', *Revue d'Histoire et de Philosophie
religieuses* (1936), Vol. xvi (1936), pp. 265-319; [R. M. Kingdom's essay
in F. Forrester Church and Timothy George (eds.) *Continuity and
Discontinuity in Church History: Essays presented to G. H. Williams*
(Leiden, 1979)].

2. Cited by Norman Sykes, *Old Priest and New Presbyter* (Cambridge,
1956), p. 76.

3. Werner Elert, *The Structure of Lutheranism* (St Louis, 1962),
pp. 255-8. For Luther's relation to the Hussites, see Karl Holl, *Gesammelte Aufsätze zur Kirchengeschichte: Vol. 1, Luther* (Tübingen, 1948),
pp. 369f.; Jaroslav Pelikan, *Obedient Rebels* (London, 1964), Part two.

4. See J. Pelikan, op. cit., p. 34 n. 2; Zwingli, *The Latin Works of H.
Zwingli*, ed. Jackson (Philadelphia, 1929), Vol. 3, p. 368 *(De Vera et
Falsa Religio)*.

5. Cited J. Pelikan, op. cit., p. 39.

6. B. C. Milner, *Calvin's Doctrine of the Church* (Leiden, 1970),
p. 133.

CHAPTER ONE: THE CHRISTOLOGICAL CENTRE (pp. 13-24)

1. J. Pelikan, op. cit., p. 14. Additional works on Luther's ecclesiology
are: E. G. Rupp, op. cit., ch. 14; ibid., 'Luther and the Doctrine of the
Church', *SJT*, Vol. ix (1956), pp. 38ff; Pelikan, *Spirit Versus Structure:
Luther and the Institutions of the Church* (London, 1968); Edmund
Schlink, *The Theology of the Lutheran Confessions* (Philadelphia, 1961);
W. Elert, op. cit., Part two, ch. 4; P. Althaus, *The Theology of Martin
Luther* (Philadelphia, 1966), chs. 21ff.; J. Headley, *Luther's View of
Church History* (New Haven, 1963); [E. Rietschel, *Das Problem der
sichtbar-unsichtbaren Kirche bei Luther* (Leipzig, 1932); F. Kattenbusch,
Die *Doppelschichtigkeit in Luther's Kirchenbegrift* (Gotha, 1928); Martin
Doerne, 'Luther's Kirchverstandnis', in *Kirchenreform I* (Gottingen, 1964),
pp. 10–41]. See also the bibliographies for parts two and three of the
present work.

2. Althaus, op. cit., p. 290.

3. Strohl, *La Pensée de la Réforme*, p. 178.

4. I am unable to trace this quotation.

5. Schlink, op. cit., p. 219.

6. P. S. Watson, *Let God be God* (London, 1947), p. 169.

7. See Pelikan, *Spirit Versus Structure*, pp. 32ff.

8. E. Troeltsch, *The Social Teaching of the Christian Churches* (London, 1931), Vol. 2, pp. 479ff.

9. Althaus, op. cit., p. 292. See also Léonard, op. cit., p. 88.

10. Cited J. S. Whale, *The Protestant Tradition* (Cambridge, 1955), p. 112.

11. See Léonard, op. cit., pp. 110ff., and the works cited for Luther's view of Church polity in part two of the present work.

12. Troeltsch, op. cit., p. 518.

CHAPTER TWO: THE CHURCH TAKES FORM (pp. 25–35)

1. E. Schlink, 'The Marks of the Church according to the Augsburg Confession', *The Coming Christ and the Coming Church* (Edinburgh and London, 1967), p. 119.

2. E. Doumergue, *Jean Calvin: les hommes et les choses de son temps*, Vol. 5 (Lausanne, 1917), p. 18.

3. Melanchthon, *Loci Communes* (1555), *Melanchthon on Christian Doctrine*, ed. C. L. Manschreck (New York, 1965), p. 270.

4. P. Fraenkel, *Testimonia Patrum: the function of the patristic argument in the theology of Philip Melanchthon* (Geneva, 1961), pp. 114f.

5. Manschreck (ed.), op. cit., p. 272.

6. Fraenkel, op. cit., p. 117.

7. See C. S. Meyer, 'Melanchthon, Theologian of Ecumenism,' *JEH*, Vol. xvii (1966), p. 202.

8. Manschreck (ed.), op. cit., p. 266.

9. See R. Stupperich, *Melanchthon* (London, 1966), p. 146.

10. Manschreck (ed.), op. cit., p. 267.

11. See E. Schlink, *Theology of the Lutheran Confessions*, p. 216; cf. Fraenkel, op. cit., p. 117.

12. See H. Strohl, *La Pensée de la Réforme*, p. 205.

13. On Calvin's ecclesiology, see: Doumergue, op. cit.; Whale, op. cit.; Milner, op. cit.; A. Ganoczy, *Ecclesia Ministrans: dienende Kirche und kirchliche Dienst bei Calvin* (Freiburg, Basel, Wein, 1968); ibid., *Le Jeune Calvin: Genèse et Evolution de sa Vocation Reformatrice* (Wiesbaden, 1966); F. Wendel, *Calvin: the Origins and Development of his Religious Thought* (London, 1965); W. Niesel, *The Theology of Calvin* (Philadelphia and London, 1956); A. Lecerf, 'La Doctrine d'Église dans Calvin', *Révue de Théologie et de Philosophie*, n.s. Vol. xvii, no. 73 (1929), pp. 256-70; J. T. McNeill, 'The Church in Sixteenth-Century Reformed Theology', *Journal of Religion*, Vol. xxii (1942), pp. 251-69.

14. Wendel, op. cit., pp. 297ff.; cf. Niesel, op. cit., pp. 195ff.

15. Cochrane (ed.), *Reformed Confessions of the Sixteenth Century* (London, 1966), pp. 124f.

16. Strohl, op. cit., pp. 211f.

17. Doumergue, op. cit., p. 30.

18. Ibid., p. 44.

19. Henri Clavier, *Études sur le Calvinisme* (Paris, 1936), p. 46; cf. Ganoczy, *Le Jeune Calvin*, pp. 334f.; R. S. Wallace, *Calvin's Doctrine of the Christian Life* (Edinburgh and London, 1959), p. 207.

CHAPTER THREE: PROBLEMS IN EVANGELICAL ECCLESIOLOGY (pp. 36-44)

1. Hans Küng, *The Church* (London, 1967), pp. 265ff.
2. Cited Elert, op. cit., p. 262.
3. Schlink, op. cit., p. 224.
4. Cited Léonard, op. cit., p. 331.
5. Ganoczy, op. cit., p. 325.
6. G. Bromiley (ed.), *Zwingli and Bullinger*, Library of Christian Classics, Vol. 24 (London, 1953), pp. 299ff.

CHAPTER FOUR: DEFINING THE CIRCUMFERENCE (pp. 45-63)

1. D. Wright, ed, *Commonplaces of Martin Bucer* (Appleford, 1972), p. 31.
2. *Latin Works of H. Zwingli*, Vol. 3, pp. 368ff.; R. Walton, *Zwingli's Theocracy* (Toronto, 1967), p. 46. See also Alfred Farner, *Die Lehre von Kirche und Stadt bei Zwingli* (Tübingen, 1930) and [Roger Ley, *Kirchenzucht bei Zwingli* (Zurich, 1948).]
3. I. Breward (ed.), *William Perkins* (Appleford, 1970), pp. 268f.
4. See David D. Hall, *The Faithful Shepherd: A History of the New England Ministry in the Seventeenth Century* (New York, 1974), pp. 25f.; A. F. Scott Pearson, *Thomas Cartwright and Elizabethan Puritanism 1535-1603* (Cambridge, 1925), pp. 220, 308ff.
5. R. Stupperich, 'Die Kirche im M. Bucers theologischer Entwicklung', *ARG*, Vol. xxxv (1938), pp.81-101; Strohl, op. cit., pp. 194, 199; J. Courvoisier, *La Notion d'Église chez Bucer dans son développement historique* (Paris, 1933), p. 68. See also T. F. Torrance, *Kingdom and Church*; W. P. Stephens, *The Holy Spirit in the Theology of Martin Bucer* (Cambridge, 1970).
6. *Commonplaces of Martin Bucer*, pp. 205f. (1550-1); Courvoisier, op. cit., p. 23; D. D. Hall, op. cit., p. 18.
7. Courvoisier, op. cit., p. 24; Léonard, op. cit., p. 189f.; J. C. McLelland, *The Visible Words of God: a Study in the Theology of Peter Martyr* (Edinburgh and London, 1957), pp. 123ff. For Bullinger's views on discipline see H. Bouvier, *Heinrich Bullinger* (Neuchâtel and Paris, 1940), pp. 83ff.
8. Knox, *Works*, ed. Laing (Edinburgh, 1846), Vol. 4, pp. 266f; Vol. 2, p. 110.
9. Frere and Douglas (eds.), *Puritan Manifestos* (London, 1954), p. 9.
10. F. H. Littell, *The Anabaptist View of the Church* (2nd edn, Boston, 1958), p. xvii. On the radical movements, see also G. H. Williams, *The Radical Reformation* (London, 1962); ibid., (ed.), *Spiritual and Anabaptist Writers*, Library of Christian Classics, Vol. 25; E. G. Rupp,

Patterns of Reformation (London, 1969); N. Cohn, *The Pursuit of the Millennium* (London, 1970).

11. Williams, *The Radical Reformation*, p. 119.

12. Littell, op. cit., p. 14.

13. Franck, 'A Letter to John Campanus', *Spiritual and Anabaptist Writers*, pp. 149ff.; Littell, op. cit., pp. 22ff.; G. H. Williams, *The Radical Reformation*, p. 257.

14. Littell, op. cit., p. 82.

15. Ibid., p. 91.

16. Cited ibid., p. 90.

17. *Spiritual and Anabaptist Writers*, p. 231.

18. Dietrich Philips in ibid., p. 244.

19. G. H. Williams, op. cit., p. 183.

20. Dietrich Philips, op. cit., p. 246.

21. Cited G. H. Williams, op. cit., p. 133.

22. Cited Littell, op. cit., p. 88.

23. Cited Williams, op. cit., p. 221 and Littell, op. cit., p. 88.

24. Littell, op. cit., p. 86.

25. Citation from Littell, op. cit., p. 87.

26. Carlson (ed.), *The Writings of Henry Barrow 1587-1590* (London, 1962), pp. 294, 317; Scott Pearson, *Thomas Cartwright*, passim; D. D. Hall, *The Faithful Shepherd*, p. 27; F. J. Powicke, *Henry Barrow and the Exiled Church of Amsterdam* (London, 1900), pp. 98, 104.

27. Carlson (ed.), *The Writings of John Greenwood and Henry Barrow 1591-1593* (London, 1970), p. 121; Scott Pearson, op. cit., p. 219; Carlson (ed.), *The Writings of John Greenwood 1587-1590, etc.* (London, 1969), p. 98.

CHAPTER FIVE: A REFORMED CATHOLICITY (pp. 64-77)

1. H. F. Woodhouse, *The Doctrine of the Church in Anglican Theology 1547-1603* (London, 1954), p. 11; Richard Bauckham, 'Hooker, Travers and the Church of Rome in the 1580s', *JEH*, Vol. xxix (1978), pp. 37-50; Gifford, cited by W. K. Jordan, *The Development of Religious Toleration in England*, Vol. 1 (London, 1932), p. 220.

2. C. J. Sisson, *The Judicious Marriage of Mr Hooker* (Cambridge, 1940), p. 8. W. Speed Hill (ed.), *Studies in Richard Hooker* (Cleveland and London, 1972) is worth consulting and contains an annotated bibliography of works on Hooker. My study *Richard Hooker and John Calvin* is forthcoming in *JEH* (1980).

CHAPTER SIX: THE WORD OF GOD AND THE WORD OF MAN (pp. 81-94)

1. Cited Stephens, op. cit., p. 197.

2. Zwingli, *De Vera et Falsa Religio, Latin Works of H. Zwingli*, Vol. 3, pp. 376, 380.

3. Bilson, *Perpetual Government of Christ's Church*, cited E. T.

Davies, *Episcopacy and the Royal Supremacy in the Church of England in the Sixteenth Century* (Oxford, 1950), p. 35.

4. Cited R. Sider, *Karlstadt: the Development of his Thought 1517-1521* (Leiden, 1974), pp. 135f.

5. Cited Stephens, op. cit., pp. 179, 181.

6. See Whale, op. cit., p. 157; Doumergue, op. cit., Vol. 2, p. 234.

7. Cited Doumergue, op. cit., p. 504.

8. Cited R. Bainton, *Here I Stand* (Mentor Books, New York and Toronto), pp. 104, 166.

9. Calvin, *Sermons on Ephesians* (Edinburgh, 1973), p. 12.

10. See Stephens, op. cit., p. 184.

CHAPTER SEVEN: THE UNIVERSAL PRIESTHOOD (pp. 95-108)

1. Rupp, op. cit., p. 315. For Luther's doctrine of the ministry see the works cited for chapter eight n. 1, below.

2. Cited Sider, op. cit., p. 137.

3. *Spiritual and Anabaptist Writers*, p. 158.

4. Cited Littell, op. cit., p. 88.

5. Cited Hall, op. cit., p. 30.

6. Cited Sider, op. cit., p. 135.

7. Elert, op. cit., p. 343.

8. Althaus, op. cit., p. 314.

9. Elert, op. cit., p. 342.

10. Helmut Lieberg, *Amt und Ordination bei Luther und Melanchthon* (Gottingen, 1962), p. 259.

11. Courvoisier, op. cit., pp. 72ff., 90, 128.

12. Littell, op. cit., p. 92.

13. Cited J. L. Ainslie, *The Doctrines of Ministerial Order in the Reformed Churches of the Sixteenth and Seventeenth Centuries* (Edinburgh, 1940), p. 7.

14. Cited Hall, op. cit., p. 9.

CHAPTER EIGHT: THE REFORMED EPISCOPATE (pp. 109-130)

1. For Luther and Melanchthon on Church polity, see: the works already cited by Elert, Althaus, Schlink, Lieberg, Ainslie, together with G. Hök, 'Luther's Doctrine of the Ministry', *SJT*, Vol. vii (1954), pp. 14-40; J. O. Evjen, 'Luther's Ideas concerning Church Polity', *Lutheran Church Review*, No. 3 (1926), pp. 207ff.; B. Gerrish, 'Priesthood and Ministry in Luther,' *CH*, Vol. xxxiv (1965), pp. 404-22; W. Pauck, 'The Ministry in the Time of the Continental Reformation', in H. R. Niebuhr and D. D. Williams (eds.), *The Ministry in Historical Perspectives* (New York, 1956); [Hausliermann, *Luther's ordnet seine Kirche, Luther-Jahrbuch*, Vol. xxxi (1964), pp. 29-46].

2. See Niesel, op. cit., pp. 199ff.

3. For Calvin on episcopacy, see [J. Pannier, *Calvin et l'episcopat* (Strasbourg, 1926)]; J. T. McNeill, 'The Doctrine of the Ministry in

Reformed Theology', *CH*, Vol. xii (1943), pp. 77-97; Milner, op. cit., esp. p. 148.

4. For the English Reformers' view of Church polity, see: Sykes, op. cit.; Davies, op. cit.; Woodhouse, op. cit., A. J. Mason, *The Church of England and Episcopacy* (Cambridge, 1914).

5. Sykes, op. cit., pp. 82ff.; see also, ibid., 'The Church of England and Non-Episcopal Churches in the Sixteenth and Seventeenth Centuries', *Theology Occasional Papers*, NS, No. 11 (London, 1948); also Woodhouse, op. cit., p. 101.

6. Mason, op. cit., p. 61.

7. P. Collinson, *The Elizabethan Puritan Movement* (London, 1967), p. 109. See W. Nijenhuis, *Ecclesia Reformata* (Leiden, 1972), esp. pp. 43ff. for documentary sources for what follows.

8. Cited Ainslie, op. cit., p. 23.

9. Cited Mason, op. cit., p. 65.

10. W. D. J. Cargill Thompson, 'Anthony Marten and the Elizabethan Debate on Episcopacy', in G. V. Bennett and J. D. Walsh (eds.), *Essays in Modern English Church History in Memory of Norman Sykes* (London, 1966), pp. 56ff.

11. See Mason, op. cit., pp. 34ff.

12. See Davies, op. cit., pp. 33ff.

13. Cargill Thompson, op. cit., pp. 59f.

14. See also Elert, op. cit., pp. 275ff.; Rupp, op. cit., pp. 338ff.

15. Whitaker, *Disputation of Holy Scripture*, p. 510.

16. J. Strype, *The Life and Acts of Matthew Parker* (1821 edn), vol. 1, p. 139, cited Cargill Thompson, op. cit., p. 47n.

CHAPTER NINE: THE GODLY PRINCE (pp. 131-150)

1. Sykes, op. cit., pp. 2f. A general introduction to political aspects of the Reformation is provided by Quentin Skinner, *The Foundations of Modern Political Thought*, Vol. 2, *The Age of Reformation* (Cambridge, 1978).

2. J. J. Scarisbrick, *Henry VIII* (Harmondsworth, 1971), p. 505.

3. See Christopher Morris, *Political Thought in England, Tyndale to Hooker* (Oxford, 1953), pp. 1, 32, 34, 117f.

4. A. F. Pollard, *Henry VIII* (London, 1919), pp. 269f.

5. G. R. Elton, *The Tudor Constitution: Documents and Commentary* (Cambridge, 1972), p. 356.

6. Ibid., pp. 364ff. See also Walter Ullmann, 'This Realm of England is an Empire', *JEH*, Vol. xxx (1979), pp. 175ff.

7. Elton, op. cit., p. 336.

8. See A. F. Scott Pearson, *Church and State: Political Aspects of Sixteenth Century Puritanism* (Cambridge, 1928), p. 12.

9. Scarisbrick, op. cit., p. 498.

10. Cited Morris, op. cit., pp. 115f.

11. Figgis, *The Divine Right of Kings*, 2nd edn. with two additional essays (Cambridge, 1922), pp. 319ff., 335.

12. Hobbes, *Leviathan* (London, 1962), pp. 375ff.

13. Additional literature: W. D. J. Cargill Thompson, 'Martin Luther and the Two Kingdoms', in David Thomson (ed.), *Political Ideas* (Harmondsworth, 1969), p. 49; ibid., 'The "Two Kingdoms" and the "Two Regiments": Some Problems of Luther's Zwei-Reiche-Lehre', *JTS*, NS, Vol. xx, pt. 1 (1969), pp. 164-85; E. M. Carlson, 'Luther's Conception of Government', *CH*, Vol. xv (1946), pp. 257-70; E. G. Schwiebert, 'The Medieval Pattern in Luther's Views of the State', *CH*, Vol. xii (1943), pp. 98-117; L. W. Spitz, 'Luther's Ecclesiology and his Concept of the Prince as Notbischof', *CH*, Vol. xxii (1953), pp. 113-41; F. E. Cranz, *An Essay on the Development of Luther's Thought on Justice, Law and Society* (Harvard, 1959); G. Wingren, *Luther on Vocation* (Philadelphia, 1957)= *The Christian's Calling* (Edinburgh, 1958); K. Holl, 'Luther und das Landesherrliche Kirchenregiment', op. cit., Vol. 1, pp. 326–380.

14. In addition to the works, already cited, by Doumergue and Niesel, see also J. Bohatec, *Calvins Lehre von Staat und Kirche* (Breslau, 1937); J. Baur, *Gott, Recht und Weltliche Regiment im Werke Calvins* (Bonn, 1965).

15. See Scott Pearson, *Church and State*, pp. 9f, 15ff., 27, 30f., 56ff.

CHAPTER TEN: THE ROYAL SUPREMACY (pp. 151-163)

1. F. Le Van Baumer, *The Early Tudor Theory of Kingship* (New Haven, 1940), p. 1.

2. Cited, Elton, op. cit., p. 344.

3. Ibid., pp. 339, 354, 350.

4. Ibid., pp. 356f.

5. See Scarisbrick, op. cit., p. 540 and passim.

6. J. W. Allen, *Political Thought in the Sixteenth Century* (London, 1928), pp. 164f.

7. Cited Morris, op. cit., p. 51.

8. Baumer, op. cit., p. 2.

9. Ibid., p. 32.

10. See Davies, op. cit., p. 88.

11. Morris, op. cit., p. 52.

12. See W. M. Lamont, *Godly Rule: Politics and Religion 1603-60* (London, 1969), pp. 44f.

13. Baumer, op. cit., p. 136.

14. Cf. Scarisbrick, op. cit., pp. 512ff.

CHAPTER ELEVEN: THE REFORMERS AND MISSION (pp. 167-179)

1. Cited Stephen Neill, *A History of Christian Missions* (Harmondsworth, 1964), p. 221.

2. Ibid., p. 222.

3. K. S. Latourette, *A History of the Expansion of Christianity: Vol. 3, Three Centuries of Advance 1500-1800* AD (New York, 1971), p. 42.

4. W. R. Hogg, 'The Rise of Protestant Missionary Concern', in G. W.

Anderson (ed.), *The Theology of the Christian Mission* (London, 1961), pp. 97ff.

5. Latourette, op. cit., p. 38.

6. Cited Neill, op. cit., p. 141.

7. Cited J. H. Parry, *The Age of Reconnaissance* (New York, 1964), p. 33.

8. Cited Neill, op. cit., p. 220.

9. Cited Gustav Warneck, *Outline of the History of Protestant Missions* (Edinburgh, 1884), p. 28.

10. H. Strohl, 'L'Église chez les Reformateurs', *Revue d'Histoire et de Philosophie Religieuses*, Vol. xvi (1936), pp. 285; W. P. Stephens, *The Holy Spirit in the Theology of Martin Bucer*, p. 159.

11. Cited E. Stauffer, 'The Anabaptist Theology of Missions', *MQR*, Vol. xix (1945), pp. 179-214.

12. Cited Littell, op. cit., pp. 109ff.

13. G. H. Williams, *The Radical Reformation*, p. 833.

14. Littell, op. cit., pp. 114f., 198 n. 30.

15. W. Elert, op. cit., p. 387.

16. Ibid., p. 388.

CHAPTER TWELVE: THE SPREAD OF THE REFORM IN CHRISTENDOM
(pp. 180-189)

1. A. G. Dickens, *The German Nation and Martin Luther* (London, 1974), p. 72; Léonard, op. cit., p. 71, citing Imbart de la Tour, *Les origines de la Réforme*, Vol. 3, p. 51.

2. Léonard, op. cit., p. 72; Dickens, op. cit., pp. 103-13; Louise Holborn, 'Printing and the Growth of a Protestant Movement in Germany from 1517 to 1524', *CH*, Vol. xi (1942), pp. 123-37; T. B. Macaulay, *The History of England from the Accession of James II*, Vol. 1 (London, 1906), pp. 42f.; [H. Gravier, *Luther et l'opinion publique* (Paris, 1942)].

3. H. J. Hillerbrand, 'The Spread of the Protestant Reformation of the Sixteenth Century: a historical case study in the transfer of ideas', *South Atlantic Quarterly*, Vol. lxvii (1968), pp. 265-86.

4. G. H. Williams, op. cit., p. 127; Littell, op. cit., p. 18.

5. G. H. Williams, op. cit., p. 130.

6. Calvin, *Sermons on the Epistles of St Paul to Timothy and Titus* (1579), pp. 746f., cited Iain Murray, *The Puritan Hope* (London, 1971), p. 84.

7. R. M. Kingdon, *Geneva and the Coming of the Wars of Religion in France 1555-1563* (Geneva, 1956), p. 51; G. R. Elton, *Reformation Europe* (London, 1963), p. 236; *The New Cambridge Modern History Vol. 2: The Reformation 1520-1559* (Cambridge, 1958), p. 224.

8. On Farel, see Louis Aubert, 'Les missions en France de divers pasteurs du pays de Neuchâtel', in *Guillame Farel 1489-1565: Biographie Novelle* (Neuchâtel and Paris, 1930), pp. 688ff. For what follows, see R. M. Kingdon, *Geneva and the Consolidation of the French Protestant Movement 1564-1572* (Geneva, 1967).

9. Kingdon, ibid., pp. 31-6.

10. On the judicial laws of Moses in Reformation theology, see my article, 'Moses and the Magistrate: a study in the rise of Protestant legalism', *JEH*, Vol. xxvi (1975), pp. 149-172.

CHAPTER THIRTEEN: THE CONVERSION OF THE JEWS (pp. 190-203)

1. Selma Stern, *Josel of Rosheim: Commander of Jewry in the Holy Roman Empire of the German Nation* (Philadelphia, 1965). On the background see S. W. Baron, *A Social and Religious History of the Jews, Vol. 13: Inquisition, Renaissance and Reformation* (New York, 1969); Simon Dubnov, *History of the Jews, Vol. 3: From the Later Middle Ages to the Renaissance* (New York, 1969).

2. Baron, *Jewish Quarterly Review*, NS Vol. xxiii (1932-33), pp. 405ff. See also on this, L. I. Newman, *Jewish Influence on Christian Reform Movements* (New York, 1925); Carl Cohen, 'Martin Luther and His Jewish Contemporaries', *Jewish Social Studies*, Vol. xxv (1963), pp. 195-204; H. H. Ben-Sasson, 'Jewish-Christian Disputation in the setting of humanism and Reformation in the German Empire', *Harvard Theological Review*, Vol. lix (1966), pp. 369-90: ibid., 'The Reformation in Jewish Eyes', *Proceedings of the Israel Academy of Sciences and Humanities* (1969-70), pp. 239ff.

3. Stern, op. cit., pp. 131ff.; Cohen, op. cit., pp. 197f.; Christopher Hill, *Puritanism and Revolution* (London, 1968), pp. 142f.

4. On Luther and the Jews, see: R. Lewin, *Luthers Stellung zu den Juden* (Berlin, 1911); K. H. Rengstorf and S. von Kortzfleisch (eds.), *Kirche und Synagogue, Handbuch zur Geschichte von Christen und Juden: Darstellung mit Quellen*, Vol. 1 (chapter by W. Maurer on the Reformation), (Stuttgart, 1968); Armas K. E. Holmio, *The Lutheran Reformation and the Jews: the Birth of Protestant Jewish Missions* (Hancock, Michigan, 1949); Kurt Meier, 'Zur Interpretation von Luthers Judenschriften', in James Atkinson et al., *Vierhundertfunfzig Jahre lutherische Reformation, 1517-1967: Festschrift für Franz Lau* (Göttingen, 1967); Martin Stöhr, 'Luther und die Juden', *Evangelische Theologie*, Vol. xx (1960), pp. 157-82; Carl Cohen, 'Die Juden und Luther', *ARG*, Vol. liv (1963), pp. 38-51; A. Siirala, 'Luther and the Jews', *Lutheran World*, Vol. xi (1964), pp. 337-57; R. Moellering, 'Luther's attitude towards the Jews', *Concordia Theological Monthly*, (1948), pp. 920ff.; (1949), pp. 45-59, 194-215, 579; E. G. Rupp, 'Martin Luther and the Jews', Robert Waley Cohen Memorial Lecture (London, 1972).

5. Holmio, op. cit., pp. 89, 91.

6. Stern, op. cit., p. 161.

7. Cited Baron, op. cit., p. 225.

8. On Bullinger's attitude to the Jews, see Joachim Staedtke, 'Die Juden im historischen und theologischen Urteil des schweizer Reformators Heinrich Bullinger', *Judaica*, Vol. xi (1955), pp. 236-56.

9. Cited Baron, op. cit., p. 252.

10. Nijenhuis, *Ecclesia Reformata*, p. 39.

11. Rupp, op. cit.

12. Cited Newman, op. cit., p. 499; see also my 'Moses and the Magistrate'.

13. Newman, op. cit., p. 585.

14. See Baron, op. cit., p. 289; cf. ibid., 'John Calvin and the Jews', in *H. A. Wolfson Jubilee Volume* (Jerusalem, 1965), English section 1, pp. 141-63; J. Courvoisier, 'Calvin et les Juifs', *Judaica*, Vol. ii (1946), pp. 203-8.

15. See Stern, op. cit., pp. 162ff.; Nijenhuis, op. cit.; H. Eells, 'Bucer's Plan for the Jews', *CH*, Vol. vi (1937), pp. 127ff.

16. Eells, op. cit., p. 135.

17. Nijenhuis, op. cit., p. 60.

18. See Peter Toon (ed.), *Puritans, the Millennium and the Future of Israel: Puritan Eschatology 1600-1660* (Cambridge and London, 1970) and Iain Murray, op. cit.

19. Stern, op. cit., pp. 215f.

CHAPTER FOURTEEN: MISSIONS TO THE HEATHEN (pp. 204-214)

1. On the background, see *The New Cambridge Modern History*, ch. xvii; Stephen A. Fischer-Galati, *Ottoman Imperialism and German Protestantism 1521-1555* (Cambridge, 1955).

2. Cited Dickens, op. cit., pp. 54f.

3. Parry, op. cit., pp. 39f.

4. G. H. Williams, *Spiritual and Anabaptist Writers*, pp. 156, 232f.

5. Ibid., *The Radical Reformation*, p. 835.

6. See K. Holl, 'Luther und die Mission', *Gesammelte Aufsätze*, Vol. 3; C. U. Wolf, 'Luther and Mohammedanism', *Moslem World*, Vol. xxxi (1941), pp. 161-177.

7. Fischer-Galati, op. cit., p. 117.

8. Additionally: G. W. Forrell, 'Luther and the war against the Turks', *CH*, Vol. xiv (1945), pp. 256-71; H. Buchanan, 'Luther and the Turks 1519-1529', *ARG*, Vol. xlvii (1956), pp. 145-59.

9. J. Pannier, 'Calvin et les Turcs', *Revue Historique*, Vol. ccxxx (1937), p. 284.

10. Elert, op. cit., pp. 394, 399.

11. Latourette, op. cit., p. 43.

12. S. H. Rooy, *The Theology of Missions in the Puritan Tradition* (Delft, 1965), p. 319.

13. Ibid., pp. 126f.

CONCLUSION: THE RELEVANCE OF REFORMATION ECCLESIOLOGY (pp. 215-225)

1. Strohl, *La Pensée de la Réforme*, pp. 5f.

2. J. T. McNeill, *Unitive Protestantism* (New York, 1930), p. 64; Gustav Aulén, *Reformation and Catholicity* (Edinburgh and London, 1960), p. 181.

3. Pelikan, *Obedient Rebels*, p. 13.

4. McNeill, op. cit., p. 89; ibid., *A History of the Ecumenical Movement 1517-1948*, eds. R. Rouse and S. C. Neill (London 1954), *ad loc.*

5. Forsyth, *The Church and the Sacraments* (London, 1917), p. 31.

6. Barth, *The Epistle to the Romans* (Oxford, 1933 and 1968), p. 36; ibid., *Church Dogmatics* (Edinburgh, 1956), Vol. iv, pp. 652ff.

7. Küng, *The Church* (London 1967), pp. ixff., 30ff., 285f.; *The Documents of Vatican II* (London and Dublin, 1966), pp. 17, 39.

8. Ramsey, *The Gospel and the Catholic Church* (London, 1936), pp. 179f.

9. Aulén, op. cit., p. 187; Barth, *Church Dogmatics*, Vol. iv, p. 1.

10. *The Documents of Vatican II*, pp. 17ff.; Küng, op. cit., pp. 92ff.

11. Tillich, *The Protestant Era* (Chicago, 1948), p. 163; Torrance, *Theology in Reconstruction* (London, 1965), p. 164.

INDEX OF SUBJECTS

(Index to the Text only)

1. GENERAL

Monasticism (religious orders), 170, 172
Moravians, the, 213

Opus operatum; opus operantis, 37, 55, 92f.
Order, power of (*potestas ordinis*), 115,
119ff., 122f., 158f.

Pacifism, 54, 56
Papacy, the (Pope, the), 1, 4, 13, 20f.,
26, 36ff., 40, 42f., 50, 72, 98, 105,
114, 128f., 133f., 138, 144f., 151, 155,
158, 161, 167, 172, 174, 195, 204,
209f., 216
Peasants' Revolt, the, 23, 51, 193
Persecution, see Suffering
Pope, the, see Papacy, the
Praemunire, 152
Preaching, see Word, the
Presbyterianism, 46, 49, 68, 103, 109,
112, 114ff., 118f., 121, 123f., 161
Priesthood of all Believers, see Universal
Priesthood
Printing, 182, 187, 214
Puritans, the, 6, 16, 18, 22, 35, 45f., 50f.,
68ff., 72f., 76, 85ff., 109, 115, 123ff.,
137, 143, 147ff., 161, 171, 182, 213

Radicals, the (Radical Reformation,
the), 3, 6, 18, 21, 25, 28f., 34, 36, 39f.,
42, 45, 47, 49, 51f., 54ff., 73, 84f.,
87, 96f., 101, 103f., 138, 175ff., 185f.,
193f., 204, 206ff.
Renaissance (Humanism), 40, 56, 170,
174, 180, 185, 192
Royal Supremacy, 132ff., 151ff.

Sacraments, the, 1, 3, 6, 8f., 14ff., 20,
22, 25ff., 36ff., 41ff., 47ff., 59, 82, 84,
87f., 91f., 94, 96ff., 99, 101, 105ff.,
110, 112, 115f., 118ff., 128, 131, 145,
149f., 158f., 161, 216, 218ff., 222
Salvation, see Justification
Satan (Devil, the), 39, 42, 50, 58, 66,
71f., 83, 89, 123, 145, 199

Schism, see Heresy
Scripture (authority of; interpretation
of), 14, 23f., 37f., 43f., 46, 51, 56f.,
59, 62, 67f., 81ff., 85ff., 89, 115f., 118,
123, 125ff., 132, 136, 141, 153f., 156,
159, 161, 185, 190, 200, 216f.
Separatists, the English, 6f., 22, 28f.,
45ff., 61ff., 68, 72f., 96, 171
State, see Magistrate
Suffering (Persecution; Cross, the), 1,
14f., 26, 39, 46, 57f., 113, 129, 175f.
Sword, power of the, see Magistrate

Things Indifferent, see *Adiaphora*
Tractarians, the, 127
Tradition, 54, 68, 153, 222ff.
Trinity, the (Trinitarianism; anti-
trinitarianism), 44, 54, 57f., 190,
198ff.
Turk, the, 1, 20, 37, 39, 72, 155ff., 167,
170f., 174, 176, 180, 191, 193f., 198ff.,
204ff.
Two Kingdoms, the, 87, 144ff., 209f.

Universal Priesthood, the, 4, 23, 57, 62,
82, 90, 94ff., 110f., 135ff., 146, 156,
163, 175, 178
Unworthiness of the Minister, the, see
Opus operatum
Usury, 40, 192, 196f.

Vocation (Calling), 62. 98, 104ff., 128f.,
141, 173, 177

Waldensians, the, 182
Women, ministry of, 99, 106
Word, the (Preaching), 3, 6, 8f., 13–51,
59ff., 81ff., 97ff., 106, 109f., 114, 116,
118ff., 128ff., 140, 158f., 168f., 178f.,
206f., 210, 212, 214f., 218, 224f.
World Council of Churches, 221

Zwickau Prophets, the, 51

2. CHURCH

Catholicity, etc., of, 2, 8, 13, 127ff., 172,
216

Christological Centre of, 2f., 5f., 21,
25f., 29, 33, 35, 43f., 48, 62, 64, 81f.,
109f., 114, 119, 126, 140, 163, 215,
217f., 220

Congregation (Gathered Church), 19,
23ff., 35, 42, 47, 49, 52f., 56, 58f.,
61ff., 101, 104f., 112

Discipline, 3, 6f., 13, 18, 22f., 27f., 30f.,
35, 40f., 45ff., 55f., 59ff., 96f., 103,
108, 221

3. LAW

INDEX OF NAMES

1. HISTORICAL: THE REFORMERS AND OTHERS

(Index to the Text only)

2. SECONDARY WRITERS
(Index to the Text and Notes)